New Frontiers in Education
A Rowman & Littlefield Education Series
Edited by Dr. Frederick M. Hess

This Rowman & Littlefield Education series provides educational leaders, entrepreneurs, and researchers the opportunity to offer insights that stretch the boundaries of thinking on education.

Educational entrepreneurs and leaders have too rarely shared their experiences and insights. Research has too often been characterized by impenetrable jargon. This series aims to foster volumes that can inform, educate, and inspire aspiring reformers and allow them to learn from the trials of some of today's most dynamic doers; provide researchers with a platform for explaining their work in language that allows policy makers and practitioners to take full advantage of its insights; and establish a launch pad for fresh ideas and hard-won experience.

Whether an author is a prominent leader in education, a researcher, or an entrepreneur, the key criterion for inclusion in *New Frontiers in Education* is a willingness to challenge conventional wisdom and pat answers.

The series editor, Frederick M. Hess, is the director of education policy studies at the American Enterprise Institute and can be reached at rhess@aei.org or (202) 828-6030.

Other titles in the series:

Working for Kids: Educational Leadership as Inquiry and Invention
    by James H. Lytle
Social Entrepreneurship in Education: Private Ventures for the Public Good
    by Michael R. Sandler
It's the Classroom, Stupid: A Plan to Save America's Schoolchildren
    by Kalman R. Hettleman
Choosing Excellence in Public Schools: Where There's a Will, There's a Way
    by David W. Hornbeck with Katherine Conner

Taking Measure of Charter Schools

Better Assessments, Better Policymaking, Better Schools

Edited by Julian R. Betts and Paul T. Hill

ROWMAN & LITTLEFIELD EDUCATION
A division of
ROWMAN & LITTLEFIELD PUBLISHERS, INC.
Lanham • New York • Toronto • Plymouth, UK

Published by Rowman & Littlefield Education
A division of Rowman & Littlefield Publishers, Inc.
A wholly owned subsidiary of The Rowman & Littlefield Publishing Group, Inc.
4501 Forbes Boulevard, Suite 200, Lanham, Maryland 20706
http://www.rowmaneducation.com

Estover Road, Plymouth PL6 7PY, United Kingdom

British Library Cataloguing in Publication Information Available

Library of Congress Cataloging-in-Publication Data
Taking measure of charter schools / edited by Julian R. Betts and Paul T. Hill.
    p. cm.
  Includes bibliographical references and index.
  ISBN 978-1-60709-358-9 (cloth : alk. paper) — ISBN 978-1-60709-359-6 (pbk. : alk.
paper) — ISBN 978-1-60709-360-2 (electronic)
  1. Charter schools—United States—Evaluation. I. Betts, Julian R. II. Hill, Paul T.
(Paul Thomas), 1943-
  LB2806.36.T37 2010
  371—dc22   2009051859

∞ ™ The paper used in this publication meets the minimum requirements of American
National Standard for Information Sciences—Permanence of Paper for Printed Library
Materials, ANSI/NISO Z39.48-1992.

Printed in the United States of America

Contents

Chapter One

Through a Glass Darkly: An Introduction to Issues in Measuring the Quality of Charter Schools

Julian R. Betts and Paul T. Hill

INTRODUCTION

Charter schools are semiautonomous public schools that receive renewable charters to operate, typically from a host school district or university. Charter schools typically do not hew to the local district's collective bargaining agreement, nor do they strictly follow the district's curriculum and pedagogical approach. In return for this semi-independence, charter schools are accountable to the host district for academic results. The host district has the option of closing down a charter school or deciding not to renew its charter agreement.

Even casual observers of education policy know that charter schools are controversial. Since 2004 there has been a widely covered debate among researchers disagreeing on the meaning of data on charter school performance (see, for example, Carnoy et al., 2005, and Henig, 2008). There have been major legislative fights over whether to permit additional charter schools in California and New York. Some school district leaders have denounced charter schools for depleting their budgets.

None of these events has stopped the growth in numbers of parents applying to charter schools. Nor has it stopped local public education leaders in New York, Chicago, D.C., and elsewhere from embracing chartering as a way to provide new options for children. State governments forced to take over collapsing school districts in Pennsylvania, California, and Louisiana have also turned to chartering.

Despite the controversy, nobody seriously expects charter schools to go away. Opponents can denounce and oppose charter schools, but they have no success in reducing the numbers of charter schools or killing the special state laws on which they are based. Even teacher unions, which in Ohio and

1

elsewhere have filed lawsuits hoping to block the growth of charters, have also decided to start charter schools of their own.

Charter schools, or something very much like them, are here to stay. This is so, not because charter schools have always been proven superior to other forms of public school or because proponents have always won the fights described above. They haven't. However, charter schools offer something that public school systems, parents, and teachers need: a way to experiment with alternative ways of teaching, motivating students, organizing schools, using technology, and employing teachers. Even in localities like Chicago and Philadelphia, where charter schools are plentiful but state law limits their further growth, district leaders are creating contract and partnership arrangements that look a lot like charters.

By exempting schools from many regulations and collective bargaining, chartering opens up possibilities for new uses of public money, teaching talent, student work, time, and technology. As we have seen, chartering also creates possibilities for failed experiments and big mistakes. On balance, however, Americans are willing to give charter schools a chance. Indeed, a 2007 nationwide poll found that 60 percent of respondents stated that they favored charter schools, compared to 35 percent who opposed and 5 percent who were undecided. Support was even higher, at 63 percent, among public school parents (Rose and Gallup, 2007).

That does not mean that citizens in general, or even charter supporters, are satisfied that the value of charter schools has been proven.

Like many other public policies, charter school laws were enacted without a great deal of thought about how their effects would be measured and judged. Proponents assumed that charter schools would perform so well that their superiority could be seen with the naked eye. Children would benefit so dramatically that parents would demand more and more charter schools, and elected officials would become strong supporters.

Opponents, also fearing that charters would be visibly effective, prepared objections of the "yes . . . but" variety. Opponents expected to attack charter schools based on discrimination in admissions and other abuses, not performance.

Everyone was surprised by how difficult it was to assess charter school performance. Somehow, it had been assumed, children would be tested and scores could be compared. But often children weren't tested, or comparison was difficult because the students at a given school changed over time, making comparisons of overall trends in average achievement of dubious value. Other problems have been that charter schools did not use the same tests as district schools, and school records didn't tell much about students' characteristics and prior educational experience.

Opponents were surprised that charter schools did not discriminate against poor and minority students; to the contrary, they served such students in disproportionate numbers. Everyone was surprised to find that many students entered charter schools with serious educational deficits. It was therefore difficult to set definite expectations for those students' performance and therefore not obvious from the simple snapshots of average school performance how much students gained from attending charter schools.

Thus, supporters and opponents—not to mention neutral public officials and citizens—faced unexpected challenges in judging charter school performance.

Researchers sought to assess charter school performance by comparing the test scores of students attending charter schools with students in regular public schools. But study results—whether they showed positive or negative effects for charter schools—were subject to withering criticism. It proved extremely difficult to find a credible comparison group against which to compare charter students' scores. Few noncharter schools served exactly the same mix of students as did charter schools, and researchers could never be sure that a given group of students attending regular public schools was a perfect match for students attending charter schools.

The 2004 dustup over charter school research illustrates how far we are from having the unambiguous evidence on charter school performance. Nobody can "win" the debate about whether students attending charter schools benefit because the data for good analysis just isn't available on a nationwide basis, although it is indeed available in certain cities and a handful of states.

THE CHARTER SCHOOL CONSENSUS PANEL

The National Charter School Research Project (NCSRP) was founded in 2004 to take a hard look at charter schools and become a trustworthy source, both of evidence about charter school performance and of ideas about how that performance can be improved. This book is a result of one of NCSRP's first initiatives, which was to assemble a consensus panel of top scholars to review charter school research and suggest ways parents, educators, and policy makers could get valid evidence about charter school performance.[1]

The Consensus Panel's first product was a white paper, *Key Issues in Studying Charter Schools and Achievement: A Review and Suggestions for National Guidelines*, published in May 2006. It considered the strengths and weaknesses of different methods for estimating how much students learn as a consequence of attending charter schools. As the white paper showed, there are three basic approaches to estimating a charter school's benefits to students:

- comparing the scores of students attending charter schools with those of students who applied to the same schools but did not get in because all the seats were taken
- comparing individual students' test scores before and after entering charter schools in order to judge whether students' learning rates were higher or lower in charter than in noncharter schools[2]
- comparing scores for students in charter versus noncharter schools, matched on the basis of students' income, race, and other educationally relevant factors (e.g., home language, immigrant status, handicapping conditions)

As the white paper explained, in theory the first method, comparing scores of charter school students with others who applied to the same schools but lost in a lottery, is best because it compares students who are on average identical in all ways (including their desire to enroll in a charter school) and are distinguished only by the luck of the draw.

The second method is also very good because it uses individual students as his or her own controls; scores are compared before and after a student transfers between a public school and a charter school.

By contrast, the third assessment method is tricky because it involves comparing different students. It can produce valid or invalid results — depending on how well researchers match up students in charter and regular public schools. Comparisons of groups with big differences in income, race, parents' education, and ESL status can be highly misleading. Valid comparisons can be difficult even if the researcher controls all relevant student characteristics. For example, if the students in a charter school have unusually committed parents or unusually high prior achievement levels, demographic matching will ignore key factors and almost certainly make the charter school look good for reasons other than the effectiveness of its program. The same point can be made in the opposite direction. A charter school may have a disproportionate number of children who left regular public schools because they were doing much worse than others of their same economic or racial group. Students remaining in regular public schools were not motivated in the same way and are therefore different.

A particularly weak, yet common, version of the third method is simply to compare average test scores in a given year across schools with rudimentary or even no controls for student characteristics across schools. Such snapshots tell us nothing about growth in achievement.

Whether one method or another can be used to assess a particular charter school or group of schools depends on local conditions and the availability of data. The first method can only be used in a locality where charter schools have lotteries with waiting lists. The second method can only be used in localities where annual test scores are kept for all students, including those who transfer between charter and district-run public schools.

The white paper noted that most of the charter school research done to date is limited by the quality of data available. Researchers are often stuck with databases that make valid comparisons difficult. The Consensus Panel suggested that readers of a study consider the quality of data on which it is based, asking questions such as:

- Does it include test scores for multiple years or just one year? A one-year snapshot can give a misleading result if, for example, students in one kind of school (charter or regular public) had higher average scores before the year in which the snapshot was taken. Though more studies use one-year snapshots than any other method, they cannot lead to results as definitive, no matter how large a database they draw from or how sophisticated the analysis. In short, a study that does not control for the academic history of the student in some way is likely to go awry.
- Does the study include detailed information about the students in charter schools? Weak data on student attributes—which can make dissimilar students look alike and similar students look different—can wreck efforts to compare performance of students from different schools.[3]
- Does the analysis include good information about factors correlated with school effectiveness? How long, for example, has the school been operating (new charter schools struggle much more than older ones), is the school financially stable, and what is the turnover rate among teachers and school leaders?
- Have students in charter schools—and students to whom they are compared—been tested in the same way? When charter school students take one test and the district-run school students to whom they are compared take another, gaps in outcomes can be due to differences in the tests rather than to school quality.

No single research method is perfect, and it is seldom possible to get ideal test scores or complete information about schools and students. Any rigorous study, for example, would try to control for the proportions of low-income students in charter versus regular public schools, but many charter schools do not participate in the free or reduced-price lunch program, a common proxy for low-income status. As a result, counts of students in the lunch program may provide rough estimates of student poverty in regular public schools but seriously underestimate the number of low-income families in charter schools. Some researchers have no alternative but to use free and reduced-price lunch counts as their measure of low-income status—but the results must then be interpreted very carefully.

Every study, in short, includes some compromises. And researchers and readers must be clear about how those compromises limit the applicability of findings in charter schools.

BEYOND THE WHITE PAPER

Though the white paper was well received for clarifying the debate about charter school performance, members of the Consensus Panel thought their work had just begun. It is one thing to say what the best research methods are and quite another to show that they make a difference in study outcomes. Similarly, it is one thing to urge researchers to use the results of admissions lotteries to find control groups but another to say how to identify a lottery that would produce a truly randomly selected control group.

The white paper left many issues unresolved, including how researchers might use outcome measures other than test scores (e.g., students' persistence in school and ability to succeed at the next higher level of education) and how studies might factor in richer information about school programs and teacher qualities. The white paper also urged researchers to consider how elected officials, funders, and others use information about charter school performance, without explaining how those parties actually used data.

Thus, immediately after publishing the white paper the Consensus Panel committed to looking much more deeply into a number of these issues. Individual panel members took responsibility for many of the needed analyses, and other scholars with special knowledge were also invited to contribute.

The result, this book, is in two parts: The first part focuses on how to improve estimates of charter schools' performance, especially their benefits to students who attend them; the second part suggests how policy makers can learn more about charter schools and make better use of evidence.[4]

PART ONE: IMPROVING RESEARCH ON CHARTER SCHOOLS

Julian Betts and colleagues lead off in chapter 2 with a new analysis of student achievement results from San Diego charter schools. Local data allow them to analyze student achievement data using alternative methods, some relatively crude (e.g., comparing averages scores of students in different schools) and some highly sophisticated (comparing test score trajectories of students before and after enrolling in charter schools). They show not only that more sophisticated methods lead to richer results but also that better methods can produce a totally different message about charter performance. In their San Diego data, naïve analyses whose methods and results resemble some of the cruder studies done on national databases prove negatively biased against finding positive charter school outcomes. It is possible that in other local contexts the bias would run in the other direction. Indeed, in their reanalysis of experimental results at one San Diego school, naïve models overstate rather than understate the true causal effect of attending the given charter school. They find that the more sophisticated models can produce the same sign and similar coefficients on the estimated effect of attending charter schools on student achievement. But the simpler models that do not incorporate value-added data are seriously biased.

Laura Hamilton and Brian Stecher discuss nontest outcomes in chapter 3. They remind readers that test scores provide incomplete information about school effectiveness and fail to capture all of the outcomes that parents and educators truly care about—students' completion of courses, graduation, ability to gain admission and succeed at higher levels of education, find productive work, and act as effective citizens. They suggest other milestone indicators that might be used to supplement test scores (e.g., attendance, teacher quality, stability of enrollment) and also identify more authentic long-term measures that can more fully represent the consequences of charter schooling. Examples of the latter include ability to take college courses without remediation, postsecondary degree attainment, employment, earnings, and civic values. Hamilton and Stecher conclude with recommendations on how nontest data might be collected and how researchers and local officials can set priorities for data gathering and dissemination in order to obtain and report on the most important of these hard-to-measure outcomes.

In chapter 4, Julian Betts reviews the existing charter school achievement studies, using the criteria for sound methods first developed by the Consensus Panel. The chapter also summarizes and analyzes results of the first studies to assess charter schools' long-term effects on student attendance, persistence in school, graduation, and college attendance. Betts concludes that the preponderance of evidence on achievement suggests that charter schools are outperforming traditional public schools but that there are important variations and some locations and subject areas/grades (e.g., math in high school) in which charter schools appear to be underperforming. There is now a small literature that models outcomes apart from test scores. These studies are small in number but provide hints that charter schools may increase the probability of graduating from high school and the probability of attending college while reducing the number of student disciplinary actions. Much more needs to be done on all research fronts.

In chapter 5 Julian Betts addresses a problem that vexes all efforts to measure the effectiveness of charter schools—whether the children whose parents choose charter schools are so different from the children in regular public schools that straightforward comparisons are impossible. Betts shows that in theoretical models low-income families choose charter schools because of their perceived greater quality (compared to the public school options available to them) but that many factors can reduce disadvantaged children's attendance in charter schools, even when school operators intend to serve such children. Low-income families, he notes, are especially sensitive to transportation issues, so school location is extremely important. Some families are discouraged from applying by requirements for parental participation in school activities. Though he concludes that many charter schools intend to serve disadvantaged minority (especially African American) populations, their actual locations and recruitment practices can favor slightly more educated and economically secure black families. Betts concludes with suggestions about how researchers can test and control for schools' selectivity bias.

Patrick McEwan and Robert Olsen take a careful look at charter school lotteries in chapter 6 and explore implications for policy and research. The authors describe why some charter schools conduct lotteries and some do not, how they conduct them, and why all lotteries are not created equal. In addition, they explore the effects that lotteries may have on equal access and stratification in public schools. Finally, they discuss lottery-based studies of charter school effectiveness, which compare student outcomes between lottery winners, who are admitted to charter schools by random chance, to lottery losers. McEwan and Olsen conclude that lottery-based studies have enormous potential when the lottery details are well understood but that they have important limitations as well. The authors conclude by noting that requirements to conduct lotteries in public may increase the transparency of lotteries and that requirements to report lottery results might help provide opportunities for both monitoring—to ensure the lotteries are truly random—and research to exploit the natural experiments that charter school lotteries provide.

In chapter 7, Paul Hill and Lydia Rainey suggest that charter school maturation should be a factor in studies of school performance. As they show, many charter schools are relatively new; moreover, charter schools consistently have lower scores in the first years after they open than at later times. Hill and Rainey apply literature from business and broader education research to show that new schools are likely to have growing pains that will depress early performance. They therefore suggest that studies of charter performance should distinguish schools in their first three years from older charters. They also consider the possibility of using school maturation measures as control factors in research or as leading indicators to alert families and authorizing agencies to possible trouble. They conclude, however, that schools mature at such different rates and in such different sequences that it is impossible to create a model of normal maturation.

In chapter 8, Dominic Brewer and June Ahn review what is known about charter school teachers and consider how data on teachers might be used to explain differences in school performance. They show that charter school teachers are younger and lower-paid than teachers in regular public schools serving similar students. Though many charter teachers have educational backgrounds generally similar to those of regular public school teachers, teacher qualifications are highly variable in charters. Similarly, teacher turnover is high and variable; moreover, the significance of turnover depends on whether charter schools have definite strategies for managing it (or simply scramble constantly to fill classrooms). Charter school teachers generally work longer hours than their public school counterparts, but schools differ between those that routinely cause teacher burnout and those that help teachers sustain needed levels of effort over a long time. To date, links between teacher factors and charter school performance have not been shown. But as Brewer and Ahn conclude, teacher factors might prove to be important in explaining variations in charter school outcomes. To the degree possible, studies of charter school performance should account for differences in teacher qualifications, satisfaction, and stability of employment.

PART TWO: HOW POLICY MAKERS
CAN MAKE BETTER USE OF EVIDENCE

In chapter 9, Robin Lake and Larry Angel review studies done on charter schools within individual states. They show that state studies are highly variable in quality but that they include many of the best studies based on following students from before to after they enter charter schools. States that keep records on individual students and have score data for every year a student is tested are in position to sponsor very sound studies. State legislators and their staff members can be excessively demanding and reasonable in turn. State legislation mandating charter studies can pose questions that cannot be answered given the low quality of data kept by their states; yet, officials generally know that definitive evidence about charter schools is not forthcoming soon. Angel and Lake suggest ways legislatures can both discipline their requests for results and upgrade the quality of data so that the answers they need will ultimately become available.

Jeffrey Henig examines controversies over the political uses of charter school research in chapter 10 and draws lessons about how policy makers might use better research as it becomes available. He provides both bad news and good news about the use of research results in policy making. The bad news is that policy makers are not well equipped to tell the difference between strong and weak studies, especially of a relatively new phenomenon like charter schools, and that institutions that could help them interpret the existing research are not serving that function as well as they should. Under such circumstances, elected officials are more likely to use studies to buttress preestablished positions than to weigh options. The good news is that the weight of research can accumulate over time, especially when the quality of studies increases and their results converge on key points. Henig concludes with recommendations to researchers who want their work used and trusted, emphasizing the need to frame the consequences of research modestly and to avoid oversimplification of findings in search of headlines.

In the final chapter, Julian Betts and Paul Hill distill lessons from all of the Consensus Panel's work. They suggest ways states and localities can improve the quality of data on which charter school studies are based and trace some of the ways charter school research influences policy. Consistent with Jeffrey Henig's conclusions, they find no hard link between research and public policy, though elected officials care enough about studies to fund them and to cite results in support of their positions. However, research results have powerful effects inside the charter school movement. Funders, school operators, and government authorizing agencies are using research aggressively, responding even to mixed study results with new quality standards for charter schools to meet. Finally, Betts and Hill note that charter school research is starting to influence the data kept on regular public schools and the ways individual schools are assessed. No Child Left Behind, for example, will require districts to measure and judge the performance of all their schools.

The ultimate result, they argue, will be that all public schools will be assessed on the same student performance standards that now apply almost exclusively to charters. However, charter schools still face much more severe consequences for perceived failures than do traditional public schools. It is true that No Child Left Behind, with its stipulation that traditional public schools that repeatedly fail to make adequate yearly progress must be reconstituted, reorganized, or converted into charter schools, brings stronger accountability to noncharter schools. But even these interventions still pale compared to the power that a chartering authority, usually a school district, has to shut down a charter school simply by refusing to renew its charter.

Student achievement tests have been used for decades, and administrators and researchers have long claimed that they were evaluating school performance. However, until recently test scores had few real consequences. Public schools were not closed if their scores were low or expanded or rewarded in any particular way if their scores were high. In the 1990s, standards-based reforms enacted by all but a few states adopted the rhetoric of performance-based accountability, but no state followed through completely. Now test scores can have real consequences, at least for charter schools that admit students by choice.

Now that the stakes have been raised, data and methods that once looked acceptable prove inadequate. As the Consensus Panel has shown, the wrong data, or the right data used wrongly, can lead to unwarranted conclusions about school success and failure. There are now real incentives for hard thinking and careful use of data. Charter school research has improved slowly but steadily over just the last five years, and it will continue improving.

NOTES

1. Consensus Panel members include Julian Betts, University of California San Diego; Dominic Brewer, University of Southern California; Anthony Bryk, Stanford University; Dan Goldhaber, University of Washington; Laura Hamilton, RAND Corporation; Jeffrey Henig, Columbia University; Paul Hill, University of Washington; Susanna Loeb, Stanford University; and Patrick McEwan, Wellesley College.

2. The full text of the white paper explains the different ways data collected for a study using this method can be analyzed.

3. However, two methods reduce the need for detailed student characteristics. Lotteries, by definition, ensure that on average lottery losers and winners will have about the same characteristics because they have been assigned to the two groups by a flip of the coin. In the second method we mentioned—using student "fixed effects" to compare individual students' performance gains when in charter versus regular schools—we do not have to compare one student to another.

4. The Consensus Panel has also published a media guide to help reporters understand the limitations of charter school studies. See Lydia Rainey, *Making Sense of Charter School Studies: A Reporter's Guide,* National Charter School Research Project (Seattle: Center on Reinventing Public Education, 2007).

REFERENCES

Carnoy, M., Jacobsen, R., Mishel, L., and Rothstein, R. (2005). *The Charter School Dust-Up: Examining the Evidence on Enrollment and Achievement.* New York: Teachers College Press.

Charter School Achievement Consensus Panel. (2006). *Key Issues in Studying Charter Schools and Achievement: A Review and Suggestions for National Guidelines.* NCSRP White Paper Series, No. 2. Seattle: Center on Reinventing Public Education.

Henig, J. (2008). *Spin Cycle: How Research Is Used in Policy Debates: The Case of Charter Schools.* New York: Russell Sage Foundation/Century Foundation.

Rainey, L. (2007). *Making Sense of Charter School Studies: A Reporter's Guide.* National Charter School Research Project. Seattle: Center on Reinventing Public Education.

Rose, L. C., and Gallup, A. M. (2007). The 39th Annual Phi Delta Kappa/Gallup Poll of the Public's Attitudes Toward the Public Schools. *Phi Delta Kappan* 89:1, September 2007, 33–48.

Part I

IMPROVING RESEARCH ON CHARTER SCHOOLS

Chapter Two

Madness in the Method? A Critical Analysis of Popular Methods of Estimating the Effect of Charter Schools on Student Achievement

Julian R. Betts, Y. Emily Tang, and Andrew C. Zau

INTRODUCTION

The Charter School Achievement Consensus Panel issued a white paper in 2006 that argued that methods that have been used to evaluate the effect of charter schools on student achievement range from poor to excellent and that most studies to date have used methods that are fair to poor. In theory, weaker methods that, for example, do not control for outside factors that influence student test scores could give quite different results than stronger methods. One could peruse the literature to study this possibility, but the problem has been that different authors not only use different methods but also different data. Because the whole point of charter schools is to give educators greater autonomy, it is reasonable to believe that the effectiveness of charter schools in boosting math and reading achievement could vary from one area to the next.[1] So if we find that a well-designed study of Texas charter schools produces different results than a poorly designed national study, are we to conclude that the quality of the research method matters, or that geography matters? It is impossible to know for sure.

In an attempt to answer this question, this paper uses test-score data from a single location, San Diego Unified School District (SDUSD), to investigate how the measured effect of charter schools on achievement varies with the method used. In earlier work, Tang and Betts (2006) study a panel of SDUSD students up through the period 2004 using student fixed-effect models and conclude that on the whole charter schools perform about equally well in terms of producing high test scores in math and reading, with some important variations related to age of the charter school, grades served, and whether the charter is a startup charter or a traditional public school that has converted to charter status. Also see Betts et al. (2006, chapter 5) for a less technical and detailed version of that work.

We study test scores on the California Standards Test, in math and reading, based on all students in SDUSD during the school years 2002–2003 through 2005–2006. Our analysis proceeds in two phases. First, each year the California Department of Education issues an Academic Performance Index score for each school in the state as an overall measure of student achievement. The API is a single number that aggregates test scores on various elements of the California Standards Test and various other outcomes, both aggregated and by student subgroup. Because this is the most commonly used starting point for public discussions of "school quality" in California today, we analyze mean API scores by taking a simple mean across charter and traditional public schools respectively.

Second, we use student-level data to estimate models of the determinants of reading and math achievement using a sequence of increasingly sophisticated models.

We find that more robust estimation methods yield vastly different results than simpler, less robust methods. Looking at trends in API scores is highly misleading due to changes in the number and type of charter schools over time and, perhaps, due to changes in the types of students attending each charter school over time.

The regression findings are even more striking. Typically, the simpler methods underestimate the effect of attending a charter school on reading and math achievement, often in quite dramatic ways. This pattern is consistent with negative selectivity bias into San Diego's charter schools, or, put more simply, with the idea that San Diego charter schools attract students with below-average achievement before they enroll. Simple methods that do not take into account students' past academic history and achievement growth trajectories can thus wrongly ascribe to charter schools low achievement that is due to poverty or to unobserved factors.[2]

NAÏVE ESTIMATES OF CHARTER SCHOOL QUALITY USING PUBLICLY AVAILABLE SCHOOL AVERAGE TEST SCORES

We start with a method that will approximate the way that many members of the public might use to assess charter schools. Namely, we take simple averages of published test scores, which in California are provided in summary form as API scores, across schools. In this way we compare charter schools to traditional public schools. Figure 2.1 shows the results. Charter schools appear to underperform traditional public schools significantly in the early years but catch up quickly, and by 2005 they have virtually erased the gap in API scores.

Now, does this pattern of underperformance and rapid catch-up tell us much about the quality of instruction at the two types of schools? On the one hand, it could be that within each charter school we have seen marked improvement in teaching methods and teacher effectiveness over the period of study, so that individual students have improved at a rate concomitant with figure 2.1. On the other hand, maybe the composition of the charter school movement in San Diego has changed over time, and with it so has the composition of the student body in charter schools. The first hypothesis is one of a dramatic increase in school quality. The second hypothesis is more consistent with selectivity bias. That is, as new charter schools open over time and others close, the types of students in charter schools is likely to change, and this could explain some or even much of the apparent improvement.

It is hard to know for sure which story is more important when all we have is school-level test scores. But we can do what economists call a shift-share analysis. The idea is to ask: "How would the mean API score of charter schools have changed over time if the sample of charter schools in San Diego had not changed after the first year?" This tells us how much student achievement has "shifted," or improved, within these original charter schools. The remainder of the improvement in average API scores will thus be due to changes in the "share" of charter schools; that is, the creation of new charter schools over time that have different test scores.

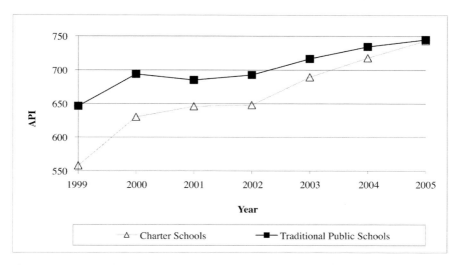

Figure 2.1.   Average API Scores of Traditional Public Schools and Charter Schools in San Diego, 1999 to 2005

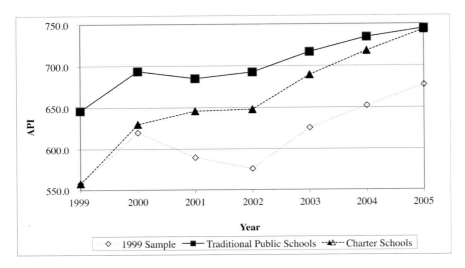

Figure 2.2.   Average API Scores of Traditional Public Schools and Charter Schools in San Diego, along with Average API Scores of Charter Schools That Existed in 1999, for 1999 to 2005

Figure 2.2 redraws figure 2.1 but adds a new line showing the average API score of the original set of charter schools over time. These original charter schools did improve over time, but not nearly as much as implied by figure 2.1. In fact, much of the apparent improvement in the quality of San Diego charter schools reflects the arrival of new charters during the period shown. On average, the new startup charter schools had test scores much higher than the original charter schools, which primarily consisted of low-performing traditional public schools that were converted to charter schools.

Table 2.1 decomposes the decrease in the API gap between charter and regular schools into the part due to changes within the preexisting schools and the part due to the creation of new charter schools. It shows that about 75 percent of the reduction in the API gap can be accounted for by the creation of new charter schools that happen to have higher test scores. Table 2.2 shows the average test scores by year for all charter schools that were in existence as of the year stated in the left-hand column. Clearly, the arrival of new charters plays a big role in the improved test scores of charter schools. Note also that the rate of improvement varies a lot from one of these cohorts to another, suggesting that idiosyncrasies of the populations of new charter schools are quite important.

This problem is not unique to San Diego at all. Rather, the opportunity for misreading of average school achievement is ubiquitous. When Nelson et al. (2004) studied National Assessment of Educational Progress achievement

Table 2.1. A Shift-Share Analysis of the Sources of Reduction in the API Gap between Charter and Traditional Public Schools, 1999–2005

API Gap, Regular vs. Charter, 1999	89
API Gap, Regular vs. Charter, 2005	2
Naïve % Reduction	98.3%
API Gap, Regular vs. Charter, 2005 Based on 1999 Set of Charters	68
% Reduction Due to Shift in Preexisting Charter Schools' Achievement	23.5%
% Reduction Due to Change in the Composition of Charter Schools	74.8%

Note: Data on API were downloaded from the California Department of Education, available at http://www.cde.ca.gov/ds/sp/ap/

data, they concluded that charter schools were underperforming. But it has since been shown that most of this gap can be explained by differences in the socioeconomic mix of students in charter schools and traditional public schools nationally. For instance, let's apply the same sort of shift-share analysis to the Nelson et al. report and test whether differences in the racial/ethnic mix between traditional public schools and charter schools can explain why charters have lower test scores in grade four math and reading. It turns out that 67 percent of the apparent gap in math and 74 percent of the gap in reading can be explained by this lone factor—differences in the racial mix.

What can we conclude from these analyses? If we are to attempt to measure charter school quality by a simple comparison of average test scores, we need to be extremely aware of the almost complete inability of this approach to assign causation. The gap in scores between charters and traditional public schools, in San Diego or nationwide, may be due entirely to variations in the

Table 2.2. Average API Scores of Charter Schools Based on Samples of Charter Schools in Operation by the Given Year

Year	1999	2000	2001	2002	2003	2004	2005
Samples of Charter Schools Based on Charters in Existence as of Given Year							
1999 Sample	557.8	620.0	589.8	576.0	625.8	652.3	677.2
2000 Sample		630.1	610.2	626.9	653.7	680.3	713.9
2001 Sample			646.0	667.2	684.9	709.3	740.2
2002 Sample				648.0	677.5	704.0	736.5
2003 Sample					689.5	714.1	746.4
2004 Sample						718.0	747.8
2005 Sample							743.4
Traditional Public Schools	646	694	685	693	717	735	745

Note: Data on API were downloaded from the California Department of Education, available at http://www.cde.ca.gov/ds/sp/ap/

initial achievement of students who enter charter schools and those who enter traditional public schools. For the same reason, at least in San Diego, most of the growth in charter school performance may be due to the changing student composition of charter schools as new schools started up. Compositional changes alone suggest it may be foolhardy to venture *any* conclusions about the relative "quality" of charter schools based on average test scores at the school level, or trends in those average test scores.

COMPARING A SEQUENCE OF INCREASINGLY ROBUST MODELS USING STUDENT-LEVEL DATA

We now turn to student-level data and estimate an increasingly rigorous series of models. The first model simply models the level of a student's test score as a function of whether he or she is in a charter. This is really quite analogous to naïvely looking at average test scores school by school. The second model adds demographic characteristics to test whether these controls change the conclusions.[3] Models 3 and 4 model individual student gains in achievement, without and then with demographic controls. Model 5 adds student fixed effects to model 4. These fixed effects remove the average value of all characteristics of the student, both observed and unobserved.

Table 2.3 shows results for reading, when we pool students across all grades, and table 2.4 shows the same for math. Tables 2.5 and 2.6 replicate these models separately for elementary, middle, and high school students.

Table 2.3. Models of Reading Achievement Using Normed CST Data from 2002 through 2006, for All Grades Combined

Dependent Variable:	(1) Test Score	(2) Test Score	(3) Gain in Score	(4) Gain in Score	(5) Gain in Score
Charter	−0.0113	−0.0098	0.0276	0.0190	0.0309
	(0.0566)	(0.0395)	(0.0117)*	(0.0118)	(0.0142)*
Observations	313535	313535	313535	313535	313535
Number of Students	125356	125356	125356	125356	125356
Controls for Student Characteristics	No	Yes	No	Yes	Yes
Student Random Effects	Yes	Yes	Yes	Yes	No
Student Fixed Effects	No	No	No	No	Yes

Notes: Standard errors in parentheses. All models allow for clustering at the school level.
* significant at 5%; ** significant at 1%
Models with student characteristics include controls for race and ethnicity, English learners, fluent English proficiency, and parental education.

Table 2.4. Models of Math Achievement Using Normed CST Data from 2002 through 2006, for All Grades Combined

Dependent Variable:	(1) Test Score	(2) Test Score	(3) Gain in Score	(4) Gain in Score	(5) Gain in Score
Charter	−0.0110	0.0025	0.0368	0.0454	0.0630
	(0.0592)	(0.0446)	(0.0240)	(0.0241)	(0.0241)**
Observations	313867	313867	313867	313867	313867
Number of Students	124309	124309	124309	124309	124309
Controls for Student Characteristics	No	Yes	No	Yes	Yes
Student Random Effects	Yes	Yes	Yes	Yes	No
Student Fixed Effects	No	No	No	No	Yes

Notes: Standard errors in parentheses. All models allow for clustering at the school level.
* significant at 5%; ** significant at 1%
Models with student characteristics include controls for race and ethnicity, English learners, fluent English proficiency, and parental education.

Table 2.5. Models of Reading Achievement Using Normed CST Data from 2002 through 2006, for Elementary, Middle, and High School Students Separately

Dependent Variable:	(1) Test Score	(2) Test Score	(3) Gain in Score	(4) Gain in Score	(5) Gain in Score
Elementary School Students Charter	−0.0456	−0.0794	0.0327	0.0306	0.0419
	(0.0844)	(0.0655)	(0.0215)	(0.0202)	(0.0262)
Observations	112473	112473	112473	112473	112473
Number of Students	61378	61378	61378	61378	61378
Middle School Students Charter	−0.0826	−0.0018	0.0133	0.0071	0.0102
	(0.1120)	(0.0575)	(0.0191)	(0.0202)	(0.0277)
Observations	108408	108408	108408	108408	108408
Number of Students	59286	59286	59286	59286	59286
High School Students Charter	0.0522	0.0401	0.0516	0.0573	0.1518
	(0.1198)	(0.1133)	(0.0192)**	(0.0210)**	(0.0270)**
Observations	92654	92654	92654	92654	92654
Number of Students	52189	52189	52189	52189	52189
Controls for Student Characteristics	No	Yes	No	Yes	Yes
Student Random Effects	Yes	Yes	Yes	Yes	No
Student Fixed Effects	No	No	No	No	Yes

Notes: Standard errors in parentheses. All models allow for clustering at the school level.
* significant at 5%; ** significant at 1%
Models with student characteristics include controls for race and ethnicity, English learners, fluent English proficiency, and parental education.

Table 2.6.   Models of Math Achievement Using Normed CST Data from 2002 through 2006, for Elementary, Middle, and High School Students Separately

Dependent Variable:	(1) Test Score	(2) Test Score	(3) Gain in Score	(4) Gain in Score	(5) Gain in Score
Elementary School	0.0662	0.0576	0.0656	0.0674	0.2919++
Students Charter	(0.1187)	(0.0950)	(0.0623)	(0.0583)	(0.0376)**
Observations	114841	114841	114841	114841	114841
Number of Students	62545	62545	62545	62545	62545
Middle School	−0.1036	0.0010	0.0356	0.0463	0.0080
Students Charter	(0.1025)	(0.0577)	(0.0280)	(0.0292)	(0.0504)
Observations	109593	109593	109593	109593	109593
Number of Students	59983	59983	59983	59983	59983
High School	0.0548	−0.0027	0.0219	0.0443	−0.0124
Students Charter	(0.0993)	(0.1019)	(0.0522)	(0.0643)	(0.0445)
Observations	89433	89433	89433	89433	89433
Number of Students	50339	50339	50339	50339	50339
Controls for Student Characteristics	No	Yes	No	Yes	Yes
Student Random Effects	Yes	Yes	Yes	Yes	No
Student Fixed Effects	No	No	No	No	Yes

Standard errors in parentheses. All models allow for clustering at the school level.
Notes: * significant at 5%; ** significant at 1%
Models with student characteristics include controls for race and ethnicity, English learners, fluent English proficiency, and parental education.
++ Model 5 for elementary students could not be run with both a student fixed effect and clustering at the school level. The results reported include a student fixed effect but do not cluster at the school level.

The main results in tables 2.3 and 2.4 tell a fairly dramatic and uniform story. The most naïve model, model 1, suggests that charter schools are underperforming traditional public schools, although the difference is not statistically significant. The addition of student demographics weakens this relation somewhat in the sense that the coefficient rises, and, in the case of math, becomes positive. But still the charter coefficient is not significant. The switch to modeling student gains (models 3 through 5) leads to a large change in the charter school coefficient, which becomes positive for both the reading and math models. In the reading model, the charter coefficient becomes significant in models 3 and 5 and is nearly significant in model 4. In these reading models, attending a charter school is significantly associated with gains in test scores about 0.03 of a standard deviation above that in traditional public schools. In the math models shown in table 2.4, the value-added specifications all yield positive charter school effects, although it is only in the fixed-effect specification that the charter variable becomes significant. The effect size is 0.06 in this case, twice that for the reading model. Another interesting pattern in the math models is that as we move to increasingly rigorous models from left to right in table 2.4, the coefficient on charter schools becomes more positive in every case.

The strong pattern here suggests that as we use increasingly rigorous methods to control for student background and student academic history, the apparent "effect" of attending a charter school on achievement flips from being negative and insignificant to positive and significant. These results strongly imply that selectivity bias materially biases downward naïve estimates of the effect of charter schools on achievement in San Diego.

Tables 2.5 and 2.6 replicate these analyses for elementary school, middle school, and high school students. Although the precision of these estimates will in general be lower because of smaller sample size, they tend to show the same patterns as the pooled results. The reading results in table 2.5 yield a positive coefficient on charter schools for all of the value-added models. Only for high schools does the charter coefficient become statistically significant. In this case the coefficient is positive and quite big, as large as 0.15 in the fixed-effect model. Conversely, the two models that model the level of test scores show negative and insignificant coefficients, or, in the case of high schools, positive but insignificant coefficients.

For the math models in table 2.6, the charter coefficient rises markedly and becomes significant in the case of elementary schools for the fixed-effect model. However, in that model we were unable to allow for both the fixed effect and clustering, apparently due to a relatively small number of school switchers, so the standard error in that model is artificially small.[4] In the higher grades, the charter indicator does not become significant. For middle schools, the familiar pattern of coefficients that become "more positive" in the more rigorous specifications appears again. At the high school level, there is no clear pattern.

A common criticism of fixed-effect models, and value-added models more generally, is that they ignore students without multiple years of achievement. Appendix tables 2.1 and 2.2 replicate models 1 and 2 using the same regression samples as in tables 2.3 and 2.4, but then repeat these models using the larger sample that is available if we include observations where we can observe the level of a student's test score but not the year-to-year gain. This is a worthwhile robustness check because the comparison of the results from the smaller and larger samples tells us something about representativeness of the sample of students with repeated observations. There is very little change in regression coefficients between samples, but in the case of both math and reading, there are some changes that suggest that students with multiple observations might have had slightly higher test scores in charter schools. Even here, the differences are quite small, on the order of less than one hundredth of a standard deviation.

Overall, we are left with a clear sense that the more rigorously a method controls for students' past histories and background, and for interstudent differences in growth trajectories (through student fixed effects), the more positive will be the estimated effect of charter schools on achievement of attendees.

COMPARING EXPERIMENTAL AND NONEXPERIMENTAL ESTIMATES FOR THE PREUSS SCHOOL

One of the charter schools in the San Diego sample, the Preuss School at UCSD, has been studied using experimental methods based on the admissions lottery. For instance, McClure et al. (2005) compare outcomes for lottery winners versus losers. These outcomes include test scores, completion of college preparatory courses, and, for a very small cohort that graduated in 2005, college attendance. This work is of particular interest because it affords us the opportunity to compare the test-score effects from the experimental analysis versus the estimated effects from the various methods we have already used here. Do we obtain similar results to the experimental analysis?

McClure et al. (2005) focus on students who were admitted to grades six and seven by lottery in fall 1999 and later years. We will focus on attempting to replicate the authors' findings about the impact of attending the Preuss School on math and reading scores. The authors test for differences in test scores in spring 2003 and 2004 between lottery winners and losers, testing separately for each cohort and test year. They find no differences in reading scores that are significant at the 5 percent or lower level between lottery winners and losers. However, they find a number of cases in which the math scores of lottery winners and losers differed significantly, at a 5 percent or lower level. In two of these three cases, Preuss students scored lower in math than did lottery losers. In a fourth case, Preuss students again had lower math scores but the difference was significant at the 6 percent level.[5]

McClure et al.'s analysis also shows extremely clearly that the Preuss School runs against the general tendency for charter schools to enroll students who are relatively low scoring. In fact, the Preuss School has some of the highest test scores of any other school in the San Diego Unified School District or the county of San Diego more generally. This is all the more surprising given that to be eligible to enroll in the school, a student must be eligible for meal assistance, and neither parent nor guardian of the student can have graduated from a university. The explanation for the pattern of positive selectivity is that the rigorous curriculum, which is single-track college preparatory, plus the school's longer-than-average school year and longer-than-average school day appear quite intimidating to all but the most ambitious students.

This positive selectivity creates an unusual opportunity to show how well the various regression methods handle selectivity bias. We would expect the less rigorous approaches, in particular models 1 and 2 that model the *level* of a student's test scores without taking into account the student's past academic history, could produce estimates of the causal effect of the Preuss School on achievement that are biased upward quite badly. Ultimately, we are interested in finding out which of the regression methods, if any, can reproduce the lottery-based evidence that Preuss students performed about the same as applicants who lost the lottery on reading, and in some cases performed worse in math than lottery losers.

Unfortunately, we cannot focus exclusively on the set of students who entered grades six and seven in 1999 and later, as did McClure et al. (2005), because California changed its official state test quite radically after 2001, so that, for instance, we are not in a position to do a fixed-effect analysis that follows those particular students from the period before they entered the Preuss School through the period that our data using the California Standards test cover, which is from 2001–2002 through 2005–2006. However, we can look at the entire set of entrants into the Preuss School for whom test scores are available during this later period.

Tables 2.7 and 2.8 replicate the reading and math models from tables 2.3 and 2.4, respectively, but replace the single dummy variable for charter schools with one dummy to indicate Preuss attendees and another to indicate attendees at any of the other charter schools in San Diego.

As shown in Table 2.7, the results for reading conform almost exactly with the above prediction. Model 1, which models the level of the student's test score without controlling for covariates, suggests that attendees at the Preuss School score about 0.2 of a standard deviation above other students attending traditional schools. But this is clearly not a causal effect of attending this particular charter school. Model 2, which adds controls for student demographics, produces an even *bigger* "effect" of attending the Preuss School, which is very close to being significant at the 5 percent level. At first this seems counterintuitive, until one realizes that by design, the school admits only students whose parents have relatively low education. (In addition, the income criterion for eligibility in practice leads to a severe underrepresentation of whites at the school.) These differences from the average demographic characteristics districtwide "fool" the regression into implying that the Preuss School does an even better job at boosting reading achievement than did model 1. Of course, what is missing here is that the Preuss School attracts unusually motivated students.

Table 2.7. Models of Reading Achievement That Distinguish the Preuss School from Other Charter Schools, Using Normed CST Data from 2002 through 2006, for All Grades Combined

Dependent Variable:	(1) Test Score	(2) Test Score	(3) Gain in Score	(4) Gain in Score	(5) Gain in Score
Preuss School	0.1951	0.3126	0.0281	0.0156	–0.1079
	(0.1320)	(0.1617)	(0.0055)**	(0.0126)	(0.0227)**
Other Charter	–0.0231	–0.0224	0.0275	0.0192	0.0351
	(0.0549)	(0.0340)	(0.0128)*	(0.0124)	(0.0147)*
Observations	313535	313535	313535	313535	313535
Number of Students	125356	125356	125356	125356	125356
Controls for Student Characteristics	No	Yes	No	Yes	Yes
Student Random Effects	Yes	Yes	Yes	Yes	No
Student Fixed Effects	No	No	No	No	Yes

Notes: Standard errors in parentheses. All models allow for clustering at the school level.
* significant at 5%; ** significant at 1%
Models with student characteristics include controls for race and ethnicity, English learners, fluent English
  proficiency, and parental education.

Table 2.8. Models of Math Achievement That Distinguish the Preuss School from Other Charter Schools, Using Normed CST Data from 2002 through 2006, for All Grades Combined

Dependent Variable:	(1) Test Score	(2) Test Score	(3) Gain in Score	(4) Gain in Score	(5) Gain in Score
Preuss School	0.1819	0.2878	0.0787	0.0885	-0.0955
	(0.1395)	(0.1531)	(0.0105)**	(0.0218)**	(0.0387)*
Other Charter	–0.0230	–0.0095	0.0320	0.0425	0.0678
	(0.0573)	(0.0409)	(0.0260)	(0.0251)	(0.0242)**
Observations	313867	313867	313867	313867	313867
Number of Students	124309	124309	124309	124309	124309
Controls for Student Characteristics	No	Yes	No	Yes	Yes
Student Random Effects	Yes	Yes	Yes	Yes	No
Student Fixed Effects	No	No	No	No	Yes

Notes: Standard errors in parentheses. All models allow for clustering at the school level.
* significant at 5%; ** significant at 1%
Models with student characteristics include controls for race and ethnicity, English learners, fluent English
  proficiency, and parental education.

In stark contrast, once we begin to model gains in student achievement, in models 3 through 5, we find that this simple way of accounting for a student's past academic achievement leads to quite different results. The coefficient in model 3 is still positive, is only about one-tenth as big as in the naïve model 2, but does become statistically significant. Adding student demographics in model 4 leads to a slightly smaller and now insignificant coefficient on the Preuss variable. Finally, when we add a student fixed effect in model 4, the coefficient for this school plummets, and in fact becomes negative and significant.

Table 2.8 shows the corresponding results for math. The patterns are highly analogous to those for reading. Models of the level of the test score suggest the Preuss School outperforms traditional public schools, with the effect in model 2 becoming almost significant. Again, changing the dependent variable to gains in test scores, to account for past history, leads to a dramatic reduction in our estimated effect of attending the Preuss School, to about one-quarter its original size. The effect, which is positive, becomes statistically significant. Adding student demographics in model 4 leads to a slightly bigger but still relatively small coefficient on the Preuss variable, which again is statistically significant. (This coefficient is bigger than that in model 3, perhaps for the same reason that model 2 provides a bigger coefficient than model 1.) As in the case of reading, the addition of a student fixed effect in model 5 leads to a negative and significant effect of the Preuss School.

HOW WELL DO THESE REGRESSION MODELS MATCH THE LOTTERY-BASED EVIDENCE?

In reading, none of the models exactly matched the conclusion by McClure et al. (2005) of no differences in reading. The simplest models, of test-score levels, yielded insignificant coefficients, but the coefficients were large, at around 0.2 to 0.3 of standard deviation. Arguably, the two models of reading gains that did not include a student fixed effect came closest to matching the lottery result, in that the estimated coefficients are tiny and fairly precise. The student fixed-effect model yielded a negative and significant effect for Preuss students. So it seems that modeling gains helps us approximate the experimental result, but adding a student fixed effect leads to estimates that are "too low."

Notably, only one math regression model could replicate the lottery-based evidence of McClure et al. (2005) that Preuss students in some cases underperformed lottery losers in math. The successful candidate was the fixed-effect model. We infer that modeling gains and at the same time adding fixed effects to control for unobserved student heterogeneity were crucial in this case.

Finally, we note that the report by McClure et al. (2005) also analyzed "one-time" events, such as whether the students completed the sequence of courses required to attend a California university or whether the students attended college after graduation. Strikingly, Preuss students who had won the lottery fared much better on these outcome measures than students who had lost the lottery. It is beyond the scope of the paper to attempt to replicate these findings. But the most convincing of the regression methods used here, student fixed effects, cannot be used to analyze one-time events, such as whether a student attends college. It is for analyses such as these that lottery data or other methods of randomization become particularly valuable.

CONCLUSION

Much of the existing charter school literature uses average test scores across schools, such as those published in newspapers around the nation every year when state departments of education release test results to infer the quality of education provided by charter schools relative to traditional public schools. These attempts are doomed to fail because they cannot reliably identify the causal effect of attending a charter school. The relative level of test scores in the two types of schools in many cases mostly reflects selectivity bias. That is, the initial achievement of students before they enter charter schools explains most of the differences. Similar problems arise when one studies trends in average test scores across schools, which can paint a quite misleading picture of trends in the relative quality of instruction provided at the two types of schools.

San Diego is an apt case of what can go wrong in these overly simple comparisons. In that city, charter schools in 1999 had test scores far below those of traditional public schools, but they virtually erased this gap by 2005. It appears that the initial gap is due to the low initial achievement of the students who attended the set of charter schools early in the period. The rapid gain in relative test scores only partly represents improvement in individual charter schools over time, with most of the narrowing achievement gap explained by rapid change in the mix of charter schools over time and differences among the students who attended the older and the younger charter schools.

In San Diego, it is no coincidence that early on charter school achievement lagged that of traditional public schools: low-performing regular schools that had been converted to charter status were especially prominent in the early years. Over time, the birth of many start-up charter schools that have had higher scores has brought charter school scores, on average, closer to those of traditional public schools.

Notably, this convergence may well reverse itself in the next decade. Under No Child Left Behind (NCLB), one of the options for schools that persistently fail to meet state requirements for Adequate Yearly Progress is to convert them into charter schools. It would be highly misleading if in the future any policy analyst summarily attributed any drop in the relative achievement of students in charter schools to a drop in the quality of education provided by charter schools. In truth, such a drop might simply reflect conversion of "failing" schools to charter status.

The same potential for misleading inferences arises in regression models. We showed that the simple approach of modeling the *level* of individual students' test scores as a function of whether the students attend a charter school suggests that charter schools underperform traditional public schools. However, more rigorous models either suggest much smaller achievement gaps or in fact suggest that charter schools in San Diego *outperform* traditional public schools.

The most important improvement to the modeling approach appears to be modeling *gains* in achievement, rather than *levels*. This change is clearly an improvement because it takes into account the past achievement of the student. But almost as important, adding student fixed effects to account for unobserved variations among students in test-score growth increases the estimated effectiveness of charter schools, and indeed often produces a statistically significant gap favoring charter schools.

Finally, our analysis of one particular charter school for which there exists experimental evidence shows that nonexperimental regression methods produce estimated effects that swing quite widely. Some models obtained larger estimated effects than the experimental approach, and others produced results that were smaller. This pattern is quite reminiscent of LaLonde's much cited 1986 paper in which he attempted to replicate experimental results on the effect of a government training program after throwing out the experimental control group and replacing it with workers from other unrelated data sets.

And yet, in our charter school results there is a consistent pattern that explains the wide variations in the nonexperimental evidence. Naïve regression models tended to overestimate the true effects, probably due to positive (ability) selection of students into this particular charter school. (Only the most motivated students are inclined to apply to a school with such a demanding curriculum and schedule.) More realistic models that examined gains in test scores, in so doing taking into account where each student was starting out academically, produced lower and more realistic estimates. Notably, the only statistical model that could replicate the lottery-based result that students at this charter sometimes underperformed lottery losers in math was the fixed-effect model. This is an accomplishment given that selectivity bias led to large positive (and probably erroneous) estimated math effects in the simpler models. But for reading, fixed-effect estimates, for whatever reason, gave results that were in fact less optimistic than the experimental evidence. One possibility is that we used a longer and bigger sample that included all students who entered the Preuss School, by lottery or not.

The overall message to policy makers from this work is that simply looking at average test scores by school, such as those commonly published state accountability programs, tells us little if anything about the relative quality of instruction across schools.[6]

Should policy makers then turn to statistical models of charter effectiveness that adjust for student background? Simple regression models that try to explain the *level* of students' test scores are almost as misleading because they fail to take into account the past academic history of the student. Regression models that instead model gains in achievement come much closer to telling us whether the quality of instruction in charter schools differs from that provided in traditional public schools. These models, after all, attempt to take into account the student's past history by focusing only on current-year gains. Still, the disparities that remain across specification in the San Diego data suggest that the research community as a whole must remain vigilant against overselling the results of any regression analysis as definitively establishing the causal effect of charter schools themselves on student achievement. And policy makers, even when examining the latest shiny statistical models, would be wise to kick the tires before buying. At least now we have a clearer picture of what to look for: models of gains in achievement rather than levels of achievement, and, perhaps, fixed effects as well to control for unobserved variations across students.

APPENDIX

Appendix Table 2.1. Does the Sample with Test Score Gains Resemble the Sample with Levels but Not Gains? Evidence from the Reading Models

	Restricted Sample		Unrestricted Sample	
	(1) Test Score	*(2)* Test Score	*(3)* Test Score	*(4)* Test Score
Charter	−0.0113	−0.0098	−0.0171	−0.0122
	(0.0566)	(0.0395)	(0.0561)	(0.0407)
Observations	313535	313535	394121	394121
Number of Students	125356	125356	154037	154037
Controls for Student Characteristics	No	Yes	No	Yes
Student Random Effects	Yes	Yes	Yes	Yes
Student Fixed Effects	No	No	No	No

Notes: Standard errors in parentheses. All models allow for clustering at the school level.
* significant at 5%; ** significant at 1%
Models with student characteristics include controls for race and ethnicity, English learners, fluent English proficiency, and parental education.

The first two columns of this table repeat models 1 and 2 from table 3, while the third and fourth columns show the same specification but use the larger sample that is made available when observations that include the level of achievement, but not gains in achievement, are added back.

Appendix Table 2.2.   Does the Sample with Test Score Gains Resemble the Sample with Levels but Not Gains? Evidence from the Math Models

	Restricted Sample		Unrestricted Sample	
	(1) Test Score	*(2)* Test Score	*(3)* Test Score	*(4)* Test Score
Charter	−0.0110	0.0025	−0.0195	−0.0005
	(0.0592)	(0.0446)	(0.0564)	(0.0451)
Observations	313867	313867	392505	392505
Number of Students	124309	124309	152950	152950
Controls for Student Characteristics	No	Yes	No	Yes
Student Random Effects	Yes	Yes	Yes	Yes
Student Fixed Effects	No	No	No	No

Notes: Standard errors in parentheses. All models allow for clustering at the school level.
* significant at 5%; ** significant at 1%
Models with student characteristics include controls for race and ethnicity, English learners, fluent English proficiency, and parental education.

The first two columns of this table repeat models 1 and 2 from table 4, while the third and fourth columns show the same specification but use the larger sample that is made available when observations that include the level of achievement, but not gains in achievement, are added back.

NOTES

1. A recent literature review by Betts and Tang (2008) provides evidence that the effects of charter schools on achievement vary across grades and geographic areas.

2. See Coley (2002) for evidence that family income is positively and strongly related to cognitive development of children just entering school.

3. This model is the closest to the reassessment of NAEP data on charter schools published by the National Center for Education Statistics in 2005. This report typically showed no differences between the performance of students at charter schools and traditional public schools, or in a few cases, lower performance among charter school students. The study explicitly warned that many unobserved factors could contribute to the test scores of students at charter and traditional public schools. Nonetheless, its release generated considerable controversy over the question of whether one can use a single snapshot of test scores to judge charter school quality.

4. Clustering does not change regression coefficients but tends to increase standard errors. For instance, in the middle and high school models with student fixed effects, without clustering the standard error on the charter variable falls from 0.05 to 0.02 and from 0.04 to 0.03, respectively.

5. Notably, the authors do find that Preuss students complete significantly more college preparatory courses, and attend universities in significantly higher rates, than do lottery losers.

6. The implications of this apparently simple statement are important and far-ranging. For instance, the requirement under NCLB that states rank schools by the percentage of students scoring above a certain point on reading and math tests in a

given year will lead to a ranking that often will have little to do with the quality of instruction in each of these schools.

REFERENCES

Betts, J. R., and Tang, Y. E. (2008). *Value-Added and Experimental Studies of the Effect of Charter Schools on Student Achievement.* Seattle, WA: National Charter School Research Project, Center on Reinventing Public Education, University of Washington Bothell.

Betts, J. R., Rice, L. A., Zau, A. C., Tang, Y. E., and Koedel, C. R. (2006). *Does School Choice Work? Effects on Student Integration and Achievement.* San Francisco: Public Policy Institute of California.

Charter School Achievement Consensus Panel. (2006). *Key Issues in Studying Charter Schools and Achievement: A Review and Suggestions for National Guidelines.* NCSRP White Paper Series, No. 2. Seattle: Center on Reinventing Public Education.

Coley, R. J. (2002). *An Uneven Start: Indicators of Inequality in School Readiness.* Princeton, NJ: Educational Testing Service.

LaLonde, R. (1986). Evaluating the Econometric Evaluations of Training Programs with Experimental Data. *American Economic Review* (September), 604–20.

McClure, L., Strick, B., Jacob-Almeida, R., and Reicher, C. (2005). *The Preuss School at UCSD: School Characteristics and Students' Achievement.* The Center for Research on Educational Equity, Assessment and Teaching Excellence, University of California, San Diego. Download at http://create.ucsd.edu/, December 2005.

National Center for Education Statistics. (2005). *America's Charter Schools: Results from the NAEP 2003 Pilot Study.* Published as part of the National Assessment of Educational Progress, The Nation's Report Card, NCES 2005–456. Washington, DC: United States Department of Education.

Nelson, F. H., Rosenberg, B., and Van Meter, N. (2004). *Charter Achievement on the 2003 National Assessment of Educational Progress.* Washington, DC: American Federation of Teachers.

Tang, Y. E., and Betts, J. R. (2006). Student Achievement in Charter Schools in San Diego. Manuscript, Department of Economics. San Diego: University of California San Diego.

Chapter Three

Expanding What Counts When Evaluating Charter School Effectiveness

Laura S. Hamilton and Brian M. Stecher

INTRODUCTION

Most studies of the effectiveness of charter schools focus on student achievement measured using test scores on district or state tests. There is good reason for this focus. Although public schools are asked to promote a variety of outcomes, most of those who conduct and use charter school research agree on the primacy of academic achievement, and state and district standardized tests typically provide the least expensive and most readily available measures of achievement. Moreover, in the current environment of standards-based accountability, the use of tests that are aligned with state content standards is arguably an appropriate way to measure schools' effectiveness at promoting generally agreed-upon learning goals.

At the same time, reliance on standardized tests of reading, mathematics, and science (the requirements of No Child Left Behind and hence the default tests in most jurisdictions) provides at best an incomplete understanding of how charter schools are affecting the students they serve. Stakeholders, including parents, educators, and policy makers, are likely to be interested in other outcomes even while acknowledging that these test scores should be important indicators of charter school success. This is particularly true when charter schools adopt goals that differ from those adopted by existing public school systems.

This chapter examines some of the problems associated with relying solely on current state or district standardized test scores to measure charter school outcomes, and it identifies additional measures that could be incorporated into a more comprehensive set of indicators of charter school effectiveness. The goal of the chapter is to describe a more comprehensive set of outcome indicators that can help inform decisions about charter schools by parents, policy makers, and others. There are already efforts under way to develop indicator systems that report more than just test scores. For example, the University of Southern California's Center on Educational Governance has developed a system for reporting on charter school performance and operations, with a strong emphasis on finances, staffing, and test scores (see Brown, Wohlstetter, and Liu, 2008). Although it does not address all of the outcomes we discuss below, it provides a good model of the type of system we envision.

Although the focus of this chapter, and of the volume in which it appears, is on charter schools, the system of outcome indicators that we describe could also be applied to traditional public schools and to measuring the relative effectiveness of charter schools and traditional public schools. In fact, to the extent that the types of data described below are valuable for a wide variety of research, evaluation, and reporting purposes beyond those that concern charter schools (e.g., evaluating professional development initiatives, providing school-level reports to parents across all public school types), the costs of gathering them might be shared among several constituencies, thereby reducing the marginal cost of evaluating charter school performance. In addition, the data gathered could prove useful not only to researchers but also to policy makers who are interested in using performance information to make decisions about schools (see Hamilton, Stecher, and Yuan, 2008, for a discussion of indicators in the context of standards-based accountability).

MEASURING THE OUTCOMES OF CHARTER SCHOOLS

Charter schools, like all public schools, are charged with promoting a variety of outcomes deemed important to society. Most of these outcomes can be expressed in terms of the characteristics students possess after they complete their education. Specifically, public education is supposed to produce well-informed, productive, and civic-minded adults. Broadly speaking, these three adjectives represent the key outcomes that public schools are entrusted to develop and that people use to judge schools' effectiveness.

Although individuals might define the term *well-informed* differently, most people would agree that well-informed students have learned how to read well and compute efficiently. In addition, they possess basic knowledge of, and appreciation for, science, history and government, and the arts. In the context of today's standards-based accountability systems, it might be said that well-informed students have mastered the domains of learning embodied in state academic content standards. For the most part these standards are comprehensive and thorough. State standards usually include basic facts and simple procedures relating to each subject (for example, the multiplication tables and the algorithm for multiplying two-digit numbers), but they also typically include broader principles and higher-order reasoning skills used at advanced levels in a subject (for example, the distributive property of operations, quantitative reasoning, mathematical problem-solving skills).

The term *achievement* is widely used to describe this broad class of outcomes, i.e., what students know and are able to do in school subjects. For many people, achievement is the most important outcome of charter schools. Certainly, more resources are devoted to measuring achievement than any other public school outcome. As discussed below, annual, large-scale, multiple-choice testing in reading, mathematics, and (in selected grades) science is the most common measure of student achievement (and school outcomes) currently available.

As students mature through their school years, they reach various milestones that provide indirect indications of their achievement, and information about these milestones could supplement test-based achievement data. Being promoted from one grade to the next on schedule, completing enough years of high school mathematics courses to fulfill the state requirement, and graduating from high school provide indirect evidence of meeting educational goals. These metrics are commonly referred to as *attainment*, and, when schools' criteria for promotion and graduation are aligned with mastery of standards, measures of attainment go hand in hand with measures of achievement.

Schools are also designed to help students become productive adults, i.e., individuals who can find and hold a job, develop a worthwhile career, and become contributing members of society. There are many ways in which schools prepare students to achieve these goals. Career and vocational courses in high school help some students find employment both during and after high school. Majorities of students take courses that prepare them for postsecondary education, where they can earn associate, bachelor's, or advanced degrees that qualify them for specific careers. Some students focus their education on athletic, musical, or artistic pursuits that enable them to pursue careers in these fields. All four types of courses and activities (vocational, college preparatory, athletic, and artistic) contribute to students' development as productive members of society.

Moreover, schools can train students to work in teams, to communicate clearly, and to have good habits of behavior, all of which are valued by employers and will enhance students' careers. The importance of promoting these skills and habits is evident in recent discussions in which they have been described as "21st century skills" (Partnership for 21st Century Skills, 2008; Silva, 2008). These attributes might be developed through regular coursework but are also likely to be affected by participation in sports and other extracurricular activities. There is no simple term, analogous to achievement, for this broad class of outcomes, but most would be included under the heading "preparation for postsecondary education and employment."

Finally, schools are tasked with producing adults who are "civic-minded." By that phrase, we mean adults who understand the history of the country, know and endorse the principles embodied in our founding documents, and respect public institutions. Such citizens participate in civic life by paying taxes, voting, and otherwise contributing to their communities. At some points in our history, serving in the armed forces or alternative service was expected of young men, and schools played a role in facilitating that service. Schools still provide information and communication in this area.

The concept of civic-mindedness is difficult to define and hence to measure. For that reason and others, civic-mindedness, or "being a good citizen," is not always part of discussions about the quality of schools. However, civic-mindedness should not be overlooked when thinking about the outcomes of charter schools since it represents an important justification for the existence of public education in this country and is often cited as an outcome that might be harmed by choice-based school attendance policies (Wolf, 2005).

The remainder of the chapter examines these three types of outcomes in greater detail and describes measures that could be part of a more comprehensive system of indicators of charter school outcomes. We begin with achievement, discussing traditional measures of student achievement—large-scale tests—and then alternative achievement measures. Following that, we explore measures of productivity and civic-mindedness. We close with a brief discussion of other features of charter schools that might be included in a comprehensive indicator system as "leading indicators" of achievement because they provide necessary conditions for promoting achievement or they are strongly predictive of achievement. These include some structural features of schools and some aspects of the educational process.

MEASURING STUDENT
ACHIEVEMENT USING LARGE-SCALE TESTS

Studies of student achievement in charter schools typically rely on district or state assessments in mathematics or reading/language arts as the primary outcome measures. As noted earlier, such measures have important advantages, and in many cases they are likely to be the best available information on student achievement in charter schools, particularly for studies that combine information across schools or districts. There are, however, dangers associated with relying exclusively on these tests.

Limitations of Large-Scale Tests

Some of the problems inherent in the use of large-scale tests for evaluating charter school effectiveness are well-known and frequently discussed in the academic and policy communities, whereas other problems tend to be considered only among certain specialized groups of researchers. Perhaps the most obvious drawback of large-scale tests stems from the limited set of grades and subjects that are tested by most states and districts. Under NCLB, states are required to administer annual tests in mathematics and reading in grades three through eight and in one high school grade, as well as science tests in at least three grade levels. Although it is common for states to require additional testing in other grade levels and/or subjects, and for districts to supplement state tests with further testing, in most cases there are still grade levels and subjects that are untested or minimally tested.

The exclusion of certain subjects and grade levels leaves users of test-score data with incomplete information about how schools are improving student achievement. As noted above, most states have academic standards in a number of subjects that are not part of NCLB testing, and test scores provide no information about achievement in these subjects. These omissions are particularly problematic for secondary schools, which emphasize a wide variety of subjects other than reading and math, and for charter schools and other public schools that have a specific focus such as arts, foreign language, or science and technology.

Another limitation associated with the range of grades tested under NCLB is that in many cases it fails to provide information about student growth during the entire time students are enrolled in a school. For instance, at the elementary level, where many schools serve students in grades kindergarten through five, the typical NCLB testing schedule provides no information until the end of third grade, when students are two-thirds of the way through their time in those schools. Again, the high school data are often even less informative—if only one grade is tested, there is no way to measure gains. Of course, many states supplement with additional grades, but very few allow a comprehensive examination of student gains from school entry to exit.

NCLB requires that assessments be aligned with state standards, so that test scores tell users about student attainment of knowledge and skills the state has deemed important. But alignment studies have demonstrated that even when standards and tests are said to be aligned, most tests capture only a subset of the content contained in the standards. Furthermore, most large-scale tests tend to emphasize the lower-level skills that are easier to test (Rothman et al., 2002). Moreover, the traditional alignment study provides no assurance that the test measures what schools are actually teaching. As with many of the other problems discussed here, the issue is especially salient for high schools because most statewide NCLB tests are not course-specific. For example, gains on a measure of general mathematics achievement are unlikely to reflect the full extent of what was learned by students enrolled in geometry or other higher-level mathematics courses.

The availability of end-of-course assessments, which are increasingly being administered by states at the high school level, can provide a more appropriate way to examine achievement in these higher-level courses. However, there are other analytic challenges associated with end-of-course tests, such as lack of universal administration and the fact that students take these tests at different times during their high school careers. These differences lessen the validity of comparisons across time or across schools based on end-of-course tests.

There are additional problems associated with test results in the context of accountability that could lead to distorted information. Most of the large-scale tests currently in use are part of accountability systems that have high stakes for educators, students, or both. A large body of research suggests that attaching high stakes to scores can lead to a phenomenon known as score inflation, i.e., gains in test scores that overstate actual improvement in achievement (Linn, 2000; Hamilton, 2003; Koretz, 2002). Test scores may not accurately reflect student knowledge of the subject if teachers shift their instruction to focus only on tested material in the format used by the test, and to devote excessive time to focused test preparation. In addition, NCLB's emphasis on reporting in terms of percent proficient may encourage reallocation of teachers' attention to particular students in ways that also distort the meaning of the information. The method for calculating AYP creates incentives to maximize the number of students who score above the proficient threshold. This incentive can lead to a focus on students who are most likely to move across the proficient threshold, called "bubble kids" by some teachers, and reduce resources or attention on students whose scores are well above or well below that threshold. There is some evidence that teachers and schools have increased their focus on students near proficient (Booher-Jennings, 2005; Stecher et al., 2008), but there is mixed evidence regarding how, if at all, this focus affects the distributions or validity of scores from state tests (Neal and Schanzenbach, 2007; Reback, 2008; Springer, 2008). Nonetheless, it is important to keep in mind not only the limited information available from a percent-proficient approach to reporting but also the possibility that it creates incentives that run counter to what we expect schools to do.

It is also worth noting that the validity of information from tests stems not only from the content of the tests but also from how scores are combined and used. For example, for many purposes, measures of student growth are likely to be more informative and lead to more accurate inferences about school performance than are status measures. The chapter by Betts, Tang, and Zau in this volume addresses this issue in the context of charter schools.

OTHER MEASURES OF STUDENT ACHIEVEMENT

One way to address the limitations of existing standardized tests is to combine information from these tests with information from other available measures of student achievement. These might include district-administered assessments that are not part of the state or district accountability system, interim or benchmark assessments, or student work samples that are gathered in a systematic way. Some of these measures, such as benchmark testing systems, are designed to provide information similar to what is obtained through state tests, but at more frequent intervals. Others, such as student work samples, can be useful for examining students' acquisition of skills and knowledge that are not measured by standardized tests, such as the ability to prepare a well-researched essay. It is critical, however, that users of this information refrain from making inferences or decisions for which these measures have not been validated. For example, scores from interim assessments might not be sufficiently reliable to support their use for public reporting or evaluation purposes.

Some supplemental measures might be especially useful for measuring aspects of achievement that are often not captured by commonly used paper-and-pencil tests. For example, school reformers, educators, and business leaders often describe the importance of generic attributes such as the ability to solve complex problems, use technology, and work collaboratively (see Partnership for 21st Century Skills, 2008). Few of these attributes are measured by the tests that are currently administered to public school students, but they are not "unmeasureable," and recent test-development efforts have moved us closer to being able to capture evidence of such skills in a reasonably cost-effective way (see Silva, 2008, for a discussion of several advances in this area). Supplemental information could also prove useful at those charter schools that have a curricular focus that does not align strongly with state standards and assessments.

Stakeholders might also be interested in scores on tests that are taken by a subset of the student population but that might be useful for examining some aspects of charter school achievement. These measures include college admissions tests and Advanced Placement exams. All of these additional measures have limitations that researchers do not face when using large-scale standardized state tests. The limitations include the selective nature of the population of students who take some of these tests, the lack of consistent measures over time for some tests, and the lack of standardized administration conditions, particularly for interim tests and work samples.

There is an additional limitation that applies to all of the achievement measures discussed so far, including large-scale tests and alternative measures. Measures from different jurisdictions, be they states or districts, cannot easily be combined. Local assessments selected by districts are not the same from one district to the next, so it is challenging to make valid comparisons using these additional measures across districts in the same state. State tests differ, as well, and it is problematic to combine results across states to try to create national estimates. Even the measures discussed in the previous paragraph that are national in scope, e.g., Advanced Placement examinations, are not administered to all students or even to the same types of students across districts or states. There is currently no measure of achievement that can provide good national estimates of charter school effectiveness. Any effort to combine information across jurisdictions using different tests will need to address differences in content, format, difficulty, severity of stakes, and other characteristics of the tests and the accountability systems in which they are embedded.

MEASURING OUTCOMES OTHER THAN ACHIEVEMENT

Although the primacy of achievement test scores in most charter school studies is understandable and generally appropriate, a complete understanding of the educational effects of charter schools requires a broader focus, including other indicators of student progress toward achievement (i.e., attainment), and indicators of productivity and civic-mindedness. Some of these outcomes can be measured while students are still enrolled in the school, or immediately after they leave, whereas others are not observed until many years after students have left the school. The relevance of these outcomes to charter school effectiveness may vary by level (elementary, secondary) but they are likely to be considered important outcomes for any family that chooses a charter school, regardless of level.[1]

Attainment

Graduation Rates

The likelihood that a student will receive a high school diploma is arguably one of the most important academic outcomes to consider when examining charter school effects. A number of methods have been developed to measure graduation rates (e.g., Greene and Winters, 2006). Each approach involves certain decisions about how to create both the numerator and the denominator — for example, whether to follow students for four, five, or more years, whether to adjust for the fact that ninth grade cohorts are often larger than other cohorts because of the relatively larger number of students who are retained in ninth grade, and how to deal with students who are missing data (e.g., because they moved out of the district or state).

Most of the current national- and state-level estimates are based on using data from successive cohorts of students; i.e., comparing the number of graduates in 2006 with the number of ninth grade students in 2002, perhaps after adjusting for the number of students likely to have been retained in ninth grade. More accurate measures of graduation rates could be developed through the use of longitudinally linked data on individual students. As more states develop data systems that provide such data, better measures of graduation rates are likely to follow. Although graduation is clearly most relevant for high school students, it might also become a long-term indicator of success in elementary and middle school. If new data systems provide a way to follow students as they move from one school to another, it will become possible to examine ways in which elementary and middle schools might differ in their production of students who will eventually graduate from high school. Recent analyses of charter schools in Chicago and Florida have taken advantage of data improvements in these jurisdictions to incorporate both graduation rates and postsecondary attendance into their examination of charter school effectiveness (Booker et al., 2008).

Retention/Promotion Rates

Examining how many students are retained in a grade, and what their characteristics are, is helpful for understanding how charter schools affect educational attainment and could be important for interpreting test-score trends. As with high school graduation rates, longitudinally linked individual student data provide the best hope for measuring promotion rates accurately. These rates are likely to vary across states and districts, in part as a function of policy differences surrounding promotion criteria.

Transfers to Other Schools

Although transfers might not be considered an outcome of interest for most schools, the numbers of students who transfer out of a school and the types of schools into which they transfer (for example, alternative schools) are particularly relevant for understanding how charter schools affect the students who attend them.

Productivity

Enrollment in College-Preparatory or Advanced Coursework

One measure of a high school's contribution to the development of productive adults is the percentage of students who complete the courses required to qualify for college admission. The economic returns from a college degree are large, and high schools can boost students' access to college and their future productivity by ensuring that they complete the necessary preparatory courses. Further, high schools can accelerate students' progress through college by offering advanced coursework, such as Advanced Placement or International Baccalaureate classes. Enrollment in advanced coursework at the secondary level can also be considered a relevant outcome to examine for elementary and middle schools. For example, middle schools that do not make algebra or prealgebra widely available might produce students who are excluded from taking the more advanced mathematics courses in high school.

College Readiness

An additional postsecondary measure that is important to examine, when possible, is the degree to which students who graduate from a particular charter school are adequately prepared for college. One way to measure this is to examine whether students enroll in remedial coursework once they get to college.

Postsecondary Educational Attainment

Where students go after they complete their K–12 schooling is probably one of the outcomes of greatest interest to parents as well as policy makers. These data have rarely been available in the past because most states do not have data systems to follow individuals through school and into postsecondary education and employment. Although the data needs are daunting, some states are developing data systems that will permit some tracking of students between K–12 education and large public institutions of higher education. These states will be able to track important postsecondary educational outcomes, including the percentage of students who attend two- and four-year colleges, the percentage who eventually receive degrees, the quality of institutions attended, and the specific degree programs pursued. In the near future, the first and second of these outcomes are the most likely to be measurable, and even these might be limited depending on factors such as how many students attend schools out of state.[2] As noted above, Booker et al. (2008)

recently conducted a charter school analysis that incorporated data on post-secondary attendance.

Employment and Earnings

Some students will choose not to attend college immediately after graduating from high school, and for these students it would be of interest to know something about the types of careers they pursue and how much they earn. Employment and earnings could also be examined for students who do attend postsecondary institutions. At present, states maintain information about employment and earnings in their unemployment insurance files and some states have begun linking these data to education data (see Carey, 2006, for an illustration of the utility of this information for evaluating postsecondary institution quality).

Enrollment in Occupational/Vocational Programs

Many students benefit from taking occupational and vocational courses while in high school, whether they drop out of school to work, go to work immediately after graduation, or enroll in postsecondary education. In fact, a large proportion of students take at least one vocational course during their high school careers. Completion of a connected sequence of vocational courses provides some students with occupational training that contributes directly to their employment and productivity. For instance, among students who enter the labor market directly after high school, taking vocational courses is associated with higher wages (Mane, 1999). Other students take high school vocational courses that connect to postsecondary technical training, in fields such as nursing or information technology, thus boosting their prospects for employment. Vocational course taking provides another indicator of a school's contribution to the eventual productivity of its students.

Civic-Mindedness

Civic Values

Critics of school choice, including charter schools, sometimes worry that the creation of schools that do not follow the common school model embodied by traditional public education will lead to citizens who are less civic-minded. On the other hand, the presence of an active, vital charter school sector could foster engagement with schools, public debate about education, and enhanced civic-mindedness on a broad scale. Although some of the desired outcomes are difficult to measure, a number of scales have been developed to capture information about specific competencies, attitudes, or activities related to civic values. Wolf (2005) summarizes his work examining civic outcomes related to school choice and describes measures of constructs such as tolerance, political participation (e.g., voting), political knowledge, and volunteerism. Many of these measures have been widely used in large-scale studies (see, e.g., Campbell, 2001), and have been shown to work well for secondary and postsecondary students as well as adults.

Civic Actions

Similarly, it might be possible to measure the extent to which charter school students or graduates engage in activities that demonstrate civic participation, such as voting or volunteering.

LEADING INDICATORS OF CHARTER SCHOOL OUTCOMES

Although this chapter focuses primarily on outcomes, there may be benefits to incorporating other measures into charter school outcome studies. In particular, some information about conditions in the schools (e.g., facilities and other inputs) and about educational processes (e.g., classroom practices) will produce a more informative picture of charter school effectiveness and might shed light on the sources of differences in outcomes among charter schools or between charter and traditional public schools. We briefly discuss selected structure and process measures.

There are some features of schools that represent preconditions necessary to support positive school outcomes that can add to studies of charter schools. The rationale for considering such indicators is that if these conditions are not present, outcomes are likely to suffer. Similarly, if the status of these conditions changes, there will likely be changes in outcomes. Some examples of key conditions in charter schools include safety, teacher quality, and class size.[3]

Safety

Unsafe and dangerous schools threaten students' well-being and interfere with their learning, so it is appropriate to measure whether charter schools offer safe havens for learning. While it is relatively easy to measure serious threats to safety that reach the level of police involvement, it is more difficult to measure the availability of alcohol and drugs, or the presence of threats, bullying, and intimidation. Several surveys and other data collection techniques have been developed to assess the severity of these problems (Juvonen et al., 2004).

Teacher Quality

Although we cannot say with certainty exactly what characteristics define effective teachers, it is clear that good teachers are necessary for learning. At a minimum, studies of charter schools should determine whether teachers have sufficient knowledge in the subject(s) they teach. Research evidence suggests that subject matter knowledge is an important characteristic of effective teachers, particularly at the secondary level. Efforts by some teacher preparation programs to maintain data on preservice teachers and follow them into the schools where they teach after they graduate could prove useful for evaluating teacher quality in a deeper way than has typically been done.

Class Size

There is some experimental evidence that class size matters in student learning, particularly in the early grades. One widely cited study suggests that students in smaller classes in kindergarten through third grade learned more than students in larger classes, and these gains persisted through high school.[4] Class size should not be confused with the overall pupil-to-teacher ratio, and care needs to be taken that measures of class size reflect the actual number of students in each classroom.

Some educational processes are strongly associated with positive outcomes, and measures of these processes can be included in evaluations of the effectiveness of charter schools. For example, most students learn through interactions with teachers, textbooks, support materials, and other students, and measures of such learning activities can predict later achievement. These process measures can be thought of as "leading indicators" that predict changes in the outcomes discussed previously. In addition, process indicators can provide information to help us understand the effects, or lack of effects, of charter schools and to explore variations in effects across different types of charter schools. The most important process measures are those that relate directly to learning, including opportunities to learn, learning time, the use of effective teaching methods, and student participation in learning. In addition, there are indirect measures of effective practice that may produce useful information about long-term effectiveness, such as parent satisfaction. Finally, we include some intermediate outcomes in the list, for they can also serve as leading indicators of achievement.

Exposure to Content

Students are unlikely to learn content they have not seen, and therefore indicators of exposure to content can reveal important information. At the elementary level, exposure to content has been measured through teacher reports of content coverage and reviews of curriculum materials. At the secondary level, exposure can also be measured in terms of access to, and participation in, courses and course sequences that lead to mastery of advanced content.

Effective Curriculum and Instruction

A school's choices regarding curriculum and instructional strategies should reflect current knowledge of what works most effectively with the students being served. Ideally, charter schools should be using textbooks and materials that have been validated through empirical research, and teachers should be using instructional approaches that have had similar study. At present, the research base for making decisions about curriculum and instruction is generally limited. Nevertheless, it is helpful to gather information about curriculum and instruction as a formative tool for thinking about charter school improvement and as a comparative tool for understanding differences in performance among charter schools and between charter and traditional schools. Information about the depth and cognitive complexity of both instructional content and pedagogy is especially important for predicting later outcomes (Gamoran et al., 1997).

Provision of Services to Students with Special Needs

Charter schools are sometimes criticized for neglecting the needs of special education students or for discouraging such students from applying. Information should be provided on the numbers and classifications of students with disabilities as well as the services provided to them. Much of this information is already available. In addition, services provided to English Language Learners (ELL) should be documented. Information about the percentages of ELL who are reclassified as non-ELL would provide evidence of success at serving these students.

Time on Task

The amount of learning time in the school day is strongly predictive of achievement. Time on task can be measured broadly in terms of the length of school day and year, but more sophisticated measures would focus on the time students spend engaged in learning activities.

Instructional Support

Learning involves more than just a teacher and a group of students. The learning process is facilitated by a variety of supporting materials and equipment, including textbooks and supplemental learning materials, supplies, and equipment for experimentation, libraries with current reference materials, access to the Internet and online resources, and supplemental staff with expertise in science, mathematics, or other complex subject matter. All these types of learning supports can be measured with relative ease.

Attendance

Students who are not present in school are unlikely to learn, and sustained poor attendance is associated with poor academic performance. Most schools have high attendance rates, in part because they are reimbursed on the basis of attendance. This incentive may even lead to inflated reports. Nevertheless, large differences in attendance rates are likely to be predictive of outcomes, and they are easy enough to obtain from existing records.

Participation in Athletic and Arts Programs

We think of participation in athletic and artistic programs as intermediate outcomes because they may lead to higher achievement and mastery of skills that have career implications. Some people would argue that all students should participate in athletic activities to train their bodies and in artistic activities to train their aesthetic sense for their own sake, and they should be measured as elements of a complete education. Whether one agrees with these claims or not, most people would agree that athletic and artistic performance opens the way to work and careers for some students and that these activities foster other desirable attributes, such as improved health, perseverance, discipline, and the ability to work in teams.

A recent study suggests that for many students, participation in sports or in leadership roles in other activities was more strongly associated with post-secondary attendance and earnings than were test scores (Deke and Haimson, 2006). Therefore, access to and participation in quality athletic and artistic programs can be considered an advance indicator of outcomes. It might also be useful to measure the strength of these programs in terms of the success of individuals and teams in competitions, both athletic and artistic. A charter school with an award-winning band or art program will be more attractive to many parents than one without.

PARENT SATISFACTION

Charter schools depend on parent satisfaction for their existence, and it seems sensible to include measures of satisfaction as an indicator of how well schools are meeting the needs of students and families. It can be difficult to interpret ratings of parent satisfaction because they are quite subjective. For example, research suggests that parents are generally satisfied with their child's school while holding negative opinions about the public schools in general. Nevertheless, strong negative ratings about a school are a sign of problems and are likely to be predictive of negative outcomes. Alternative indicators of satisfaction, such as the length of "wait lists" to enroll in a school, might provide a more objective indicator of satisfaction.

SETTING PRIORITIES

The preceding sections provided a long list of measures that could be useful for a variety of purposes related to charter schools and to public education more generally. Of course, this long wish list is unlikely to become a reality any time in the near future, so it is worth considering which measures deserve highest priority. This decision should combine feasibility and cost considerations with the likely value or importance of the information for understanding how schools are performing.

Clearly achievement is of central importance to almost anyone interested in charter school performance, and achievement test-score data in reading and mathematics are already being gathered at all levels of the system. A first priority for improving the evaluation of charter schools (and the public education system in general) would be to broaden the academic content that is regularly measured through traditional methods. Science testing is a requirement of NCLB beginning in 2006–2007, and it might be beneficial to have regular measures of other subjects as well, including history, social studies, foreign languages, etc. This measurement would not necessarily have to take place every year or for every student; using matrix sampling, alternative year testing or alternative grade testing can keep the testing burden reasonable and minimize the likelihood that the tests will exert negative effects on instruction.

Another priority should be to develop data-collection approaches that make existing test-score data accessible and useful for analytic purposes while simultaneously exploring ways to improve the validity of information from test scores.

A third priority is the accurate collection of information falling under our "attainment" heading: graduation rates, promotion rates, and transfer. Some of this information is already required under NCLB and many state laws, though its quality varies.

Once the achievement and attainment measures are in place and integrated into a usable data system, districts and schools should start exploring the feasibility of gathering information on productivity, civic values, and on some of the leading indicators—particularly exposure to content and quality of curriculum and instruction—while states and large districts should work with other organizations toward the goal of developing a data system that tracks students into their postsecondary years. A system with all of the components we discussed may not be attainable for many years, but the list provides a number of fruitful directions that can be pursued at all levels of the education system.

Another factor that could be considered when evaluating priorities is the extent to which each of the indicators provides information that is redundant with other indicators. For example, if test scores were highly correlated with postsecondary outcomes, one might conclude that the latter do not need to be collected since we already gather the former. However, most of the correlations among the outcomes (where these have been measured) are not so high as to suggest redundancy. Moreover, the nature of relationships between test scores and other outcomes is likely to change as the role of testing changes. In particular, we do not know how well the high-stakes, standards-based assessments that states are administering predict later outcomes or how the predictive power of these tests is likely to change as schools increasingly align their curriculum and instruction with those tests. It is also not clear how well some of the leading indicators, such as exposure to content, will predict either test scores or postsecondary outcomes. Several years' worth of data from a comprehensive system would be needed before conclusions about redundancies could be made with confidence.

RESPONSIBILITY FOR DATA GATHERING

Any recommendation for new data collection should be accompanied by a discussion of who bears the responsibility for gathering the data. Although there are a number of ways in which responsibility could be assigned, some data types are probably best gathered at the state level, whereas others could be most effectively collected at a lower level of the education system.

Logical candidates for state-level efforts include data that are already part of statewide systems and those that combine information across multiple schools or contexts. These include scores on state achievement tests as well as some of the postsecondary outcomes that would require coordination with other large databases. By contrast, individual schools are probably in the best position to maintain information about other testing programs, such as SAT, ACT, and AP, and about college applications and acceptances. Graduation rates and other measures of attainment might require school-level input but should be coordinated at the district or state level and should be informed by standardized instructions for recording the information. Coordination with state-level databases is particularly important for determining whether students dropped out or transferred to another school.

Some of the additional data sources we discussed require the administration of surveys or other data-collection instruments. These probably require the combined efforts of school and district-level staff, with monitoring from an outside body to ensure data quality and reduce the likelihood of inaccurate reporting. Clearly a comprehensive data-gathering effort requires the cooperation of educators, administrators, and other staff at all levels of the system, along with appropriate monitoring and oversight activities.

CONCLUSION

This chapter listed a wide variety of outcomes and processes that are relevant for understanding how charter schools affect the students who attend them. We recognize that it is unrealistic to expect that all of this information will be available for any school in the near future. The list was intended in part to help users of information about charter schools understand how to put the available information—such as test scores—in context. Most studies and reports on charter school performance are limited to a small number of indicators of success, and a lot more information would be needed to gain a full understanding of how well charter schools are performing. Nonetheless, increasing availability of high-quality data, information, and dissemination systems are likely to provide opportunities to expand stakeholders' access to indicators of charter school performance, so it is worth thinking about what a comprehensive indicator system should include.

In this final section we discuss a few key issues that will have to be addressed as we move forward with efforts to increase access to information about charter school performance.

The first obstacle, mentioned several times in this chapter, is lack of data. Some of the outcomes and processes we discussed are not currently measured in most cases, and when they are measured, they may not be measured well. Other outcomes and processes might be measured, but we lack the data infrastructure to link these measures to other student information in a way that will allow us to interpret them accurately. For example, although there are student records that indicate whether a student received a diploma, these records are of limited value if they are not part of a larger data system that allows us to track students over time. Many states and districts are engaged in efforts to improve their data systems, and these efforts are likely to be enhanced by national initiatives such as the U.S. Department of Education's pilot program to allow states to explore the use of growth models for AYP calculations.

Developing data systems that follow students from the K–12 system into college and the workplace is an especially challenging endeavor, but some states are beginning to explore methods for doing so. One such effort is being carried out by the Texas School Project at the University of Texas at Dallas, which is developing a database to follow high school seniors into postsecondary institutions.[5]

A second concern stems from the well-known problem, discussed earlier, that performance measures are often corrupted, particularly when high stakes are attached to them. One of the advantages of a system that uses multiple measures of school performance is that it is more resistant to corruption than a system based on a single or a small set of measures (Koretz, 2003). Still, it is important for developers of indicator systems to devise strategies for monitoring the validity of the measures over time, and in cases where corruption is evident or likely, to develop audit mechanisms to detect it. The problem of test-score inflation provides a good example of the kind of corruption that can occur, but the other measures discussed in this chapter might also be manipulated and should be monitored.

Another issue that must be addressed is the fact that different stakeholder groups are likely to value different types of information. District administrators who are using information to decide whether to expand the number of charter schools in their districts are likely to be interested in a somewhat different set of measures than parents who are deciding whether to send their children to a charter school. State policy makers who are considering legislation related to the establishment or governance of charter schools may have still different priorities. It is possible that a comprehensive system of indicators could meet the needs of all users, but it is more likely that in order to provide stakeholders with information that will help them make good decisions and to avoid information overload, different sets of indicators will need to be provided to different groups. Therefore, any comprehensive system of indicators should be accompanied by a flexible system of reporting that allows reports to be tailored to specific purposes.

We discussed earlier the problem of corruption that can occur when high stakes are attached to a few prominent outcome measures. By including a specific outcome in the system, policy makers are sending a message about the importance of that outcome, and this message is likely to influence educators' behaviors. An opposite problem can occur if too many outcomes are identified as important. Educators' efforts can be so diffuse that they lose their potency. Developers have to walk a fine line between comprehensiveness and focus, striving to identify a "valid, useful and parsimonious set of indicators" (Shavelson, McDonnell, and Oakes, 1989, p. 9). The set of outcome measures should reflect an understanding of how schools operate and the goals that society has for its public schools.

A final, related issue is the fact that one goal of the charter movement is to promote diversity in curricular focus. We need to consider the extent to which we expect the same outcomes of all charter schools and in what instances we are willing to accept differences that result from variation in curriculum, instruction, or other school characteristics. We probably want to see a high level of reading and math proficiency regardless of whether a school focuses on a college-preparatory curriculum or on the arts, but other outcomes might be expected to vary. Charter schools with a thematic focus, such as business, health, or technology, may reasonably be expected to achieve different outcomes than charter schools with a more general focus.

Perhaps the right approach is to think about a common core of outcomes supplemented by a focused set relating to the school's theme or emphasis. Again, a comprehensive set of indicators that allows for customization might be a way of addressing the fact that there is a core set of outcomes that should be of interest for all schools and an additional set that might be of primary interest for certain types of schools.

Charter school outcomes are rich and varied, and the reading and mathematics test scores currently produced by states provide at best an incomplete picture of their effectiveness. The message of this chapter is that it is possible to expand the way we measure school outcomes to better reflect the goals of charter schools, thus providing more useful information for students, parents, school administrators, and policy makers, all of whom make decisions that influence the success of charter schools.

NOTES

1. Although we do not discuss research methodology in this chapter, it is worth pointing out that some of the approaches used to evaluate achievement outcomes (such as student "fixed-effects" models) cannot be used for one-time events such as high school graduation. High-quality analyses will require sophisticated longitudinal modeling approaches; e.g., survival analysis for graduation rates, comparisons of trajectories for earnings.

2. A good example of an attempt to use information about postsecondary outcomes is the study of the Preuss School at the University of California San Diego. Research-

ers interviewed lottery winners and losers and compared them on several measures of postsecondary preparation and attainment (McClure et al., 2005).

3. Other structural features such as school size are likely to be of interest to some stakeholders, but we focus here on a small number of structural features that are most likely to be related to outcomes.

4. The experimental evidence is strong. See Jeremy D. Finn and Charles M. Achilles, "Answers and Questions about Class Size: A Statewide Experiment," *American Educational Research Journal* 27, no. 3 (1990): 557–77. The real-world evidence is limited because few places have done class-size reduction well. For example, in California there was a marked decline in the average preparation of teachers after implementation of a class-size reduction program, which may have reduced potential benefits.

5. See http://www.utdallas.edu/news/archive/2006/student-tracking-database .html.

REFERENCES

Booher-Jennings, J. (2005). Below the Bubble: "Educational Triage" and the Texas Accountability System. *American Educational Research Journal*, 42, 231–68.

Booker, K., Sass, T. R., Gill, B., and Zimmer, R. (2008). *Going Beyond Test Scores: Evaluating Charter School Impact on Educational Attainment in Chicago and Florida.* Santa Monica, CA: RAND.

Brown, R., Wohlstetter, P., and Liu, S., (2008). Developing an Indicator System for Schools of Choice: A Balanced Scorecard Approach. *Journal of School Choice* 2(4), 392–41.

Campbell, D. E. (2001). Making Democratic Education Work. In P. E. Peterson and D. E. Campbell (Eds.), *Charters, Vouchers, and Public Education* (pp. 241–67). Washington, DC: Brookings.

Carey, K. (2006). *College Rankings Reformed: The Case for a New Order in Higher Education.* Washington, DC: Education Sector.

Deke, J., and Haimson, J. (2006). *Valuing Student Competencies: Which Ones Predict Postsecondary Educational Attainment and Earnings, and for Whom?* Princeton, NJ: Mathematica Policy Research, Inc.

Gamoran, A., Porter, A. C., Smithson, J., and White, P. A. (1997). Upgrading High School Math Instruction: Improving Learning Opportunities for Low-achieving, Low-income Youth. *Educational Evaluation and Policy Analysis,* 19, 325–38.

Greene, J., and Winters, M. (2006). *Leaving Boys Behind: Public High School Graduation Rates.* Center for Civic Innovation. Civic Report No. 48. Download at http://www.manhattan-institute.org/pdf/cr_48.pdf.

Hamilton, L. S. (2003). Assessment as a Policy Tool. *Review of Research in Education,* 27, 25–68.

Hamilton, L. S., Stecher, B. M., and Yuan, K. (2008). *Standards-based Reform in the United States: History, Research, and Future Directions.* Washington, DC: Center on Education Policy.

Juvonen, J., Le, V., Kaganoff, T., Augustine, C. H., and Constant, L. (2004). *Focus on the Wonder Years: Challenges Facing the American Middle School.* Santa Monica, CA: RAND.

Koretz, D. (2002). Limitations in the Use of Achievement Tests as Measures of Educators' Productivity. In E. Hanushek, J. Heckman, and D. Neal (Eds.), *Designing Incentives to Promote Human Capital.* Special issue of the *Journal of Human Resources,* 37:4 (Fall), 752–77.

Koretz, D. (2003). Using Multiple Measures to Address Perverse Incentives and Score Inflation. *Educational Measurement: Issues and Practice,* 22:2, 18–26.

Linn, R. L. (2000). Assessments and Accountability. *Educational Researcher,* 29:2, 4–16.

Mane, F. (1999). Trends in the Payoff to Academic and Occupation-specific Skills: The Short and Medium Run Returns to Academic and Vocational High School Courses for Non-college-Bound Students. *Economics of Education Review,* 18:4, 417–37.

McClure, L., Strick, B., Jacob-Almeida, R., and Reicher, C. (2005). The Preuss School at UCSD: School Characteristics and Students' Achievement. La Jolla, CA: Center for Research on Educational Equity, Assessment and Teaching Excellence, UCSD.

Neal, D., and Schanzenbach, D. W. (2007). *Left Behind by Design: Proficiency Counts and Test-based Accountability.* Washington, DC: American Enterprise Institute.

Partnership for 21st Century Skills. (2008). *21st Century Skills, Education, and Competitiveness: A Resource and Policy Guide.* Download at http://www.21stcentury skills.org/documents/21st_century_skills_education_and_competitiveness_guide .pdf, September 26, 2008.

Reback, R. (2008). Teaching to the Rating: School Accountability and the Distribution of Student Achievement. *Journal of Public Economics,* 92, 1394–1415.

Rothman, R., Slattery, J. B., Vranek, J. L., and Resnick, L. B. (2002). *Benchmarking and Alignment of Standards and Testing.* CSE Technical Report 566. Los Angeles: Center for Research on Evaluation, Standards, and Student Testing.

Shavelson, R., McDonnell, L., and Oakes, J. (Eds.). (1989). *Indicator Systems for Monitoring Mathematics and Science Education.* R-3570-NSF. Santa Monica: RAND.

Silva, E. (2008). *Measuring Skills for the 21st Century.* Washington, DC: Education Sector.

Springer, Matthew G. (2008). Accountability Incentives: Do Schools Practice Educational Triage? *Education Next,* 8:1, 74–9.

Stecher, B. M., Epstein, S., Hamilton, L. S., Marsh, J. A., Robyn, A., McCombs, J. S., Russell, J. L., and Naftel, S. (2008). *Pain and Gain: Implementing No Child Left Behind in California, Georgia, and Pennsylvania, 2004 to 2006.* Santa Monica, CA: RAND.

Wolf, P. (2005). School Choice and Civic Values. In J. R. Betts and T. Loveless (Eds.), *Getting Choice Right: Ensuring Equity and Efficiency in Education Policy* (pp. 210–44). Washington, DC: Brookings Institution Press.

Chapter Four

The Effect of Attending Charter Schools on Achievement, Educational Attainment, and Behavioral Outcomes: A Review

Julian R. Betts

INTRODUCTION

This chapter reviews the research on whether charter schools affect student outcomes. Understandably, in this era of accountability and state testing, the bulk of research to date has focused foursquare on student test scores. However, as economists often point out, test scores are related only weakly to adult outcomes such as earnings and whether students graduate from high school or attend college. The prior chapter by Laura Hamilton and Brian Stecher provides a rich framework for thinking about the diverse goals of public education, listing many outcomes beyond test scores that researchers might want to study. Researchers are just now beginning to look at the effect of attending a charter school on some of these other outcomes. The final section of this chapter will review work on these alternative outcomes, which so far have focused mainly on variants of educational attainment, such as high school graduation.[1]

AN UPDATE ON THE LITERATURE ON CHARTER SCHOOLS AND ACHIEVEMENT

Betts and Tang (2008a, b) provide an overview and a more detailed description, respectively, of a meta-analysis of all work on charter schools and achievement that they could find published as of mid- to late 2008. They made the decision to focus on studies that had used either lottery data or value-added models that take into account students' past test scores, based on evidence in chapter 2 and as outlined by the Charter School Achievement Consensus Panel (2006), because these methods are more likely than weaker methods to produce unbiased estimates of the causal effect of attending a charter school on student achievement. Remarkably, of roughly seventy studies they considered, only thirteen studies conformed to these two approaches—three lottery-based studies and ten value-added studies.

Betts and Tang found evidence that in some grades and locations charters outperformed traditional public schools, and in other grades and locations they underperformed. Overall, when weighting studies by the number of charters in each study, they found more evidence of positive achievement effects of charter schools than negative, but again the results varied by grade and subject.

One can summarize the literature by examining the percentage of studies that found significant negative or positive results. Alternatively, one can calculate the overall distribution of effect sizes. (Effect sizes in this context refer to the predicted number of standard deviations by which test scores would change in one school year if a student switched to a charter school.)

Betts and Tang found that the majority of estimated effects of charter schools are positive. This imbalance is sometimes mild, but in some cases, such as for reading scores in elementary schools and for math scores in middle schools, the literature strongly suggests that charter schools are outperforming traditional public schools. There are important exceptions. Charter high schools appear to underperform significantly in math. In several cases of specific grade spans and test subjects, Betts and Tang find considerable evidence of both positive and negative effects of charter schools, with variations by geographic location.

Betts and Tang (2008b) provide cautions about the dangers of drawing nationwide conclusions from the studies they examined because of the relatively narrow geographic coverage of the studies they included. The states studied included Texas, Florida, North Carolina, Delaware, and Idaho. Other studies included four districts in California, charter schools in New York City, and three charter schools in Chicago. They report that their pessimistic results for high school math derive from Texas, Idaho, Delaware, and a small number of large urban districts in California.

Another way to look at the data is to study the effect sizes rather than the signs of the estimated effects. Table 4.1, reproduced from Betts and Tang (2008b), shows the median effect sizes for math and reading by grade span studied. The three columns show results when we weight each study equally, when we weight each study by the number of charter schools in the study samples, and when we weight by the product of the number of charter schools and the number of years of data included in the study. A weakness of the first (unweighted) approach is that it gives equal importance to a study of one charter as it gives to a statewide study of 1,000 charter schools. The two

Table 4.1. Median Effect Sizes on Math and Reading Scores from Attending a Charter School Based on Studies Examined by Betts and Tang (2008b)

		(1) *Unweighted*	*(2)* *Weighted by #* *of schools*	*(3)* *Weighted by # of* *schools* x *#* of years
All studies	Math	0.0305	0.00519	0.00519
		(19)	(1,277)	(6,044)
	Reading	0.0197	0.0175	0.0220
		(16)	(1,243)	(5,976)
Elementary	Math	0.0863	0.0807	0.0807
		(6)	(300)	(1,854)
	Reading	0.039	0.086	0.086
		(5)	(288)	(1,830)
Elementary and	Math	0.0807	0.0807	0.0807
Combined		(7)	(367)	(2,256)
Elementary/Middle	Reading	0.0363	0.086	0.086
		(6)	(355)	(2,232)
Middle	Math	.00519	.00519	.00519
		(5)	(226)	(1,879)
	Reading	−.00460	.0220	.0220
		(4)	(213)	(1,853)
Middle and	Math	0.00519	0.00519	0.00519
Combined		(5)	(232)	(1,927)
Middle/High	Reading	0.00659	0.0220	0.0220
		(4)	(219)	(1,901)
High	Math	−0.0206	−0.215	−0.0155
		(4)	(190)	(369)
	Reading	0.0592	−0.163	0.0592
		(3)	(181)	(351)

Source: Betts and Tang (2008b), Table 5. Number of studies, number of represented schools, or number of represented schools times years in parentheses.

weighting schemes gives a more representative picture of what happened at the "typical" charter school or in the typical charter school year.

The first pattern apparent in the table is that regardless of the weighting scheme, in most cases the median effect is positive. This supports the vote-counting analysis referred to above: there are far more positive findings than negative findings. The only exception is at the high school level, in which the median effect is negative for math scores regardless of weighting and negative for one of the cases of reading. Again, this closely matches the patterns of significance discussed earlier.

While generally positive, the median effect sizes tend to be small. In all cases but two, the absolute value of the median effect size is less than 0.10, or less than 1/10 of a standard deviation of a test score. This is true for all of the unweighted median effects as well as the weighted effects when the number of schools times the number of years serves as weight. Again, the only exception is at the high school level, and only under one of the weighting schemes.

It is important to put these effect sizes into context. Betts and Tang (2008b) point out that the effect size for both math and reading in elementary schools is 0.08, or 8 percent of a standard deviation. They calculate that a student with median test scores—ranking fiftieth out of a hundred students—would be predicted to move up to about the forty-seventh rank out of one hundred students after one year at a charter school. Over several years of such gains, a student could move up markedly. For comparison purposes, Clotfelter, Ladd, and Vigdor (2007) estimate that in North Carolina, reducing class size by five students is associated with gains in achievement of 1.0 percent–1.5 percent of a standard deviation.

Several new studies have appeared since the review of the literature conducted in 2008 by Betts and Tang. Zimmer, Gill, Booker, Lavertu, Sass, and Witte (2009) report on value-added modeling of math and reading achievement in Texas, Ohio, Chicago, Denver, Milwaukee, Philadelphia, and San Diego. In the cases of Texas and San Diego, this work updates work done by some of these authors and other researchers, and in the other locations this report produces the first value-added knowledge of which I am aware.

The authors emphasize their middle and high school results because they have relatively few elementary school students who switch between charter schools and traditional public schools. In these "non-elementary" models, in five of seven cases there was no statistically significant difference between reading and math gains in charters versus traditional public schools. But charter schools in Chicago underperformed in reading, and in the Texas sample charter schools underperformed in both math and reading. In each of these negative cases the effect size was in the range of -0.08 to -0.09.[2]

One other recent study, which in this case uses the ideal method of comparing lottery winners and losers, examines charter schools in Boston. Abdulkadiroglu et al. (2009) found that the estimated effect of attending a charter school for one year was positive and quite large. For example, they estimated effect sizes of 0.17 and 0.16 for English language arts in middle and high school and effect sizes of 0.54 and 0.19 for math in middle and high school. All effects were significant at the 5 percent or lower levels. As the authors point out, a gain of 0.54 standard deviations in a single year is very large.

Overall, the new results fit quite well with the earlier literature as reviewed by Betts and Tang (2008a, b)—there is a mix of results, with the earlier nonlottery results being slightly more negative than the earlier work and the Boston study being among the most positive results found to date.

EVIDENCE ON OUTCOMES OTHER THAN TEST SCORES

Several papers have started to look at student outcomes other than academic achievement as proxied by test scores. This literature is just in its infancy, but already the results strongly hint that test scores do not fully capture all of the effects of attending a charter school on individual student outcomes. The bulk of this work has focused on various measures of educational attainment; that is, measures of how much education each person obtains.

EMERGING EVIDENCE ON EDUCATIONAL ATTAINMENT

A central problem in analyzing years of education, or whether a student graduates from high school or enters college, is that we observe a person's (final) level of education only once. With test scores, which we observe repeatedly, we can compare student performance before and after he or she enters a charter school, using a student fixed effect value-added model. Even if we do not have the minimum of three test scores needed for this model, we could use just two test scores to measure how much students improve in different school environments. We cannot use these "value-added" models for outcomes such as high school graduation. The closest we can come is to model, for instance, whether a person graduates while controlling for observable student characteristics at some earlier point in time. The chances that unobserved differences across students are driving the results rise exponentially.

For precisely this reason, lottery data that allows comparison of outcomes between lottery winners and losers is particularly useful in the context of "once only" variables, such as high school or college graduation. If the only thing that separates lottery winners and losers is the luck of the draw, then on average we expect students in these two groups to have the same probability of reaching a given level of education. If statistically significant differences emerge, we can be quite confident that winning or losing the lottery has caused these differences in educational attainment.

Unfortunately, there has been only one lottery-based study of the effects of charter schools on educational attainment, and that study examines only one California charter school. McClure, Strick, Jacob-Almeida, and Reicher (2005) use admission lotteries at the Preuss School at UCSD to examine the effect of winning a lottery on student achievement and educational attainment. They did not find big differences in test scores between lottery winners and losers, but they did observe large differences in a variety of measures of educational attainment. First, they studied how many college preparatory courses the students completed and found large differences emerging as early as grade ten, in favor of lottery winners.

The authors also surveyed lottery losers in the graduating class of 2005 (who had enrolled in traditional public schools in San Diego) when they reached grade twelve. Part of the survey asked about the students' plans for college. The survey found a striking gap in planned college attendance. Among the Preuss School attendees (the lottery winners), 90.3 percent were set to enroll in a four-year college in the fall, and 9.7 percent were planning to enroll in community college. Only 66.7 percent of respondents from the group of lottery losers planned to attend a four-year college in the fall, a gap of about 23 percent.

An issue with this comparison is that just under two-thirds of students in the group that did not win the lottery replied to the survey. By assuming either that none of the nonrespondents, or alternatively, that all of these nonrespondents were intending to enroll in college, we obtain a range of 42.1 percent to 78.9 percent as the possible range for the actual four-year college enrollment in this comparison group. Regardless, then, the lottery winners were more likely to enroll in college than the lottery losers at this school.

The remaining studies of educational attainment do not use lottery data and so potentially suffer from bias caused by omitted variables. For instance, if students who attend charter schools are more motivated than are students who attend traditional public schools, then greater educational attainment among charter students could simply reflect variations in unmeasured motivation.

Zimmer, Gill, Booker, Lavertu, Sass, and Witte (2009) examine the association between educational attainment and charter school attendance in a variety of locations. One of the approaches they take to reduce the self-selection among charter students is to focus on students who attend a charter school in grade eight, and then to compare educational attainment within this subsample between students who later attend high school charter schools and those who attend traditional public high schools. Because of onerous data requirements, this analysis is limited to Chicago and Florida.

In Chicago, the authors estimate that attending a charter high school is associated with a 7 percent increase in the probability of graduating from high school and a 10 percent increase in the probability of attending a community college or four-year college. The corresponding figures for Florida are 12–15 percent and 8 percent. The limitations of this method are that we cannot be sure that limiting the analysis to students who attended charter schools in grade eight removes unobserved variations among students who, after all, come to different decisions about whether to attend charter public high schools.

Another perhaps more convincing approach implemented by these same authors uses instrumental variables to take into account students' endogenous choice of whether to attend a charter school. The central idea is to replace the variable indicating actual charter school attendance with a predicted charter attendance variable, which is created by using various measures of the proximity of other local charter schools. These models produced even bigger estimates. For instance, the probability of graduating from high school is predicted to rise when attending a charter high school by about 15 percent in Florida and about 32 percent in Chicago. The estimated changes in probability of attending a two- or four-year college are 18 percent and 14 percent in Florida and Chicago, respectively. On the surface these estimates seem high. On the other hand, the Preuss School results, which use the more convincing lottery method, suggest a 24 percent boost in the probability of attending a four-year college.

These are all strong results, but the results are limited to one school in San Diego and charters in Chicago and Florida. In principle, it would be simple to extend these sorts of analyses to other states and cities, at least for high school graduation.

EVIDENCE ON ATTENDANCE AND BEHAVIOR

Imberman (2007) studies two outcomes that are more closely related to student behavior than student achievement: attendance and suspensions from school (combined with more serious disciplinary actions). He studies an unnamed, large urban school district. He finds significant reductions in student disciplinary infractions among those who attend charter high schools. A natural concern, of course, is that charter high schools may suspend or otherwise discipline students less often for a given behavior, perhaps because of lower disciplinary standards or a lower probability of catching students violating the behavior code. Still, the differences are quite large. For instance, the baseline model suggests a change of -0.36 infractions per student, which is large compared to the average number of infractions per student in traditional public schools of 0.42 infractions.

Imberman also models the percentage attendance rate. The baseline model shows no relation between charter school attendance and attendance rates. However, in models that also control for lagged charter school attendance, a small positive relation between attending a charter two periods ago and attendance in the current period arises.

CONCLUSION

The rapidly growing literature on charter schools and achievement still contains a surprisingly small number of studies that use convincing value-added or experimental (lottery) methods, but this subsample of studies is growing steadily.

The achievement results neither confirm the worst fears of charter critics nor fulfill the greatest hopes of charter supporters. There is ample evidence that some charter schools outperform traditional public schools and that others underperform. Overall, the evidence to date supports the notion that positive effects are somewhat more common than negative effects. High school math scores are a weak point for charter schools, while charter schools most typically outperform traditional public schools in elementary school reading tests and middle school math tests. But even with some excellent recent additions to the literature, we are still surveying a literature that completely ignores the majority of U.S. states. In many states, policy makers have to choose between rigorous evidence from other states or districts and less rigorous or even no evidence on the influence of charter schools in their own location.

Researchers are just beginning to examine outcomes other than test scores. Studies in three different locations suggest that attending a charter high school is associated with significantly higher educational attainment. A study in an unnamed urban district suggests that disciplinary infractions fall when students switch to charter schools. There is also weak evidence that those who switch to charter schools eventually exhibit slightly higher attendance rates.

None of these models of nonachievement outcomes has been estimated in a sufficiently wide range of school districts to know whether the results generalize, but the results are certainly very promising. They suggest that the call by Hamilton and Stecher in the previous chapter for researchers to investigate a broader set of student outcomes could prove prescient.

NOTES

1. I thank Jon Christensen for his insights on the literature.
2. In the sample that included primary schools for Ohio, the overall charter effect was negative for both reading and math. This result appeared to derive from some "virtual" charter schools that educate students at a distance, typically through the Internet.

REFERENCES

Abdulkadiroglu, A., Angrist, J., Cohodes, S., Dynarski, S., Fullerton, J., Kane, T., and Pathak, P. (2009). *Informing the Debate: Comparing Boston's Charter, Pilot and Traditional Schools.* Boston: The Boston Foundation.

Betts, J. R., and Tang, Y. E. (2008a). Charter Schools and Student Achievement: A Review of the Evidence. In Robin J. Lake (Ed.), *Hopes, Fears and Reality: A Balanced Look at American Charter Schools in 2008* (pp. 1–8). Seattle: National Charter School Research Project, Center on Reinventing Public Education.

Betts, J. R., and Tang, Y. E. (2008b). *Value-Added and Experimental Studies of the Effect of Charter Schools on Student Achievement: A Literature Review.* Seattle: National Charter School Research Project, Center on Reinventing Public Education.

Charter School Achievement Consensus Panel. (2006). *Key Issues in Studying Charter Schools and Achievement: A Review and Suggestions for National Guidelines.* NCSRP White Paper Series, No. 2. Seattle: Center on Reinventing Public Education.

Clotfelter, C. T., Ladd, H. F., and Vigdor, J. L. (2007). How and Why Do Teacher Credentials Matter for Student Achievement? Cambridge, MA: National Bureau of Economic Research Working Paper 12828. Download at http://www.nber.org/papers/w12828.

Imberman, S. (2007). *Achievement and Behavior in Charter Schools: Drawing a More Complete Picture.* Unpublished manuscript, University of Houston.

McClure, L., Strick, B., Jacob-Almeida, R., and Reicher, C. (2005). *The Preuss School at UCSD: School Characteristics and Students' Achievement.* The Center for Research on Educational Equity, Assessment and Teaching Excellence, University of California, San Diego. Download at http://create.ucsd.edu/.

Zimmer, R., Gill, B., Booker, K., Lavertu, S., Sass, T. R., and Witte, J. (2009). Charter Schools in Eight States: Effects on Achievement, Attainment, Integration, and Competition. Santa Monica, CA: RAND Corporation.

Chapter Five

The Selection of Students into Charter Schools: A Critical Issue for Research and Policy

Julian R. Betts

INTRODUCTION

This chapter discusses how and why students enrolling in charter schools are likely to be unrepresentative of students in their district. This question holds great political and policy relevance. It is relevant to charter school politics because simple snapshot comparisons of test scores at charter schools and traditional public schools have dominated the debate about whether charters are faring well. But if the students in charter schools are quite different from students in traditional public schools, then naïve comparisons of test scores are almost meaningless.

For instance, if parents are more likely to switch their students into charter schools if they are having trouble at school, then average test scores of charter enrollees would necessarily be lower than in regular public schools. But this would say nothing about the quality of charter schools. This is an example of students self-selecting into charter schools in nonrandom ways. Conversely, charter school operators may indirectly select students through their decisions about where to locate their schools. Critics of charter schools sometimes claim that charter schools are "skimming off" high-achieving students, but others claim that charters tend to locate in less affluent areas, and therefore they primarily enroll disadvantaged students who arrive at school less ready to learn.

The question of who attends charter schools has policy relevance for two reasons. First, policy makers do care about how the quality of charter schools compares to that of traditional public schools as it may influence the number of charter schools that are allowed to renew their charters or the number or type of new charter schools that receive charter agreements. It is impossible to know the answer to this "quality" question unless researchers understand the initial achievement of students before they enter charter schools. Second, charter schools, as a new form of choice, have the potential to alter the distribution of educational outcomes among types of students, whether defined by family income, socioeconomic status, or race and ethnicity. Are charters primarily serving underserved populations? Or are they merely providing services to affluent students who already had more choices among schools through choosing a school by moving into an affluent area or by paying to attend a private school?

This chapter will survey both the theory and the empirical evidence on who attends charter schools. The main text will discuss the theoretical issues in fairly nontechnical terms but with the goal of showing that even the simplest models yield ambiguous results concerning who self-selects to attend charter schools. This ambiguity is compounded by the additional uncertainty about where charter school operators decide to locate their schools. The upshot is that the question of who attends charter schools is ultimately an empirical question, the answer to which could vary from location to location.

TWO SIMPLE MODELS OF HOW THE DECISION TO ATTEND A CHARTER SCHOOL COULD DEPEND ON FAMILY INCOME

A family's income has been shown by many studies to predict student achievement quite well. For example, Coley (2002) documents large differences in cognitive development between kindergarten students from affluent and less affluent families. This matters for analysis of charter schools because differences in test scores between students at charter schools and traditional public schools could largely reflect differences in family income that are typically only poorly measured by researchers.

We now consider two simple models. Mathematical versions of the models appear in the appendix. One of the main lessons from these models is that we must think about both the demand for charter schools and the supply of charter schools. The latter is an important point—the decisions charter operators make about where to locate their schools could profoundly affect who applies.

Model 1

Suppose that two parents are thinking of sending their child to a charter school. In comparing the value of this choice relative to sending their child to the local neighborhood school, they might be weighing two countervailing factors. On the one hand, they may perceive the charter school to have higher quality, but on the other hand they would rather not send their child to a distant school. If the value of the gain in school quality outweighs the perceived costs of having to transport their child across town, the parents may decide to apply to the charter school.

Now, consider how variations in family income might affect these calculations. Suppose that low- and high-income families value the academic quality of a school equally.[1] Similarly, we assume for now that family income does not influence the relative importance of school quality versus distance. However, a lower-income family might perceive a greater gain in quality from attending a given charter school simply because its local school was not as good as the local school for more affluent families. This difference suggests that charter schools will primarily attract lower-income families, which have more to gain in relative terms.

Nonacademic aspects of charter schools provide a second reason why charter schools may appeal to low-income families for nonacademic reasons. For instance, if a charter school offers a violence-free environment and low-income families are more likely to feel that their local neighborhood school is violence-prone, again, they would be more apt to apply to the charter school than a high-income family would.[2]

Now, what about the negative effect of the extra distance between a student's home and the charter, relative to his local school? How would family income affect this cost? This depends crucially on where charter school operators decide to open a school. If charter schools are more likely to locate in less affluent areas of a city, then the distance to the charter school may in fact be lower for the low-income family. If this holds, then the lower-income family will have higher benefits from attending *and* less distance to travel. Together, both factors suggest that low-income families will be more likely to attend the charter school.

But on the other hand, if charters tend to locate in more affluent areas, then low-income families could be less likely to apply because they would have to travel a greater distance. This works in the opposite direction to the differential effects of gains in school quality, which overall makes it uncertain whether low-income families would gain more or less from switching.

We conclude that the decision by charter school operators about where to locate has the potential to decide whether low-income students are over- or underrepresented in charter schools. But lower-income families may perceive bigger quality gains from switching their child to a charter school.

Model 2

Model 2 is only slightly more complex than model 1. Again, we assume that family income is the source of all non-random selection of students into charter schools. We add two sensible complications to the above model. The relative importance of distance relative to school quality may be higher for low-income families than for high-income families. To see this, suppose that a low-income and a high-income family would both have to transport their child fifteen miles to attend a given charter school, compared to one mile to their respective neighborhood schools. The low-income family may lack the private transportation to get their child halfway across town, making this a much more costly move for this family. This wrinkle in the model suggests that, if the other factors were equal, then there would be "positive selection" into charter schools, meaning that high-income students would be overrepresented in charter schools.

Kleitz et al. (2000) report on a survey of 1,100 parents who had enrolled their children in Texas charter schools. The paper, which seeks to test whether demographic groups differ in the factors that they consider when choosing a school, provides direct evidence that low-income families may be particularly sensitive to sending their children to distant schools. The authors find that nonwhite and low-income charter school parents place higher-than-average importance on the location of the charter school, with 79 percent of low-income parents listing school location as important or very important compared to only 63 percent of high-income parents.

The second complication we add is to consider the costs to families of volunteering in charter schools or otherwise participating in activities such as the Parent Teacher Association. If low-income families lack the private transportation needed for parents to attend school activities, or if they lack the time to attend, then they will gain less from switching their child to the charter school than will a high-income family. Low-income families may lack the time to participate in these activities if, for instance, the low-income family is a single-parent family or if adults in the low-income family must hold multiple jobs to make ends meet. High-income families could be more likely to have one spouse voluntarily staying at home. They may also view the charter school's requests that parents become involved in the school as a *relatively* small imposition because their default local school, which happens to be in an affluent area, itself makes quite high demands on parental time, at least compared to local schools serving low-income families. On the other hand, if some of these school activities would require parents to come to the school during working hours, it could be that high-income parents would be less likely to want to participate due to higher wages forgone.

Overall, we are left with four different factors influencing a family's decision to send its child to a charter school. The first factor, the gain in perceived quality between the charter school and the local school, suggests that low-income families will dominate. The second factor, the extra distance to the charter school, will increase or decrease the relative probability of low-income versus high-income students attending the charter, depending on whether charter school operators tend to locate in low-income or high-income areas. The third factor, the relative cost of transporting one's child to a charter school, probably favors high-income students being overrepresented in charter schools. The final factor, the relative costs to parents of participating in school activities, could favor either type of family, but it probably favors high-income students becoming overrepresented in charter schools.

There is no way to know which of these four competing factors will dominate.

There are additional sources of ambiguity that we have yet to discuss. For example, we have assumed that low-income and high-income parents make decisions based on the same information sets. If low-income parents lack contacts with other parents whose children attend schools of choice, they may know less about quality differences between the default local school and the schools of choice. It therefore becomes possible that low-income parents are less sensitive than high-income parents to differences between local schools and charter schools. Schneider, Teske, and Marschall (2000) provide indirect evidence that information sets can indeed vary demographically. These authors report that parents from disadvantaged backgrounds are relatively more likely to use official sources of information when choosing schools for their children while advantaged parents are more likely to rely on information obtained from other parents. The implication is that affluent parents benefit from relatively abundant information networks.

Yet another source of ambiguity stems from the possibility that the academic quality of a given charter or local school could vary depending on the characteristics of the given student. An obvious example of this is that if schools group students by ability, and if the quality of instruction varies by ability group, then a given school might be quite attractive for students in one part of the achievement distribution and rather unattractive for students from another part of the achievement distribution.

There are three essential lessons we distill from this analysis. First, it becomes an empirical question as to whether low-income families will be over- or underrepresented in charter schools. Second, the locational choices made by charter school operators could prove to be decisive in practice. Third, even though we have considered student selection that relates to a single variable, family income, even this apparently simple modeling exercise reveals a complex set of countervailing factors.

The question of selection of students into charter schools is important because selectivity might bias simple analyses of charter school quality that are based on comparisons of average test scores at charters and noncharters.

Selection Based on Variables Apart from Income

The above section assumes that one variable, family income, is the sole dimension along which students self-select into charter schools. It seems likely that other characteristics, such as parental education, race and ethnicity, and attitudes about multicultural mixing, could influence parents' choice of schools for their children. Social scientists have yet to make much headway at assessing multiple sources of selection into charter schools. But it seems reasonable to conclude that the overall determinants of selectivity bias could be even more complex than painted above. Moreover, the direction of bias could vary from city to city and indeed from school to school within a district.

Another strong possibility, almost a certainty, is that students self-select into schools based upon *unobservable* factors. These might include the student's own motivation and the parents' attitudes about education. It is quite unlikely that any sort of survey-based data set that social scientists would collect would capture these influences particularly well. The combination of selection on multiple variables and the fact that some of these are unobservable makes it very uncertain whether those who select into charter schools will be academically stronger or weaker than those who remain in regular public schools.

DO CHARTER SCHOOLS CREAM SKIM IN PRACTICE?

It should be clear that observations of the relative racial or income mix of charter and regular public schools alone cannot tell us whether there is going to be positive or negative selection into charter schools in an academic sense. But it remains important as a first step to study this question.

The evidence appears to be that charter school students are more likely to be economically disadvantaged and more likely to be nonwhite than students in regular public schools. An AFT study of National Assessment of Educational Progress data makes this point clearly. The study, by Nelson et al. (2004), purported to show that charter schools were underperforming regular public schools, but the report was widely criticized for having failed to control for selection into charter schools. What the report did achieve accurately was a portrayal of who attends the two types of schools. Figures 5.1 and 5.2 show that charter school students at the grade four level in 2003 were about 15 percent less likely to be white and 8 percent more likely to be eligible for free/reduced-price meal assistance, relative to their counterparts in regular public schools.

Many studies of achievement in the two types of schools have also reported demographic breakdowns of students in charters and regular public

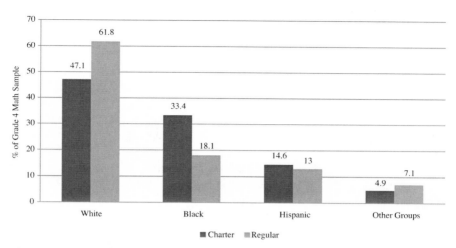

Figure 5.1. **Racial/Ethnic Composition of Grade Four Schools Participating in 2003 National Assessment of Educational Progress Math Test** *Source:* Nelson et al. (2004), page 11.

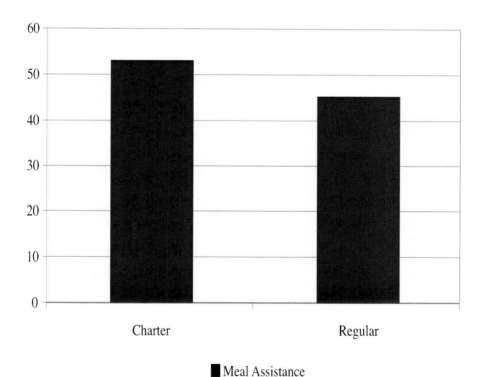

Figure 5.2. **Percentage of Students Eligible for Free/Reduced-Price Meals in Schools Participating in 2003 National Assessment of Educational Progress Math Test** *Source:* Nelson et al. (2004), page 7.

schools, and the results are broadly similar but often vary in details. For instance, in their Texas study, Booker et al. (2004) report that charter school students were far more likely to be black, and very slightly less likely to be Hispanic, than students at traditional public schools. Overall, 78 percent of charter students were black or Hispanic compared to 55.8 percent of students in traditional public schools. However, the percentage of students who were limited English proficient at charter schools was 6.7 percent versus 14.6 percent in traditional public schools. Bifulco and Ladd (2006) report that in a North Carolina charter school students were more likely to be nonwhite but were less likely to have parents who had a high school diploma or less. Sass (2006) finds a mixed picture in Florida, where charter school students were more likely to be black, about equally likely to be Hispanic, but less likely to be receiving free/reduced-price meal assistance and slightly less likely to be limited English proficient, in special education, *or* gifted education.

In California Zimmer et al. (2003) find that "charter school students are more likely to be black and less likely to be Hispanic or Asian, but no more or less likely to be white." A study of school choice in San Diego by Betts et al. (2006) finds that charter school students are less likely to be white or Asian but more likely to be black or Hispanic, compared to students at traditional public schools. Additionally, 66 percent of charter students were eligible for free/reduced-priced meals compared to 56 percent of students in regular schools.

Ross (2005) performs a panel analysis of the locational decisions of charter schools in Michigan and concludes that charter schools are more likely to locate in predominantly black neighborhoods. Fully 49 percent of charter students in her Michigan sample were black, compared to 20 percent in traditional public schools; figures for Hispanic students were 3.3 percent and 3.8 percent, respectively. On the other hand, just over 25 percent of charter school students were eligible for meal assistance, compared to 34 percent in regular public schools.

Many of these studies are consistent with the possibility that charter schools attract relatively high concentrations of nonwhite students but that this is partly counterbalanced by some positive, or at least neutral, socioeconomic sorting into charter schools. Henig and MacDonald (2002) model the locational decisions of charter school operators in Washington, D.C. They find that charters are much more likely to open in areas with above-average shares of blacks and Hispanics. However, within these neighborhoods D.C. charters are most likely to open up in areas with relatively high home ownership rates and middle incomes rather than low or high incomes.

I interviewed Larry Rosenstock, CEO of High Tech High (HTH) School and HTH Learning in San Diego, about how the High Tech High family of charter schools has made locational decisions in California. The schools currently enroll 2,700 students in seven schools. The management of HTH schools has earned California's only statewide charter from the state Board of Education, and it now intends to open up several "villages" of charter schools throughout the state in the next few years. CEO Rosenstock told me that the ideal location for a new HTH charter school is "on the cusp" of at least one low-income area, but not so far away from more affluent areas that the location would preclude interest from middle- and high-income families as well.

One federal program that may encourage charter school operators to open up charter schools in less affluent areas is the New Markets Tax Credit (NMTC), which pays investors a cumulative 39 percent in tax credits over a seven-year period in return for investments in lower-income areas that meet certain criteria. One possible use of NMTCs is as a tax break for philanthropists to buy land for a charter school. High Tech High School in San Diego is using NMTCs to pay for new campuses.

Beyond locating near or in lower-income areas, HTH schools have implemented other practices to promote demand from lower-income families. At High Tech High in San Diego, for instance, students from lower-income families receive free passes for the city's public transportation system. Admission lotteries are performed on a zip code–by–zip code basis to ensure representation from all parts of the city, and in cases in which the number of applications from a given zip code exceeds the allotment for the zip code, students who are eligible for meal assistance receive preferences in the lottery.

High Tech High and its affiliated charter schools provide examples of charter operators that have intentionally chosen a location designed to attract lower-income students and which supplement this locational emphasis by other means.

The Green Dot Public Schools, a charter school operation in Los Angeles, provides another example of a charter school operator that has focused on areas serving relatively disadvantaged families. This pattern became even more clear in January 2007 when Green Dot applied to Los Angeles Unified School District to directly take over failing schools in some of the district's most impoverished neighborhoods (Boghossian, 2007).

None of the studies or anecdotal examples can show conclusively that charters overall attract students who have lower test scores than do students at regular public schools, but the weight of evidence points clearly in that direction, at least when we consider race. But we must be very careful here not to equate race and test scores. Within racial groups, for instance, there could be positive test-score selection in the sense that families with relatively high achievement could be the most likely to apply.

Indeed, another notable pattern in the papers listed above is that in some cases charter schools enrolled relatively few whites but appeared to have attracted students with relatively high socioeconomic status, defined either in terms of meal assistance eligibility or parental education. This is suggestive of quite complex forms of selection into charter schools where different measures suggest both negative and positive selection of students into charter schools. As another example, the fact that typically charter school students are disproportionately nonwhite suggests negative selection, but the mix of nonwhite students in some cases implies that fewer of these students are limited English proficient.

IMPLICATIONS FOR RESEARCH DESIGN

The simplest models of the effect of charter schools that simply compare means or that use linear regression models do not attempt to correct for selectivity bias. None of these approaches is likely to yield reliable results. But there are clear shades of gray among the types of research that could be attempted here. Models of gains in achievement are likely to tell us more about the causal effects of charter schools than simple snapshots of test score levels because they implicitly net out of the equation the student's past academic history. Similarly, models that control for observable student characteristics are likely to get us closer to understanding the causal effect of charter schools on achievement. But neither method should be viewed as anything close to foolproof due to the possibility of nonlinear interactions among observables and the role of both observables and unobservable variables in determining who decides to attend a charter school.

Two commonly used methods of controlling for selectivity bias are Heckman's method and propensity score matching. Both methods are two-step approaches in which the researcher estimates the probability of a student switching into a charter school in step 1. If the decision to attend a charter depends on unobservable variables, as seems likely, then neither method will produce unbiased estimates of the causal effect of attending a charter school. Additional challenges to these methods are the occasionally crosscutting forms of selection related to different measures of socioeconomic status and the variations from one geographic area to another.

Two methods that do hold out greater hope of handling selectivity bias are experimental methods that use lotteries to create treatment and comparison groups and student fixed-effect models that compare individual students before and after switching between charter and regular public schools. Chapter 2 in this volume by Betts et al. covers in great detail the relative strengths and weaknesses of these two methods. But it is worth pointing out here the different ways in which these approach the problem of selectivity.

The experimental method relies on the random process through which applicants to a charter school are assigned to the admitted pool and the rejected pool. There will still be selectivity bias, but on average it should be balanced between the pools of lottery winners and losers, and so a simple difference in achievement between these two groups will remove the selectivity bias. McEwan and Olsen (in this volume) discuss in great detail lotteries and potential problems that could bias estimated effects of charter schools even in this research design.

The student fixed-effect method is tantamount to mean-differencing the data so that the coefficient on charter schools is identified by switches between charter and regular public schools by each student, obviating the need to make comparisons across students. This method completely removes selectivity bias if the factors that determine whether a student attends a charter school do not change over time. This may or may not hold true. For instance, if a student has an unusually bad year academically, it may prompt his parents to switch him from traditional public schools into a charter school or vice versa. This can lead to biased estimates. For example, suppose that students are likely to move into charter schools if parents mistake a random one-year drop in achievement gains for a long-term problem with the student's current school. Any recovery in test scores the next year through "regression to the mean" may be wrongly attributed as a positive effect of charter schools on achievement. Conversely, if parents of a charter school student mistakenly react to a temporary drop in achievement gains by moving their student to a regular public school, this would downwardly bias the estimated effect of charter schools.

Bifulco and Ladd (2006) test for the possibility that negative test score trends induce shifts into charter schools using data from North Carolina, and they do not find evidence that this is a problem. Using panel data from San Diego, Tang and Betts (2006) test for negative shocks inducing flows of students both into and out of charter schools. They do not find consistent evidence of transitory dips in performance immediately before either switches into or out of charter schools.

IMPLICATIONS FOR POLICY MAKERS

The models we discussed earlier in this chapter established that lower-income families might have a stronger preference for charter schools than would higher-income families, although if charter operators locate schools in more affluent areas, it could be more affluent parents who express stronger demand for charter schools. Overall, both theory and evidence suggest that the self-selection of students into charter schools is an ambiguous and complex process.

This self-selection of students matters a great deal for researchers for reasons stated above. But do we care about self-selection of students from a more policy-oriented perspective? The answer is almost surely yes.

In a very real sense, the forgoing advice to researchers to avoid doing research on "charter school quality" that ignores student selection is very important for policy makers and charter school operators as well. These latter actors operate on a different and more public stage, and it is incumbent upon them to educate the public that comparing the levels of test scores across schools says little about the relative quality of instruction provided at different schools.

One prominent example is the requirement in the federal No Child Left Behind (NCLB) law that states must create standards for proficiency in math and reading, test students' mastery of these standards, and then report to the public the percentage of students in each school who are proficient. The strong tendency of charter school operators to open schools in areas serving relatively nonwhite populations will tend to lead to relatively low "percentage proficient" scores for these schools. It would be careless at best, and dishonest at worst, to claim that low levels of student proficiency in such cases pointed to a failing school.

There are other reasons why policy makers should care about the issue of selectivity bias.

Consider first the opposite type of selectivity bias: Suppose that in some school districts we found that charter schools enroll more than a fair share of high-income students. This could be interpreted as the charter movement acting to resegregate the nation's schools along socioeconomic, and perhaps even racial, lines. Second, to the extent that a student's peers at a school influence that student's learning, if high-income students are flocking to charter schools, it could leave the lower-income students who remain behind worse off academically.

So, if society values integrated schools for the sake of integration alone or because integration will benefit low-income students academically, we need to consider some policies that might encourage low-income students to apply to charter schools. Five types of policies come to mind, each of which could encourage negative income selection into charter schools:

1. Charter schools could adopt an academic focus that makes allowances for underperforming students, such as remediation programs, special education programs, and programs for English learners.

2. Charter schools could adapt a cultural focus that appeals to low-income families, for instance, by emphasizing multicultural activities.
3. Convenient, safe, and cheap public transportation could make attending a distant charter school more attractive to low-income students. More directly, provision of free school buses to and from charter schools could level the playing field. Indeed, the demand from less affluent families for a spot in a charter school could mushroom if public transportation to that school is subsidized.
4. A low cost of living in the local area could free up parent time for school-related activities, including transporting their children to the school and volunteering at the school. Thus, public policies that on the surface have nothing to do with education could have important effects on who attends charter schools. For instance, housing subsidies targeted at the poor might achieve some of these goals.
5. Policies that induce charter schools to locate in less affluent areas could be quite influential in determining the overall income mix of students in charter schools. Betts et al (2006) discuss the potential of differential student vouchers that pay higher subsidies for students with lower socio-economic status as a way of encouraging *all* schools to seek out and enroll underserved students.

Another possibility that could encourage charter operators to open up in low-income areas are grants to adapt buildings in low-income areas into school sites. One important example of such a program is the aforementioned NMTC, which High Tech High School in San Diego is using to pay for new campuses. States could implement similar programs and could target the tax credits more specifically to educational facilities than does the NMTC program.

More radically, both states and districts could alter school funding formulae to provide charter schools, or indeed *all* schools, with relatively more funding if they serve relatively educationally disadvantaged populations.

CONCLUSION

The issue of how students select into charter schools is crucial both for research and for policy making. Both politicians and policy makers want to know how the quality of education provided by charter schools compares to that in traditional public schools.

Naïve comparisons of average test scores at charter schools and traditional public schools are likely to yield quite misleading information about the relative quality of instruction provided at the two types of schools. Better models will look at gains in achievement while controlling for observable student characteristics. But neither of these additional design elements is likely to remove selectivity bias.

To illustrate the complexities, we developed two simple models in which family income was the sole variable determining selection. But even here, although the preponderance of evidence suggests that low-income and low-scoring students are more likely to switch into a charter school, the overall direction of selectivity bias is theoretically uncertain. Selection is an even more complex process than intimated by these models because many characteristics of students and their families in addition to family income, only some of which social scientists can observe, likely influence the decision to attend a charter school.

This complexity is compounded by the endogenous decisions of charter school operators about where to locate. In Michigan, D.C., and elsewhere, we have clear evidence that charter operators seek out neighborhoods that are disproportionately black. But Henig and MacDonald (2002) and others also find evidence of crosscutting selection that makes it hard to predict whether charter schools will tend to attract students who have lower or higher achievement than that of students who remain in traditional public schools.

Lessons for researchers are fairly apparent. Researchers should model gains, not level of test scores. They should also include observable characteristics of students and their families as explanatory variables. But neither of these steps will fully remove selectivity bias. Student fixed-effect models and, better yet, experimental evidence, are likely to reduce selectivity bias from estimates of the effects of charter schools.

These ideals may not always be met, especially when a government body wants a quick answer to the question of charter schools' effects on achievement but is not able to provide researchers with ideal data. At this point, it becomes incumbent upon researchers to state clearly and repeatedly that their analyses may not come close to establishing the causal effect of charters on achievement.

For policy makers, they would be wise to have a keen awareness of the pitfalls of overly simple comparisons between charter and traditional public schools. As for policy reforms, attention should be focused squarely on incentives. The dual challenge is to design stronger financial incentives for charter school operators to open up in relatively disadvantaged areas and incentives for families from across the socioeconomic spectrum to send their children to charter schools.

APPENDIX

The main text presents two models of the decision to attend a charter school and then examines how changes in family income might alter the desirability to the family of moving a child to the charter school. Here we present these simple models mathematically and derive the comparative statistics.

Parents must counterbalance their wish to put their child into a school they perceive as better than their local school against the additional distance that their child must travel to and from school. We can represent this trade-off with the following equation, which shows the perceived gain in family well-being should the student switch from the local school to the charter school, where the term Δ refers to the change in the given variable if the student switches to the given charter school from his or her default local school:

$$\Delta \text{Wellbeing} = \Delta \text{Quality} - a \Delta \text{Distance}$$

Here, α is a number indicating the relative importance of distance versus school quality. The larger is α; the more important is distance relative to school quality.

Suppose that we normalize the utility of attending the local neighborhood school to zero. Then the family will switch to the charter school if the (relative) utility of attending the charter, $U_{charter}$, > 0. This utility depends on the gain in school quality perceived by the family from a switch to a charter, less a weighting factor α (> 0) times the change in distance from the family's home to the charter school relative to the distance to the local neighborhood school.

$$
\begin{aligned}
U_{charter} &= \Delta Qual - \alpha \Delta D \\
&\equiv Qual_{charter} - Qual_{local}(I) - \alpha \left(D_{charter} - D_{local}(I) \right)
\end{aligned}
$$

where I is family income. The ΔQual term is decreasing in income I because the quality of the local school is likely to be lower for a lower-income family:

$$\frac{\partial Qual_{local}(I)}{\partial I} > 0$$

Thus

$$\frac{\partial U_{charter}}{\partial I} = 0 - \frac{\partial Qual_{local}(I)}{\partial I} - \alpha \frac{\partial \Delta D}{\partial I}$$

so that the first term is negative and the second term is either negative if the
charter school is located closer to low-income families than high-income
families or positive if the opposite holds. In the first case the low-income
family is more strongly attracted to the charter school than the high-income
family is, and in the second case it is ambiguous which family will be more
strongly attracted to the charter school.

Model 2 simply adds on to this model the possibility that α depends negatively on income I, on the grounds that added income makes it easier for a
family to find a way to transport its child to a charter school, and a second
term that depends on the change in the number of volunteer hours the parents
are expected to do should they switch their child to the charter school, ΔV:

$$U_{charter} = \Delta Qual - \alpha(I)\Delta D - \beta(I)\Delta V$$

Here β(I) is positive and could either increase or decrease with family income
as explained in the text. Differentiating with respect to family income:

$$\frac{\partial U_{charter}}{\partial I} = \frac{\partial \Delta Qual}{\partial I} - \frac{\partial \alpha(I)}{\partial I}\Delta D - \alpha(I)\frac{\partial \Delta D}{\partial I} - \Delta V \frac{\partial \beta(I)}{\partial I} - \beta(I)\frac{\partial \Delta V}{\partial I}$$

$$\qquad\qquad - \qquad\qquad + \qquad\qquad +/- \qquad +/- \qquad +/0$$

We have explained why the first term is likely to be negative. The second
term is likely to be positive because distance is less of a barrier to high-
income families. The third term could be positive or negative depending on
whether the charter school is more closely situated to the high-income or
low-income family, respectively. The sign of the fourth term is uncertain
because high-income families may be more or less sensitive to an increase in
required parent volunteer time. Unless high-income families are sensitive to
the higher opportunity cost of taking time off working, their resources probably make them less sensitive to a demand to increase time away from work,

and so this fourth term would be positive. The final term will be positive if the local school serving the high-income family has higher parent volunteer requirements than the local school serving the low-income family and will be zero if the two schools had identical requirements.

NOTES

1. Several studies of parental preferences suggest that demographic groups vary little in that they typically list school quality as the most important factor parents are looking for in school choice programs. See Kleitz et al. (2000) for evidence based on a survey of charter school parents in Texas. Similarly, Schneider, Teske, and Marschall (2000) report on a survey that asked parents what thing they thought was most important for their child's education. High teacher quality was far and away the most commonly chosen response among demographic groups.

2. Kleitz et al. (2000) and Schneider, Teske, and Marschall (2000) both report evidence that disadvantaged families place higher weight on safety when choosing schools. For instance, the former report that 81 percent of low-income parents rated safety as important or very important in a survey of Texas charter school families, compared to 68 percent of high-income parents. This gap probably does not reflect a difference in underlying preferences so much as a reaction to differences in the safety at these parents' local schools. Notably, this same survey finds almost no difference in the percentage of low-income and high-income parents who identified educational quality as important or very important (96 percent and 95 percent, respectively).

REFERENCES

Betts, J. R., Rice, L. A., Zau, A. C., Tang, Y. E., and Koedel, C. R. (2006). *Does School Choice Work? Effects on Student Integration and Achievement.* San Francisco: Public Policy Institute of California.

Bifulco, R., and Ladd, H. F. (2006). The Impacts of Charter Schools on Student Achievement: Evidence from North Carolina. *Education Finance and Policy* 1:1 (Winter), 50–90.

Boghossian, N. (2007). Mayor Opens Floodgates: LAUSD Reform Proposals Pile Up After He Sparks Debate. *LA Daily News*, January 27.

Booker, K., Gilpatric, S. M., Gronberg, T., and Jansen, D. (2004). Charter School Performance in Texas. Manuscript, Private Enterprise Research Center at Texas A&M University.

Coley, R. J. (2002). *An Uneven Start: Indicators of Inequality in School Readiness.* Princeton, NJ: Educational Testing Service.

Henig, J. R., and MacDonald, J. A. (2002). Locational Decisions of Charter Schools: Probing the Market Metaphor. *Social Science Quarterly* 83:4, 962–80.

Kleitz, B., Weiher, G. R., Tedin, K., and Matland, R. (2000). Choice, Charter Schools, and Household Preferences. *Social Science Quarterly* 81:3 (September), 846–54.

Nelson, F. H., Rosenberg, B., and Van Meter, N. (2004). Charter School Achievement on the 2003 National Assessment of Educational Progress. Washington, DC: American Federation of Teachers. Download at http://www.aft.org/pubs-reports/downloads/teachers/NAEPCharterSchoolReport.pdf.

Sass, T. R. (2006). Charter Schools and Student Achievement in Florida. *Education Finance and Policy* 1:1 (Winter), 91–122.

Schneider, M., Teske, P., and Marschall, M. (2000). *Choosing Schools: Consumer Choice and the Quality of American Schools.* Princeton, NJ: Princeton University Press.

Tang, Y. E., and Betts, J. R. (2006). Student Achievement in Charter Schools in San Diego. Manuscript, Department of Economics. San Diego: University of California San Diego.

Zimmer, R., Buddin, R., Chau, D., Gill, B., Guarino, C., Hamilton, L., Krop, C., McCaffrey, D., Sandler, M., and Brewer, D. (2003). Charter School Operations and Performance: Evidence from California. Santa Monica, CA: RAND Corporation.

Chapter Six

Admission Lotteries
in Charter Schools

Patrick J. McEwan and Robert B. Olsen

INTRODUCTION

The best school choice reforms promote parental choice and competition and minimize stratification of students by race, income, or ability (Hsieh and Uquiola, 2006; McEwan, 2000; 2004). In light of these goals, charter schools seem an appealing policy alternative because state-specific laws facilitate new schooling options and parental choice but also restrict the ability of charter schools to admit students selectively. A common restriction is a requirement that schools admit students by lottery when they have more applicants than they have space or legal authority to accept. The majority of charter schools are subject to state lottery requirements, but surprisingly little is known about the prevalence, features, and effects of charter school lotteries.

Lotteries have received increasing attention because they are a linchpin in some researchers' efforts to identify the impact of attending a charter school (e.g., Hoxby and Rockoff, 2004). Admission lotteries provide an opportunity to conduct a "natural" experiment, since charter school applicants are randomly assigned to a treatment condition in which they are offered admission to a charter school, or a control condition, in which they are not offered admission to a charter school. Natural experiments facilitate credible research on whether charter school admission or attendance causes improvements in student outcomes. This chapter broadly examines the phenomenon of charter school admission lotteries, with four goals:

1. *To describe why charter schools conduct lotteries.* In particular, the chapter focuses on state and federal rules that require charter schools to conduct lotteries when they face oversubscription of applicants and on the sources of excess demand that lead some charter schools to be oversubscribed.

2. *To describe how charter schools conduct lotteries.* Details of lottery implementation shed light on student access to charter schools, and they inform research that relies on admission lotteries.
3. *To assess the role of lotteries in charter school policy.* We consider both the intended outcomes of lottery rules (i.e., equal access) and unintended outcomes (i.e., gaming behavior that could undermine the intended outcomes).
4. *To assess the role of lotteries in research on charter school effects.* The chapter describes the well-known benefits of lotteries for securing credible estimates of charter school effects but also emphasizes the lesser-known challenges of generalizing the results to other students, schools, and contexts.

WHY CHARTER SCHOOLS CONDUCT LOTTERIES

State and federal charter school regulations require many schools to admit students by lottery when they face excess demand. This section describes these regulations, considers the conditions that give rise to excess demand, and speculates on charter schools' incentives to conduct lotteries even when not required to do so.

State Regulations

State charter school laws and related state education codes include provisions that govern admissions to charter schools. These provisions are probably the single most important reason for the existence of charter school lotteries. State regulations address which students can be given preference in admissions, which students can be excluded from the schools (if any), and whether charter schools are required to conduct a lottery if they receive more applicants than they can accommodate.

California's state charter school regulations provide a representative example of how states require lotteries when charter schools face excess demand (for excerpts from five other state laws, see table 6.1, at the end of this chapter):

> A charter school shall admit all pupils who wish to attend the school. However, if the number of pupils who wish to attend the charter school exceeds the school's capacity, attendance, except for existing pupils of the charter school, shall be determined by a public random drawing. Preference shall be extended to pupils currently attending the charter school and pupils who reside in the county except as provided for in Section 47614.5. Other preferences may be

Table 6.1.   Selected Excerpts from State Charter School Regulations

Arizona Revised Statutes Education Code: 15-184	A charter school shall enroll all eligible pupils who submit a timely application, unless the number of applications exceeds the capacity of a program, class, grade level, or building. A charter school shall give enrollment preference to pupils returning to the charter school in the second or any subsequent year of its operation and to siblings of pupils already enrolled in the charter school. A charter school that is sponsored by a school district governing board shall give enrollment preference to eligible pupils who reside within the boundaries of the school district where the charter school is physically located. If capacity is insufficient to enroll all pupils who submit a timely application, the charter school shall select pupils through an equitable selection process such as a lottery except that preference shall be given to siblings of a pupil selected through an equitable selection process such as a lottery.
Florida State Education Code: 1002.33	The charter school shall enroll an eligible student who submits a timely application, unless the number of applications exceeds the capacity of a program, class, grade level, or building. In such case, all applicants shall have an equal chance of being admitted through a random selection process.
Ohio Revised Code: 3314.06	(H) That, except as otherwise provided under division (B) of this section or section 3314.061 [3314.06.1] of the Revised Code, if the number of applicants exceeds the capacity restrictions of division (F) of this section, students shall be admitted by lot from all those submitting applications, except preference shall be given to students attending the school the previous year and to students who reside in the district in which the school is located. Preference may be given to siblings of students attending the school the previous year.
Texas Education Code: 12.117	(a) For admission to an open-enrollment charter school, the governing body of the school shall … fill the available positions by lottery; or subject to Subsection (b), fill the available positions in the order in which applications received before the application deadline were received.
	(b) An open-enrollment charter school may fill applications for admission under Subsection (a)(2)(B) only if the school published a notice of the opportunity to apply for admission to the school. A notice published under this subsection must: (1) state the application deadline; and (2) be published

Table 6.1.   (*Continued*)

	in a newspaper of general circulation in the community in which the school is located not later than the seventh day before the application.
Michigan Revised School Code: (380.501–380.507)	If there are more applications to enroll in the public school academy than there are spaces available, pupils shall be selected to attend using a random selection process. However, a public school academy may give enrollment priority to a sibling of a pupil enrolled in the public school academy. A public school academy shall allow any pupil who was enrolled in the public school academy in the immediately preceding school year to enroll in the public school academy in the appropriate grade unless the appropriate grade is not offered at that public school academy.

permitted by the chartering authority on an individual school basis and only if consistent with the law (California Education Code 47605).

Based on the ten states with the largest number of charter schools, table 6.2 summarizes regulations that affect 75 percent of charter schools and 76 percent of charter school students (U.S. Charter Schools, 2006). In descending order, these states include California, Arizona, Florida, Ohio, Texas, Michigan, Wisconsin, Pennsylvania, Colorado, and Minnesota. Table 6.2 shows that seven states require charter schools to admit students by lottery if they face excess demand. While the language of the regulations is general, their intent is clear. Charter schools with an excess of applicants are not allowed to choose students selectively or admit students in the order in which they apply. (Table 6.2 can be found at the end of this chapter.)

Even so, none of these ten states requires charter schools to fill *all* open slots via lottery. Charter schools in nine of the ten states can give preference to siblings of current students. In practice, this means that siblings who apply are admitted as long as the school has space to admit additional students. Seven of the states allow charter schools to give preference to students from a specific geographic area. In states like California that allow regular public schools to convert to charter status, this stipulation may be designed to ensure that students who live within the school's boundaries—students who would have been admitted automatically before the school was granted a charter—will still be able to enroll in the school. More generally, they allow charter schools to give preference to students who live in the community in which they are located. Geographic provisions rarely provide lottery exemptions to local students, but they can make it much less likely that nonlocal students will be admitted to a school facing excess demand.

Some states, including Florida and Texas, allow charter schools to give preference to children of adults with a direct link to the school—children of board members and employees in Florida and children of founding families and employees in Texas. Families involved in submitting the charter application to start a new charter school may often be motivated by the education of their own children, so it is not surprising that charter schools would want—and sympathetic states would permit—preferences for children of founding families.

We know little about the extent to which states or charter school authorizers monitor and enforce compliance with lottery rules. There are at least two approaches to monitoring a lottery. First, states and authorizers could observe lotteries to ensure that they meet standards. Second, they could request data on lottery results that would allow them to check for systematic differences between lottery winners and losers that would be unlikely if the lottery were truly random. We are not aware of any states or authorizers that take active steps to monitor charter school lotteries, but a systematic effort to collect data on charter school oversight was beyond the scope of this chapter. Some state provisions encourage a fair and self-monitoring process, such as California's requirement of public lotteries. However, we have no information on the extent to which the California Department of Education enforces this provision.

It is possible schools would conduct lotteries even in the absence of state regulations. Charter schools might choose to implement lottery admissions to preserve public support for charter schools or to implement a simple and fair admissions process. Since the overwhelming majority of charter schools face regulatory constraints, it is hard to ascertain how schools would behave in their absence.

However, charter schools face incentives that might discourage lottery admissions in the absence of regulatory constraints. First, like other public schools, they are subject to the performance requirements under No Child Left Behind. This might lead them to favor higher-scoring students in the admissions process. Second, like other public schools, funding for charter schools is typically based on the number of students enrolled in the school in the fall. This might lead them to admit students as they apply to fill open slots as rapidly as possible. Both of these incentives may be especially large for charter schools operated by for-profit entities, which may be able to raise revenues by maximizing enrollment and lower costs by selecting stronger students who are less costly to educate.[1] Third, charter schools with a specific mission, curricular focus, or instructional approach may prefer students who they believe will be best served by the particular educational package provided by the school. Therefore, it seems likely that most charter schools would use other techniques to admit students if not bound by lottery regulations.

Federal Regulations

Many charter schools receive supplementary funding from the federal Charter Schools Program. This program was originally designed to support charter schools during their first three years of existence. However, when the program was reauthorized in 1998, program eligibility was broadened to include charter schools even after their first three years to support the dissemination of promising practices (Finnigan et al., 2004).

The Charter Schools Program requires schools receiving start-up funding to conduct lotteries if they face excess demand. This would seem to provide an incentive to charter schools to conduct lotteries, even if they are located in states that do not require them. However, there are two reasons to suspect that this incentive may be fairly weak. First, most grant funding is awarded to states that, in turn, award funding to individual schools. It seems unlikely that states that do not require lotteries vigorously enforce the rule associated with the Charter Schools Program.

Second, it seems equally unlikely that the federal government vigorously enforces the lottery requirement, either for grants made to states or grants issued directly to charter schools. The most likely avenue for the U.S. Department of Education to monitor compliance with the lottery requirement is through its performance reporting system. While the 2005 performance report for the program alluded to "on-site monitoring by ED," the only pieces of information reported are the number of states with charter school legislation and the number of charter schools in operation—information that could be obtained without active monitoring of the lottery requirement.

Excess Demand

State and federal rules on lotteries only apply when there is excess demand for available positions. There is no empirical evidence on the factors responsible for excess demand, leaving us to rely on theory and informed speculation. Broadly speaking, we can divide these factors into two categories: (1) factors controlled partly or entirely by charter school personnel, (2) external factors, beyond the control of schools.

Charter schools can increase student demand for admission to the school—and thus the number of applications received—in at least four ways: (1) by making investments to increase the school's quality; (2) by taking steps to reduce the costs of attending the school; (3) by marketing the school more aggressively; and (4) by streamlining the application process or delaying the application deadline.

Investing in the School's Quality

Some charter schools probably experience excess demand for the same reason that some restaurants have long waits: they are perceived to be better than competing alternatives. Some of these quality differences can be directly affected by choices the schools make, including decisions about curriculum, instruction, and discipline. Others are more difficult to influence, especially given lottery admissions, including the attributes of potential peer groups.

Reducing the Cost of Attendance

Charter schools cannot charge tuition or application fees. But parents incur indirect costs to send their children to a charter school. For example, parents must transport children to school, and many charter schools require parental participation in student learning and school activities, often formalized through a "contract." Charter schools can reduce the cost of attendance by providing transportation and reducing parental participation obligations.

Marketing the School More Aggressively

Schools can influence the number of applications they receive through their efforts to market the school. These efforts can take many forms, from advertisements to open houses. Schools with excess supply face incentives to market more aggressively to reach capacity and increase their funding. Schools facing excess demand may still see benefits to additional recruiting if parents or authorizers associate excess demand with the quality of the school.

Tweaking the Application Process

Some charter schools require parental attendance at an information session, interviews with the applicant, and an extensive application completed and submitted in January or February. Others simply require a name and telephone number by late spring. Charter schools can increase the number of applicants they receive by making applications available earlier or selecting a later application deadline. In addition, charter schools can also boost applications by streamlining their admissions process.

Some charter schools facing excess demand can expand to meet this demand. Charter schools face two constraints on growth. First, the number of students served by a charter school is sometimes constrained by the charter, which can be amended with the approval of the charter school authorizer. Second, the number of students served by a charter school is constrained by the school's ability to obtain additional space and hire additional teachers. Given variation in state laws, authorizer practices, teacher labor markets, and charter school funding, charter schools may vary considerably in their ability to expand their capacity to meet excess demand.

Finally, excess demand is partly determined by external conditions in local schooling markets. A relevant external condition is the existence of barriers to starting new charter schools when demand exceeds supply. In many markets, excess demand for a product quickly leads to the emergence of competing producers to absorb the demand. In local schooling markets, entry costs and constraints in some states and communities mean that charter school expansions will occur slowly or not at all. Entry costs include investments in school buildings and related infrastructure, which are not always covered by states. Outright constraints include caps on the number of charter schools or rigorous school authorization procedures that deny some school applications.

Therefore, supply constraints may be just as important in generating excess demand for charter schools as demand-side factors. Consider two charter schools, A and B, that have equally good reputations, have identical application procedures, and receive exactly the same number of applications. If School A faces supply constraints in meeting demand but School B does not, then only School A will face excess demand. For example, School A may have access to less classroom space than School B. This difference may reflect short-run constraints, like those associated with a short-term lease. However, it may also reflect differences across states in whether regular public school districts are required to provide excess space in public schools to charter schools or differences in local capital markets that affect opportunities to borrow money to build new school buildings. This example reveals that there are many possible reasons why charter schools may face excess demand.

HOW CHARTER SCHOOLS CONDUCT LOTTERIES

To our knowledge, there is no high-quality, representative evidence on how charter schools conduct lotteries. Some schools describe their lottery procedures on web pages, but most do not. In addition, some descriptions raise as many questions about how the lottery works as they answer. In describing charter school lotteries, we rely on information gleaned from observing a small number of charter school lotteries, talking with other researchers who also observed a small number of charter school lotteries, and extracting information from a small number of charter school websites.[2] This information is not a substitute for systematic evidence. However, given how little is known about charter school lotteries, even anecdotal observations may be informative.

Lottery Settings

It appears that most charter school lotteries are held at the school outside of school hours. In addition, most lotteries are public and parents are invited to attend, even though most states do not require it. Lottery dates and locations are sometimes provided on school web pages in a section on application procedures. In other instances, the information may be provided to the parents at school information sessions or when applications are submitted.

Well-attended public lotteries are held in auditoriums, cafeterias, or other large spaces to accommodate parents. Private lotteries may be held anywhere in the school since there may be only a handful of school staff operating the lottery and recording the results. In some cases, charter school lotteries are conducted by the district.

Definition of Lottery Groups

Lotteries are invariably more complicated than a random drawing from a single applicant group. First, schools typically identify students that are granted lottery exemptions and are automatically admitted, space permitting. For example, many charter schools appear to take advantage of state provisions that allow them to exempt siblings from the lottery. Others exempt siblings of graduates of the school, and many charter schools exempt children of staff and founding families. Lottery participants vie for the remaining open slots.

Second, many charter schools admit students in multiple grade levels each year, though in our experience openings at the school tend to be concentrated in lower grades. For example, charter middle schools offering grades six to eight would be expected to have the most openings in grade six and a smaller number in grades seven and eight to replace students who transfer to another school. Thus, many charter schools conduct separate lotteries within groups defined by grade level. The probability of being admitted to the school via lottery can vary greatly by grade level depending on the number of open slots and the number of applicants by grade.

Third, some charter schools use additional student characteristics to group students within grades. Schools then conduct lotteries within these smaller groups, and the selection probability may vary across groups. For example, some charter schools (perhaps a very small number) conduct separate lotteries for each "sending" school or designated public school to avoid situations where the charter school admits a disproportionate share of the applicants from any particular school. We do not know if any charter schools divide applicant pools and lotteries by race or sex, but we would expect such provisions to face legal restrictions.

Lottery Implementation

Once lottery groups are defined, schools determine the number of students that can be admitted from each lottery group. In most cases, this means that schools determine how many students can be admitted to each grade level after accommodating currently enrolled and lottery-exempted students. After drawing up a list of remaining student applicants within each lottery group, schools implement a random drawing. While some use computerized algorithms to assign random numbers, the vast majority use a lower tech but equally valid approach. For private lotteries, randomly drawn slips of paper may simply contain the name of the applicant. For public lotteries, students are more often assigned lottery numbers, and those lottery numbers are drawn sequentially until all lottery numbers have been drawn.

The outcome is a list of students in order of their drawing. For example, if fifty students were included in the lottery for the initial grade and the school is able to admit thirty-five by lottery, the first thirty-five students will typically be notified that they have been admitted. The remaining fifteen are typically assigned to a waiting list in the order of their lottery draw. Some of these students may be offered admission if some of the first thirty-five decline the offer to enroll or if some lottery-exempt students decide to enroll elsewhere.

This stylized description of the lottery process misses some of subtleties that are more or less important, depending on your perspective. For example, it is not uncommon for siblings who apply to a charter school in the same year to receive some special consideration. If the siblings are applying to the same grade level, they may share the same lottery number and be selected as a pair in the lottery, or they may be entered separately with provisions to admit both siblings if at least one receives a high enough lottery draw to be admitted. If the siblings are applying to different grade levels and being entered into separate lotteries, the school may have provisions to "make space" for the sibling who would not have been admitted based on her lottery draw if her sibling was admitted to the school via lottery at a different grade level.

Waiting-List Management

Schools manage their waiting lists to ensure that they can fill open slots that become available in the school. In theory, the admissions process after the lottery date is straightforward: wait-listed students are offered admission if everyone ahead of them has already been offered admission and if a slot opens up in right grade level. There are potential complicating factors, though we have little evidence on their importance. One complication involves siblings who enter a charter school lottery together. If one sibling is admitted to the school by lottery and the other is not, some charter schools move the second sibling to the top of the waiting list for the respective grade to which she applied. It is also possible that a student from a lottery-exempted group, applying after the lottery date, would be placed at the top of the waiting list.

It seems plausible that waiting-list management provides schools with a modest opportunity to "cherry-pick" preferred students. Some charter schools commit to a formal notification process that gives all families equal opportunity to respond and accept an offer of admission from the waiting list. However, our impression is that the process is usually informal and that notification of admission from the waiting list comes more commonly in the form of a telephone call. The number of calls made to the household, attempts to reach parents at work, and the number of days allowed for a response before moving to the next student on the waiting list may all influence the likelihood that a parent responds to and accept the offer of admission. There is certainly scope for minor selective admissions to be implemented following the lottery. Even so, the amount of information that charter schools have about their applicants may be modest, particularly at schools that only require parents to leave their child's name, grade level, and telephone number.

How Many Charter Schools Conduct Lotteries?

Perhaps surprisingly, there is no reliable evidence on the prevalence of lotteries or even the prevalence of excess demand in charter schools today. All available estimates are too old to be informative, conceptually flawed, or both. The most credible estimates are based on charter schools in operation in 1996 and 1998, estimates that are much too old to be informative today. According to these estimates, 74 percent of charter schools in 1996 reported that student applications exceeded capacity, and 39 percent of these schools reported using a lottery (RPP and the University of Minnesota, 1997, p. 20), implying that 29 percent of charter schools in 1996 admitted students by lottery.

More recent estimates of excess demand suffer from serious flaws, and we have found no more recent estimates of the prevalence of lotteries in charter school admissions. The Center for Education Reform, an organization that advocates for charter schools, conducts an annual charter school survey. In their 2005 survey, they found that 56 percent of charter schools have waiting lists.

However, the response rate for the survey was only 30 percent (The Center for Education Reform, 2005). In addition, schools that maintain waiting lists do not necessarily face excess demand since schools that have received applications but have not made final admissions decisions may perceive the list of applicants as their waiting list. As a result, there is no credible information on the prevalence of excess demand or lotteries since 1998, since which time the number of charter schools has expanded from about 1,100 to almost 3,500 (RPP International, 2000; U.S. Charter Schools, 2006).

LOTTERIES AND CHARTER SCHOOL POLICY

Lottery rules are common in charter school legislation, so one might presume that they are intended to achieve a common policy goal. Nonetheless, policy goals are rarely specified in detail or evaluated by researchers. This section makes educated guesses about the intended policy outcomes of mandated lotteries as well as potential unintended outcomes.

Intended Policy Outcomes

In any choice-based school reform, including charter schools, the composition of students in "new" choice schools is jointly determined by the demand-side choices of parents and the supply-side behavior of schools. Parents make choices, guided by their preferences, about whether to apply to a new school, where to apply, and whether to accept an offer of admission. A common concern is that parents with higher incomes or greater access to information will be most likely to apply to schools and accept offers (though it is also possible that parents with lower-quality public school alternatives will exercise choice). On the supply side of the market, charter schools make decisions about which students to admit, either initially or from a waiting list, and there is some concern that "creaming" behavior will lead schools to choose higher-scoring students.

The simplest policy goal of lottery regulations is to ensure that admissions are fair and nondiscriminatory in the presence of excess demand (of course, nondiscrimination laws apply even in the absence of lottery admissions). A related implication is that lotteries may reduce the likelihood that the introduction of charter schools would exacerbate interschool stratification of students by income, race, or ability. Charter school laws regulate the supply side of the market by diminishing the scope for creaming behavior by schools.

Of course, even with such regulations, the applicant pool may still be "selective" because of demand-side choices by parents. However, lottery regulations could also indirectly affect the demand side of the market. If parents know that charter schools must admit students by lottery if they are oversubscribed, then it may encourage applications from students unlikely to be admitted to highly selective schools. (Imagine how the applicant pool to Harvard would change if it replaced selective admissions with a lottery!)

Research on stratification is hard-pressed to identify the specific contribution of lotteries to increasing or decreasing interschool stratification. At best, research has identified the *net* effect of introducing charter schools on stratification across public and charter schools, inclusive of demand-side and supply-side effects (at worst, research summarizes poorly interpreted descriptive statistics, with little causal meaning attached).

In one careful study, Dee and Fu (2004) assess how the percent of white non-Hispanic students in Arizona public schools changes in response to the statewide introduction of charter schools. To address the possibility that other circumstances could explain shifting racial composition in public schools, they used public schools in neighboring states, like New Mexico, where charter schools were not aggressively implemented. They find that the introduction of charter schools reduced the proportion of white students in Arizona public schools by 2 percent, on average. However, it cannot be determined whether this figure would have been even larger (or smaller) if Arizona did not require lottery admissions.

Unintended Policy Outcomes

Lottery requirements also have unintended consequences that could blunt the intended impact of lotteries on stratification and undermine other policy goals (such as increasing achievement). We must emphasize that there is little systematic evidence on any of these responses, and we view this as an inventory of potential impacts that should be fully examined by researchers.

First, it is possible that schools, especially those with a strong incentive to engage in selective admissions, could cheat on a lottery by manipulating its outcomes (i.e., transferring a preferred, "losing" student to the admitted group).[3] This seems quite unlikely when the lottery is conducted publicly, but it is certainly possible in other contexts, given the wide variation in the extent and quality of monitoring and enforcement. If precise records on lottery applicants were to be maintained, it would be a simple matter to verify the randomness of selection by comparing baseline attributes of winners and losers within each lottery group. In the absence of cheating, one would not expect any average differences, although statistical noise could occasionally introduce differences that could be mistaken for lottery manipulation.

Second, it is possible that schools engage in gaming behaviors that modify the composition of the applicant pool (even if actual selection of winners occurs via a random lottery). A particular concern is that gaming behavior could discourage or exclude some parents from the applicant pool. This sort of behavior would be far more difficult for researchers to identify, and there is considerable ambiguity as to whether some behaviors violate state and federal rules.

Prior sections identified several possible gaming responses. First, schools could time the applications process, including deadlines, to exclude "late" applicants. Second, schools could make the applications process more costly (i.e., requiring essays or attendance at specific information sessions). Third, schools could make school attendance more costly (and discourage applications from some parents) by mandating parental participation in school activities or other "contractual" obligations. Fourth, schools could make greater efforts to contact some families on the waiting list in the event that slots become available when the lottery is completed. Wait-listed parents may also lobby to have their child bumped ahead of others, a phenomenon that occurs in admissions offices of many schools.

Third, lottery requirements prevent charter schools from selecting the students that would benefit the most. As a result, these requirements may reduce charter school effectiveness. However, lottery requirements also prevent charter schools from responding to the incentives they face under No Child Left Behind (NCLB) and selecting the students likely to score highly on state assessments and graduate from high school. Since there is no empirical evidence on whether charter school impacts are relatively large or relatively small for these students, it is unclear what effects lottery requirements have on charter school effectiveness and the net benefits of charter schools.

Fourth, lottery requirements could have general equilibrium effects on local schooling markets. At a given moment, suppose there are "potential" charter schools that only exist on the drawing boards of their creators. Further suppose that potential charter school administrators must decide whether or not to enter the schooling market based upon many factors, including the cost of educating potential students and the amount of discretion they would have in all aspects of the school, including admissions decisions. A binding lottery admission reduces the scope of charter schools, whether for-profit or non-profit, to choose the applicants that are the least costly to educate or to choose the applicants they would prefer to serve. Therefore, lottery requirements may discourage some potential charter schools from entering the market.

LOTTERIES AND CHARTER SCHOOL RESEARCH

Randomized control trials (RCTs) have been used to measure the impact of educational interventions ranging from class size reduction to whole school reform. In school choice, RCTs have been used to examine the effects of private school voucher programs in New York City, Washington, D.C., and Dayton, Ohio (Howell and Peterson, 2006; Krueger and Zhu, 2004). In these studies, eligible applicants were randomly assigned to a treatment group that was offered a private school scholarship or a control group that was not. The advantages of RCTs are well-known (Barrow and Rouse, 2005). Because of randomization, there are no systematic differences between members of the treatment and control groups, and impact estimates based on a mean comparison between the groups are free of selection bias.

In many cases an RCT cannot be conducted, but assignment to a treatment or control condition is nonetheless random because of administrative rules. The mandated use of lottery admissions in choice schools provides just such a "natural" experiment. A growing number of studies employ lotteries to estimate the impact on student outcomes of attending charter schools in Chicago (Hoxby and Rockoff, 2004); magnet schools in New York and San Diego (Crain, Heeber, and Si, 1992; Betts et al., 2006); open enrollment schools, including magnet schools, in Chicago (Cullen, Jacob, and Levitt, 2006); and private schools in Colombia and Milwaukee (Angrist et al., 2002; Angrist, Bettinger, and Kremer, 2006; Rouse, 1998).[4]

In the remainder of this section, we address four questions about the emerging body of lottery-based research on charter and choice schools. First, what is the internal validity of lottery-based studies? That is, can they establish whether charter schools *cause* changes in student outcomes? Second, what is the external validity of lottery-based studies? That is, can their results be generalized to other students, schools, and settings? Third, how feasible are lottery-based studies, and what are the obstacles to implementation? Fourth, what contributions can lottery-based studies make in examining the effects of charter schools?

Internal Validity

In nonexperimental studies of charter school impacts, researchers compare the outcomes of students that apply and are accepted to charter schools with those of students that do not apply. The danger is that students in each group are different—perhaps in their ability or motivation—and that such differences, rather than charter school attendance, explain later differences in outcomes. Researchers make sophisticated statistical attempts to control for such differences, but nonexperimental studies, by their nature, do not provide airtight conclusions about the causal impact of attending a charter school.

In lottery-based studies of charter school impacts, researchers compare the outcomes of lottery winners and losers, respectively (all of whom applied to the charter school). Because assignment to each group is random, as in an RCT, and not determined by selection on observed or unobserved attributes of students, we are assured that the only systematic difference between the two groups is their exposure to the treatment. Hence, any later differences can be confidently attributed to the charter school admission treatment.

One caveat is that a simple comparison of students in treatment and control groups does not typically yield an estimate of actually *attending* a charter school. In fact, many lottery winners will decline an offer, and some losers may enroll in a different charter school. Thus, a comparison of student outcomes across lottery winners and losers yield an estimate of the "intent-to-treat," or the effect of being offered admission to a charter school. As it turns out, this is often relevant to policy makers, who can almost rarely mandate compliance with a social policy. Even so, researchers can use additional statistical methods to obtain estimates of the effect of actually attending a charter school, at least among a subset of lottery winners that accepted the offer of admission.

In principle, lottery-based studies should have the same internal validity as RCTs. The main difference between the study designs involves the degree of control over the randomization process. Randomization is not rocket science, and there is no reason to think that schools and districts are any less capable of conducting a random drawing than university researchers. However, charter schools actually conduct rather sophisticated experiments—constrained by the practical demands of operating a school and complying with rules—in which probabilities of being offered a position in a charter school can vary dramatically from student to student. First, experiments are usually conducted *within* each school and *within* grades in a given school. Second, many students are exempted from lottery procedures or given additional preferences by grouping students into additional lottery strata.

This is not a problem, as long as researchers using the natural experiment are able to fully ascertain and account for such differences. In practice, researchers conducting lottery-based studies must first be able to identify students who were not included in the lottery and exclude them from the analysis. This may include some students who were not eligible to attend the charter school because of where they lived or some other reason; it is likely to include students who were exempted from the lottery and admitted because they were siblings of current students in the school or for some other reason.

Researchers must then identify students who *were* included in the lottery and determine their probability of winning the lottery. The most straightforward way of doing so is to simply identify the smallest lottery groups to which each student belongs (i.e., second-graders applying to Northside Charter in fall 2006). In some examples cited previously, the lottery groups are further divided by zone of residence or other attributes.

However, siblings who apply to same schools in the same year, as discussed earlier in the chapter, can complicate matters. The probability that each sibling applying to the same school is admitted will depend on how the school treats these siblings in their lottery—whether they share the same lottery draw or have different draws—and whether it is school policy or practice to admit one sibling if the other receives a sufficiently high lottery draw to warrant admission. Under certain circumstances, charter schools policies can effectively give preference through higher admissions probabilities to families who submit applications for two children instead of one.

Our experience suggests that to adequately distinguish between the systematic and random components of charter school lotteries, it is sometimes necessary to attend the lottery, identify the students who participated in the lottery, confirm that the lottery was truly random, and identify any idiosyncrasies that influenced students' selection probabilities. This may not be necessary when lotteries are conducted by the district using computer programs that assign random numbers. In contrast, it may be critical for lotteries conducted by schools, in private, and without substantial documentation. It may also be important for publicly conducted lotteries in order to ensure a proper record of the lottery results (which is later merged with data on student attributes and outcomes). At any point in time, charter schools can provide information on the students currently enrolled and the students currently on their waiting list.

However, because charter schools are not typically required to report the results of their lotteries to the state, district, or authorizing agency, it may be difficult to obtain an accurate record of the lottery results from the school after the lottery has been conducted. The best opportunity to obtain a complete and accurate record of the lottery is probably on lottery night, and the only guarantee of obtaining that record is by attending and recording the results.

In addition, lottery-based studies must account for admissions from the waiting list. An important question for researchers conducting lottery-based studies is whether students admitted from the waiting list should be treated as lottery winners or as lottery losers—or excluded from the analysis entirely. The right answer might depend on how early students are admitted from the waiting list. Students admitted from the waiting list shortly after the lottery was held may value their admissions to the school as much as initial lottery winners: if so, they may accept these offers at the same rate as initial lottery winners, and it would seem natural to treat these students as lottery winners. However, one could imagine a scenario in which charter schools offer admission to students from their waiting list so late that the probability of acceptance is very low, and it might make more sense to treat these students as lottery losers.

Hoxby and Rockoff (2004) excluded students admitted to a charter schools from waiting lists after the lottery from the analysis, but they tested whether their findings were robust to alternative approaches. To our knowledge, no serious attempt has been made to identify a technically justifiable approach to this particular challenge, which is faced by all studies that rely on school- or district-based lotteries.

While many and perhaps most charter school lotteries are public, the process of working through the waiting list is inherently private: parents are notified if *their* children are being offered admission, not when *other* children are offered admission. Therefore, while we have no evidence suggesting that charter schools do anything other than admit students from the waiting list in the order of their lottery draws, it is worth noting that charter schools manage their waiting lists without outside scrutiny or regulation. To compute internally valid estimates of charter school impacts, researchers must be able to fully reconstruct the initial lottery assignment and the subsequent process of waiting-list management.[5]

A useful illustration of these points is provided by research on the Milwaukee Parental Choice Program (see especially Rouse, 1998). It suggests that lottery-based studies that cannot fully account for variation in the selection probability fall short of an RCT. In the Milwaukee program, participating private schools were required to admit voucher recipients by lottery when they were oversubscribed. Unfortunately, the Milwaukee Parental Choice Program public release data files do not include enough information to compute the probability of winning a lottery and being offered a position at a participating private school.

Rouse (1998) identified three major inadequacies in the data. First, there was no information on which schools conducted lotteries in which grade levels. Students who applied to schools in grade levels where the number of slots available was greater than the number of applicants were admitted without a lottery. Since these students were effectively not randomized, they should be excluded from the analysis, but they cannot be identified with the data available. Second, there is no information on whether particular students were exempt from the lottery. Rouse notes that siblings were admitted without having to participate in a lottery. Third, the information available was inadequate to determine the exact schools and grade level to which a student applied. Researchers have used "imputed" lotteries, but Rouse correctly notes that the information available for imputation was inadequate to identify these schools with much confidence.

In contrast, Cullen, Jacob, and Levitt (2006) were able to obtain very rich data on magnet school lottery results in Chicago, and it appears that they were able to effectively use these data to account for variation in the probability of being randomly selected for admission. The authors note that the lotteries in Chicago are typically conducted within lottery groups defined by combinations of school, grade, gender, and race, in order to help achieve desegregation goals. They were able to obtain data on this level of detail from the Chicago Public Schools, and they used the data to control for the lottery in which students participated. In addition, the data they obtained on lottery results allowed them to identify "lotteries" without any losers and exclude these students from the analysis.[6]

A key difference between the lotteries in Milwaukee and Chicago is whether the schools or district managed the lottery process. In Milwaukee, the private schools that accepted the vouchers managed their own lottery process. Therefore, it is probably not surprising that the public-use data lacked the lottery details necessary to support a study with internal validity on par with an RCT. In contrast, in Chicago, the authors focused on the twenty-seven of forty-five high schools for which the district managed the lottery, and they indicate that the district only maintains information on lottery outcomes for these schools. Therefore, if the authors had tried to include the other eighteen high schools in their study, they would have faced the same problem that researchers faced in Milwaukee.

Unfortunately from a research perspective, most charter schools conduct their own lotteries and are not required to report their lottery results to any party. In Hoxby and Rockoff (2004), the authors appear to have obtained the lottery results either from the schools themselves or from the Chicago Charter School Foundation, which granted the charters to the three schools included in the analysis. However, most charter school lotteries are conducted by the schools themselves, and the local school district will not typically have access to charter school lottery results.

Even when perfect data on the lottery results are unavailable, lottery-based studies may still have higher internal validity than many nonexperimental studies. It is possible that the largest source of selection bias in charter school results from comparisons of charter school students with students who *never applied* to a charter school and are very different from applicants in observed and unobserved ways. If a lottery-based study is able, at least, to restrict the analysis to students who applied to one or more charter schools, it may still serve to greatly reduce selection bias.

External Validity

The most common criticism of RCTs and, by corollary, lottery-based natural experiments, is that their findings have less external validity. While this is not always true—RCTs can be based on representative samples of students or schools—it is true that many RCTs and all natural experiments are designed around opportunities to randomize, which occurs when students or schools volunteer or are required to subject themselves to randomized assignment. In charter schools, this occurs when the schools face excess demand. Put simply, we can only extrapolate lottery-based findings to "similar" students, subject to lottery assignment, that attend "similar" charter schools in "similar" settings. The remainder of this section takes a closer look at students, schools, and settings to assess the external validity of lottery-based studies.

Lottery-based studies only examine the effects on students that have chosen to apply to charter schools. There may be systematic differences between charter school applicants and nonapplicants. The results of lottery-based studies of charter school effects may not be generalizable to nonapplicants for a variety of hard-to-test reasons. However, it is important to recognize that this is also a limitation of many alternative types of charter school studies, including studies based on longitudinal student-level data that estimate models with student fixed effects. Furthermore, if the policy question of primary interest is whether charter schools have positive effects on the outcomes of the students *they currently serve*, this should be viewed as a minor limitation. This limitation looms larger if the primary policy question was whether policy makers should support a large expansion of charter schools that enlarges the applicant pool.

Not all charter schools face excess demand and conduct lotteries, and it is surely safe to say that not all charter schools are equal in quality. If higher-quality charter schools are more likely to face excess demand and conduct lotteries, lottery-based studies will be weighted toward "better" charter schools, as defined by the students and parents who choose them. If parents place a high value on academic gains, and parents can obtain enough information to identify the charter schools that are most effective at boosting student achievement, then we might expect oversubscribed charter schools to yield larger impacts on student achievement and related outcomes than other charter schools.

However, parents who choose charter schools may value other school attributes, like discipline and safety, as much as or more than academics. Furthermore, while parents can obtain systematic evidence on academic *outcomes* at different schools, the only evidence on the *impacts* of specific schools is anecdotal in nature. Therefore, we should not assume that oversubscribed charter schools produce larger academic gains than other charter schools.

In addition, the quality of nearby alternative schooling options may vary across charter schools, and low-quality alternatives may boost demand for charter schools. We would expect greater demand for charter schools in areas where regular public schools have a bad reputation. If increased supply were unable to keep pace with demand, then we might find a larger fraction of charter schools conducting lotteries in these areas than in others, and lottery-based studies would be weighted toward the charter schools in these areas. If the bad reputation of the public school alternatives in these areas were warranted—that is, indicative of poor performance in boosting students' academic performance—then we would expect to find larger impacts of attending charter schools in these areas.

It is important to recognize that there is no empirical evidence on the relationship between charter school quality, the quality of nearby local public schools, and the likelihood that the charter school conducts a lottery. Since the impacts that charter schools have on student outcomes depend on both the quality of the charter schools themselves and the quality of the best alternative options, it seems plausible that charter schools that conduct lotteries are more effective in boosting student outcomes than charter schools that do not conduct lotteries. However, given the lack of evidence, little can be said with confidence about the extent to which we can generalize the results from lottery-based studies of charter schools to the broader population of charter schools, including those that do not conduct lotteries.

There are two general responses to these challenges. The most relevant to site-specific, lottery-based studies is that researchers should take great care in describing the students, charter schools, and local schooling contexts—including public school alternatives—that contribute to their study. In the absence of such descriptions, readers cannot make reasoned judgments about whether study results can be generalized.

More generally, it suggests that the greatest benefits from lottery-based studies will emerge after many have been conducted among diverse student groups, in a wide array of charter schools, and across multiple cities and states. This will diminish the inherent subjectivity in making generalizations. Perhaps an even better approach to addressing the challenges in generalizing from lottery-based studies is to conduct a large, multisite, lottery-based study to generate evidence on the variability in impacts across charter schools while eliminating or at least reducing variability in the estimates due to differences in study implementation that can occur across multiple lottery-based studies. The Mathematica-IES evaluation is a good example of such a study.

Feasibility of Research Using Lotteries

One of the main advantages of lottery-based studies is feasibility. RCTs on the effects of charter schools are not likely to be feasible because this would require schools to relinquish control over a central feature of their admissions process to the researchers conducting the evaluation. Even if this were legally permissible and allowed by the charter school's authorizing agency, it is unlikely that a charter school principal would agree to forgo their usual lottery procedures and "subcontract out" randomization to an outside organization just to facilitate an evaluation. Therefore, if we want studies of charter school effectiveness with the potential of having internal validity comparable to an RCT, lottery-based studies are probably the only option.

In addition, lottery-based studies do not require the longitudinal data needed to estimate models of student fixed effects or compute test score gains. They do not even require data on student characteristics beyond those used to define different lottery strata or groups for the same reasons that randomized experiments do not require this information: if the lottery is truly random, simple differences in means within groups can provide unbiased estimates of causal effects.

However, there are two reasons why measures of prior achievement and other background characteristics are valuable even in lottery-based studies. First, if lottery losers are more likely to leave the school system, there may be systematic differences between the lottery winners and lottery losers for whom the study can obtain follow-up data, and unadjusted differences in outcomes between lottery winners and lottery losers may provide biased estimates of the effects of school choice. This bias can be reduced by controlling for background characteristics and prelottery measures of achievement in the analysis. Second, this information can be used to check—or, if the researchers observed the lottery, double-check—if the lottery was truly random. If the differences between lottery winners and losers are larger than one would expect by chance, this would cast doubt on whether the lottery created two groups without any systematic prelottery differences.

The Potential Contribution of Research Using Lotteries

Given the pros and cons of lottery-based studies, what can they contribute to our understanding of charter school effectiveness? On one hand, the potentially low external validity of lottery-based studies of charter schools is a cause for concern. On the other hand, the most credible alternative tested to date—studies based on models of student fixed effects—may have less internal validity.[7]

In this context, lottery-based studies can make three contributions. First, they can contribute some "data points" on charter school effectiveness that are not subject to selection bias. In that sense, they should provide a common ground over which both charter school advocates and opponents can agree. If a lottery-based study is conducted correctly and documented in a way that makes this clear, then it almost surely provides the best evidence of charter school effectiveness for those charter schools included in the study and for any population of charter schools that the sample can be argued convincingly to represent.

Second, lottery-based studies may be a credible way to compare the effectiveness of different types of charter schools. While oversubscribed charter schools of any type may be unrepresentative of all charter schools of that type, oversubscribed charter schools may be equally unrepresentative for all types of charter schools. If so, the relative effectiveness of different types of charter schools can be estimated without bias using only schools that conduct lotteries.

Third, lotteries have been underexploited for testing the internal validity of nonexperimental methods. If we discover that lottery-based studies yield more or less favorable estimates than studies based on student fixed effects, for example, it will be impossible to understand the source of the differences as long as the studies were conducted in different settings. The only way to estimate the selection bias in nonexperimental studies would be to embed a nonexperimental analysis within a lottery-based study to see if nonexperimental methods and the experimental methods—those based on comparisons between lottery winners and lottery losers—yield similar results. This type of comparison has been discussed and tested in Hoxby and Murarka (2006).[8]

How difficult is it to embed an analysis based on student fixed effects, for example, into a lottery-based study? Lottery-based studies typically require an agreement with the local school district or state to allow the research team to track the outcomes of lottery participants using student-level longitudinal data. If this agreement were also crafted to cover data for a comparison sample of district students, then it would be possible to estimate a fixed-effects model of charter school effectiveness. The fixed-effects analysis would require more years of data than a typical lottery-based study. In principle, a lottery-based study would need only data for two years—the year before the lottery to test for preexisting differences and some year after the lottery to measure effects—but a fixed-effects analysis of test score gains would require at least three years of data and would benefit greatly from additional years. However, several researchers have been able to obtain the longitudinal data necessary to estimate charter school effects based on models of student fixed effects, and districts or states willing to share two years of data to support a lottery-based study may be willing to share data for enough years to support a credible analysis based on student fixed effects.

CONCLUSION

In this paper, we have described why charter schools conduct lotteries, how they conduct them, how these lotteries are regulated and enforced, and how they can be used for research purposes to estimate the effects of attending a charter school. In conducting this research project, we have reached the following conclusions:

1. *Charter school lotteries are not extremely complicated, but they are more complicated than some might think.* At many charter schools, some students are exempt from the lottery. The likelihood of admissions in a charter school lottery can depend on whether separate lotteries are conducted by grade; the treatment of siblings applying to the school concurrently; where the family lives; and other factors that vary across charter schools.
2. *Charter school lotteries are largely unregulated.* While state and federal regulations require most charter schools to conduct lotteries when they face excess demand, the regulations are not much more specific than that. There is no systematic evidence on the number of charter schools facing excess demand and the number of charter schools conducting lotteries, and it does not appear that states or the federal government take an active role in enforcing lottery requirements.
3. *Charter school lotteries provide great opportunities to learn about the effects of attending a charter school.* These lotteries generate natural experiments that allow researchers to overcome the selection bias faced by most research designs. However, it is critically important to fully understand the lottery process—to distinguish the random component of the process from the systematic components—and to have complete data on lottery results.

The states and the federal government have at least two options for increasing the transparency of charter school lotteries. First, they could require charter school lotteries to be conducted in public. Public lotteries provide parents who apply to the school on behalf of their children with the opportunity to verify that the lottery was fair. California's charter school law includes this requirement; other states (and the federal Charter School Program) could adopt the same requirement. This may be an appealing policy option because the regulatory costs would be low.

Second, they could require more extensive reporting of lottery procedures and results. This would include a complete description of lottery procedures. Our experience suggests that charter schools typically do not document their lottery process in enough detail to fully distinguish the systematic components of the process, such as the treatment of siblings, from the random components. The state, authorizers, or the federal government could require charter schools to provide this documentation. In addition, these entities could require annual reporting of lottery results at the student level. This might include: (1) a complete list of student applicants, including a unique identifying code for

Table 6.2. Summary of State Regulations on Charter School Admissions for Ten States

State (# of charter schools)	Lottery required if oversubscribed?	Lottery required to be public?	Nonenrolled students who receive admissions preference	Students who can be excluded from admission	Relevant state law or code
California (574)	Yes	Yes	Siblings Students from a specific geographic region	None	California Education Code: 47605
Arizona (499)	Yes	No	Siblings Students from a specific geographic region	Students who have been expelled from other schools	Arizona Revised Statutes Education Code: 15-184
Florida (338)	Yes	No	Siblings Students from a specific geographic region Children of board members Children of employees	Students who fail to meet artistic, academic, or other standards (as specified in charter)	Florida State Education Code 1002.33
Ohio (268)	Yes	No	Siblings Students from a specific geographic region	None	Ohio Revised Code 3314.06
Texas (241)	No	N/A	Siblings Children of founders Children of employees	Students with criminal records	Texas Education Code 12.117; Texas Administrative Code 100.1207
Michigan (216)	Yes	No	Siblings	None	Michigan Revised School Code: 380.501–380.507
Wisconsin (160)	No	N/A	Students from a specific geographic region	None	Wisconsin Statutes: 118.40
Pennsylvania (114)	Yes	No	Siblings Students from a specific geographic region Children of founders	None	Act 22 of 1997: Section 1723
Colorado (113)	No	N/A	Siblings Children of founders	None	Colorado Revised Statutes: 22-30.5-101–115
Minnesota (102)	Yes	No	Siblings Students from a specific geographic region	None	Minnesota 124D.10

Sources: U.S. Charter Schools (2006), and state regulations cited in last column.
Notes: Charter schools in Florida and Wisconsin may give preference to students based on where they live provided that this process does not distort the ethnic/racial balance stated in the charter.

each student if available and allowed by state law; (2) the lottery groups to which each student belongs (i.e., lottery-exempted, second-grade lottery applicants, third-grade applicants, etc.); (3) the initial lottery results within each group (i.e., whether a student wins or loses, and whether a student is assigned to a wait list); (4) the subsequent lottery results, including the offers of admission to wait-listed students and acceptance decisions of initial lottery winners and students admitted from the waiting list.

Data on lottery results are potentially useful for lottery monitoring and research when merged with student records data on demographic characteristics, prior test scores, and other information. The combination of lottery results and student records data would be useful in conducting simple lottery audits. If the lottery was random within strata, then the average characteristics of lottery winners and losers within strata should not be statistically different. Significant differences—especially across several lottery strata or admission years—might either suggest that the documentation provided on the lottery process is inaccurate or insufficient or that schools are cheating the lottery and enrolling the students they would prefer to enroll. While regulators should not assume that significant differences between lottery winners and losers indicate cheating, these differences might warrant further investigation.

In addition, well-maintained lottery records combined with data on test scores facilitate lottery-based studies on the effects of attending charter schools on student achievement, such as Hoxby and Rockoff (2004) and the Mathematica-IES study. Preexisting data on lottery results would obviate the need for large additional data collection efforts to support research. It may also help us to avoid the vitriolic debates that accompany studies with imperfectly observed lotteries, like the Milwaukee voucher program (Rouse, 1998). High-quality data might have other research uses as well. For example, they might facilitate better research on the role of charter school policy, including policies regarding lotteries, in affecting student sorting and stratification.

In summary, charter school lotteries are an important tool to help policy makers ensure open access to charter schools. They also have enormous research potential if they are properly understood. The limitations involving the generalizability of findings from lottery-based studies of charter schools should not be minimized, but neither should they be used as an excuse to squander the research opportunities that charter school lotteries provide in a policy area rife with strong opinions but short on compelling scientific evidence.

NOTES

1. Because many schools in Chile are managed by for-profit entities but are not subject to lottery requirements, an examination of the Chilean educational system

may shed light on how U.S. charter schools would behave without such requirements. In Chile, more than a third of school enrollments are in publicly funded and privately managed schools that are subject to many public regulations. They are not subject to lottery admissions requirements, however, and surveys suggest that a large proportion of schools consider test scores, prior behavior, and parental interviews when making admissions decisions (see McEwan, 2001, and the citations therein).

2. For example, one of the authors of this chapter, Robert Olsen, participated in the design and early implementation of the National Charter School Evaluation, which is being conducted by Mathematica Policy Research, Inc., for the U.S. Department of Education's Institute of Education Sciences (IES). The study team observed the lotteries of the charter schools participating in the evaluation to ensure that they were truly random. However, the lotteries observed by any individual member of the study team was a small and unrepresentative sample of the lotteries conducted by the schools participating in the evaluation, which was a relatively small and nonrandom sample of charter schools nationwide.

3. In a similar vein, recent research has found evidence on teacher or administrator cheating on tests in 4 to 5 percent of elementary school classrooms in Chicago (Jacob and Levitt, 2003). Cheating is higher when administrators are subject to high-powered incentives. Since charter schools are subject to many of the same accountability incentives, it is at least conceivable that other forms of "cheating," like lottery manipulation, could occur in a minority of cases.

4. The Mathematica-IES evaluation, which was described earlier and is based on a much larger number of charter schools, is ongoing and will yield findings over the next few years.

5. In many cases, it may not be possible to fully describe the systematic and random components of the process used to admit students from the waiting list. In these cases, it would seem safest to design the analysis around the events we know to be random, such as the lottery number drawn in a public lottery observed by the researcher. This lottery number could be used in two ways. First, researchers can measure the effect of winning the initial lottery by comparing initial lottery winners to initial lottery losers. Second, researchers can measure the effect of enrolling in a charter school using the random lottery number as an instrumental variable (for example, see Angrist, Imbens, and Rubin, 1996).

6. Perhaps the only detail not addressed in the paper was the treatment of wait-listed students. We suspect that students admitted from the waiting list were treated as lottery winners. However, in this study as well as other studies based on district lotteries, it is unclear how students admitted from the waiting list were treated in the analysis, and the district's procedures for admitting students from waiting lists was not documented in the paper.

7. The chapter by Betts, Tang, and Zau in this volume compares lottery-based estimates of the effects of winning a lottery to attend the Preuss School in San Diego with nonexperimental estimates. The nonlottery results are fairly close to the lottery results, especially when value-added results are used.

8. Informal communications with IES staff associated with the National Charter School Evaluation indicate that IES is considering adding this type of analysis to the evaluation if resources permit

REFERENCES

Angrist, J., Bettinger, E., Bloom, E., King, E., and Kremer, M. (2002). Vouchers for Private Schooling in Colombia: Evidence from a Randomized Natural Experiment. *American Economic Review* 92:5, 1535–58.

Angrist, J., Bettinger, E., and Kremer, M. (2006). Long-term Educational Consequences of Secondary School Vouchers: Evidence from Administrative Records in Colombia. *American Economic Review* 96:3, 847–62.

Angrist, J., Imbens, G., and Rubin, D. (1996). Identification of Causal Effects Using Instrumental Variables. *Journal of Econometrics* 71:1–2, 145–60.

Barrow, L., and Rouse, C. E. (2005). *Causality, Causality, Causality: The View of Education Inputs and Outputs from Economics.* Working Paper WP-05-15. Chicago: Federal Reserve Bank of Chicago.

Betts, J., Rice, L. A., Zau, A. C., Tang, Y. E., and Koedel, C. R. (2006). *Does School Choice Work? Effects on Student Integration and Achievement.* San Francisco: Public Policy Institute of California.

Center for Education Reform. (2005). *Annual Survey of America's Charter Schools: 2005 Data.* Downloaded October 29, 2006, from http://www.edreform.com/_upload/ncsw-numbers.pdf.

Crain, R. L., Heebner, A. L, and Si, Y.-P. (1992). *The Effectiveness of New York City's Career Magnet Schools: An Evaluation of Ninth Grade Performance Using an Experimental Design.* Berkeley, CA: National Center for Research in Vocational Education, UC-Berkeley.

Cullen, J. B., Jacob, B. A., and Levitt, S. (2006). The Effect of School Choice on Participants: Evidence from Randomized Lotteries. *Econometrica* 74:5, 1191–1230.

Dee, T. S., and Fu, H. (2004). Do Charter Schools Skim Students or Drain Resources? *Economics of Education Review* 23, 259–71.

Finnigan, K., Adelman, N., Anderson, L., Cotton, L., Donnelly, M., and Price, T. (2004). *Evaluation of the Public Charter Schools Program: Final Report.* Washington, DC: Report to the U.S. Department of Education.

Howell, W., and Peterson, P. (2006). *The Education Gap: Vouchers and Urban Schools.* Washington, DC: Brookings Institution Press.

Hoxby, C., and Murarka, S. (2006). *Methods of Assessing the Achievement of Students in Charter Schools.* Working Paper, National Center on School Choice, Vanderbilt University, September 2006.

Hoxby, C., and Rockoff, J. E. (2004). *The Impact of Charter Schools on Student Achievement.* Unpublished manuscript, Harvard University.

Hsieh, C.-T., and Urquiola, M. (2006). The Effects of Generalized School Choice on Achievement and Stratification: Evidence from Chile's Voucher Program. *Journal of Public Economics*, 90, 1477–1503.

Jacob, B. A., and Levitt, S. D. (2003). Rotten Apples: An Investigation of the Prevalence and Predictors of Teacher Cheating. *Quarterly Journal of Economics* 118:3, 843–77.

Krueger, A. B., and Zhu, P. (2004). Another Look at the New York City School Voucher Experiment. *American Behavioral Scientist* 47:5, 658–98.

McEwan, E. K., and McEwan, P. J. (2003). *Making Sense of Research.* Thousand Oaks, CA: Corwin.

McEwan, P. J. (2000). The Potential Impact of Large-scale Voucher Programs. *Review of Educational Research* 70:2, 103–49.

McEwan, P. J. (2001). The Effectiveness of Public, Catholic, and Non-religious Private Schools in Chile's Voucher System. *Education Economics* 9:2, 103–28.

McEwan, P. J. (2004). The Potential Impact of Vouchers. *Peabody Journal of Education* 73:3, 57–80.

Rouse, C. E. (1998). Private School Vouchers and Student Achievement: An Evaluation of the Milwaukee Parental Choice Program. *Quarterly Journal of Economics* 113:2, 553–602.

RPP International and the University of Minnesota. (1997). *A Study of Charter Schools: First-year Report.* Washington, DC: U.S. Department of Education. Downloaded October 29, 2006, from http://www.ed.gov/pubs/charter/index.html.

US Charter Schools. (2006). *State Information.* Downloaded October 29, 2006, from http://www.uscharterschools.org/pub/uscs_docs/sp/index.htm.

Chapter Seven

Charter School Maturation as a Factor in Performance Assessment and Accountability

Paul T. Hill and Lydia Rainey

INTRODUCTION

Charter schools are new schools. The oldest charter school is fifteen years old; the average age is under five years. Nationwide, three out of four charter schools did not exist before their charter was granted (one out of four charters existed before, as a public or private school).

New charter schools appear to have special problems. Some close before ever teaching a class or during their first year of operation. Moreover, charter schools that survive their first year often have relatively low test scores, which tend to improve over time, a phenomenon that has been documented using diverse methods (see Booker, Gilpatric, Gronberg, and Jansen, 2004; Hanushek, Kain, Rivkin, and Branch, 2005; and Bifulco and Ladd, 2005). Research on schools run by Edison, a for-profit contractor that runs many charter schools as well as some schools under direct contract from school systems, shows not only that new school scores improve over time but also that scores of children attending a new school decline in the first year (Gill et al., 2004; see also Loveless, 2003, pp. 27–36, 34). The first-year decline could be an artifact of changing tests or simple disruption of children's educational routines (see, for example, Hanushek, Kain, and Rivkin, 2004, pp. 1721–46), but the growth over time is more likely related to the schools' development as organizations.

This chapter explores the implications of school newness for research on charter school effectiveness, especially for studies that compare scores of students in charter schools and district-run public schools, which on average are much older. It also suggests how we can learn more about problems associated with newness and the processes of school maturation. A better understanding of charter school maturation could both help outcomes researchers—by allowing researchers to take better account of the special problems of newness—and authorizers and other groups concerned about school quality—by helping them distinguish between normal maturation problems and abnormal developments that may indicate serious problems.

THE POSSIBLE SIGNIFICANCE
OF SCHOOL NEWNESS AND MATURATION

Research on the effectiveness of charter schools needs to consider factors that might affect student outcomes. Thus, for example, researchers take account of students' family backgrounds. Many studies have shown that low-income students and students from disrupted families generally score lower on tests and have more difficulty in school than students from more advantaged families. The same is true of students whose home language is not English and of children who suffer from handicapping conditions.

Any analysis of charter school outcomes that did not consider such factors could be invalid because differences in the outcomes associated with one school versus another could be due to unknown differences in student body composition. Studies that do not consider the consequences of student characteristics have the burden of proof to show that any outcome differences they find are validly attributable to school, not student, effects.[1]

Much the same is true of other factors. School funding is often cited as a factor related to performance: schools that have very different amounts of money to spend have different opportunities to hire good teachers and make other investments that can determine productivity. Similarly, as some have argued, differences in schools' regulatory environment should be considered. Some argue that if government is withholding support from one kind of school and maintaining a supportive environment for another kind, any comparisons of school outcomes could be tainted—students in the school experiencing harassment might learn less, not because their school is less capable, but because it is prevented from performing as well as it can.

Analysts are just starting to consider such factors, and it is not yet clear exactly how much difference they make. But as in the case of student characteristics, the burden of proof would be on the analyst who argued that differences in school outcomes were not caused by such factors.

This chapter asks, and to the degree possible with existing evidence answers, whether school maturation (the process by which a school clarifies its mission and instructional method so that teachers and parents know how the school expects to operate and what their role is) is another such factor. It tries to answer this question in three ways: by analogy to the literature on start-up businesses, analysis of the experience of people who have started charter schools, and review of the literature on school performance and coherency.

The answer we reach is that charter schools definitely pass through a maturation process but that some move vastly more quickly than others and there appears to be no standard sequence of events. It does not seem possible to create a common maturation scale or time line on which all new schools could be reliably placed. Thus, it seems unlikely that researchers could include a few simple maturation measures in a survey so they could be factored into data analysis, like other easily measured variables such as students' race and teachers' experience. If there is any generally useful measure of school maturation, it is probably simply school age — less or more than three years old.

However, we conclude that maturation is a factor that can and should be considered by people who deal with charter schools on a one-on-one basis. We provide a way authorizers and funders can assess a school's maturation and identify issues in urgent need of attention.

THE PROBLEM OF SCHOOL MATURATION

The argument that charter schools will be efficient and effective because they have incentives to perform well and freedom to find and use the most effective methods still might prove correct. However, like most market-based predictions, it applies only in the long run. It does not say there will not be failures, perhaps as many as in the case of new small businesses. It only says that markets allow entrepreneurs to learn over time so that strong entrants are continuously improved and the weakest competitors go out of business and are replaced by new ones. Over time the average quality of all competitors rises.

The whole idea of charter schools is new, so even if it proves to be a mechanism for steady improvement of public schools, the improvement process has barely begun. Entrepreneurs are just learning how to improve charter schools founded only a few years ago, and there are efforts to learn from early failures.

Case-based studies of charter schools suggest that many change over time, resolving conflicts, benefiting from the departure of the least compatible staff and parents, and learning how to present themselves accurately to potential recruits. These possibilities make it impossible to ignore maturation as a factor in the effectiveness of charter schools.

However, we know very little about how charter schools work internally, and we know more about what pulls charter schools apart than what pulls them together.[2] The teachers, principals, and parents who are quickest to transfer to charter schools are unusual in many ways and may have hopes and expectations that are difficult to reconcile with school effectiveness. For example, parents and teachers fleeing violent or chaotic public schools might be willing to settle for safety and order even if instruction is no better than in district-run schools (see Teske, Fitzpatrick, and Kaplan, 2007, who suggest that parents seek safety first and feel free to look for more instructionally specific attributes of schools only after safety is assured). At least some of the staff members who move from public schools to charter schools may be seeking the freedom to teach as they like. Socially progressive principals and teachers who staff many charter schools might regard individual exploration as a unifying principle more important than instructional coherency.

If school maturation is a real phenomenon, it surely takes time. Staff members who previously worked in different kinds of schools must learn new habits and unlearn old ones. Parents, board members, and administrators as well as teachers have their own personal reasons for choosing a charter school, and these are unlikely to be perfectly aligned on the school's first day. All parties have to reconcile their diverse expectations and learn to work together—and in some cases, learn they can't work together and either give up or split into more compatible groups.

Unfortunately, though all school districts have opened new schools at one time or another, scholars have paid little attention to the problems of school start-up.

WHAT WE CAN LEARN FROM START-UP BUSINESSES

Any organization that produces a complex good or service requires effective collaboration and thoughtful adaptation to problems as they arise. Understanding that new businesses are particularly vulnerable, venture capitalists have created *incubators* that allow prospective companies to clarify their goals and procedures, develop financial and quality control systems, and test the market appeal of their products in a safe environment before entering the marketplace.[3]

While incubators help businesses get off the ground, there has also been research on the subsequent development of new businesses. Though analysts' schemes differ slightly, many identify five basic phases:

- Entrepreneurial: One or a few individuals with many new ideas seek resources, look for a market niche, follow many opportunities at once, and use weak and informal methods of coordination.

- Early growth: New individuals are brought into the business, sense of intimacy and dedication is sustained, coordination remains informal, and company members make extreme commitments of time and energy.
- Growth to full size: Replacement of founders, formalization of rules and procedures, explicit structure and specialization, bounded personal responsibility, emphasis on efficiency and maintenance.
- Maturity: Elaboration of structure, division into major units, decentralization of operations, termination of unproductive activities, renewal; or, in some cases, failure to adapt to market challenges.
- Decline and failure: hamstrung by processes, internal structure, cost structure, slowness to adapt.

Businesses move through these phases at different rates, and some never make it past the entrepreneurial or early growth steps. The transition between stages is usually painful and risky: organizations bring in new people and become more formal out of necessity, and people accustomed to less formal ways of working are often uncomfortable (Schumwinger, 2000). Every business that does well enough to survive and grow must eventually separate itself from the founding entrepreneurs, whether because the founder ages out or because the founders' charismatic style and preference for informality becomes a threat to company success (Greiner, 1972). This is a particularly crucial event. Businesses that do it too late, or that make the wrong choice of successor, can die.

Founders leave the organizations they have started for many reasons—whether to continue seeking the excitement of building something new or because their intuitive and informal leadership styles are poorly matched to the needs of an organization that has grown to need systems and stability. For whatever reason, founders often depart in times of crisis, and organizations become unstable and performance can drop (Adizes, 1979). One person interviewed for this paper noted that foundations often will not give new grants to nonprofits during the first year after the founders depart.

Literature on business and nonprofits emphasizes the relationship between the board and management, which, as we shall see, is especially vital in charter schools. Though some small businesses start as sole proprietorships and eventually develop boards of directors, all charter schools must have boards from the day they open. Board-management relationships can be unstable, especially in new businesses where the board represents investors and managers are driven by ideas. Undisciplined management can bring the board to micromanage; overly intrusive boards can drive out entrepreneurs before the business is ready to succeed without them. Even in very healthy companies, when it comes time to stabilize and professionalize, boards often intervene to drive out the founding entrepreneurs.[4] Such events are always deep crises, even (or especially) when they address problems that must be solved.

These general findings apply well to charter schools, as we will discuss immediately below. However, we failed to find in the literature anything specific about a maturation issue that greatly concerns charter school leaders: *how long it takes for a start-up to become competent at producing its product or service.* Businesses' production problems vary in complexity: some are as simple as operating a machine that stamps out widgets, and others are as complicated as writing software or performing open-heart surgeries. Some businesses use proven technologies, and others must invent their methods and train people for unique tasks. It is, therefore, impossible to say how long it should take before a business masters the technical and organizational challenges presented by its product and market niche.

Based on our interviews with individuals who have started charter schools, the first three phases of business development fit almost perfectly. Charters that have failed did so because they could not manage enough of the financial, human resource, and work coordination tasks to enter the third phase.

Charter schools typically start with a small group of people, often just one person with passion and an idea. The first few individuals drawn into the school are often inspired by the original vision and eager to work communally, rather than in a formal structure. As the group grows large enough to operate a school, it must bring in people who did not share the start-up experience, and it must develop clear enough employment and financial systems to keep employees and deliver on promises made to parents. Most charter schools struggle at this phase, and some collapse during it (for a review of these developmental processes, see Hill and Lake, 2003).

People experienced with charter schools also emphasize the importance of board-founder relations. The requirement that every charter school must have a nonprofit board leads to severe political and managerial challenges. As in business, board-management conflicts can destabilize and even destroy the school. Even when boards are disciplined and stay within their roles, the inevitable departure of the founder is at least as traumatic and life-threatening for a charter school as for an entrepreneurial business.

Charter school boards are problematic like the boards of other small non-profits (see, for example, Ryan, Chait, and Taylor, 2003). The sheer number of such boards in urban areas forces the recruitment of many people who have little experience with either the service being delivered or the role of a board member. As a result, many charter school boards are composed of people who have little time to give after they have met job and family obligations and little expertise to offer. Many such boards often suffer from role confusion, as inexperienced board members struggle to learn the difference between responsible oversight and intrusive micromanagement.

According to an early national survey of charter schools, 27 percent of new charter schools and 17 percent of existing ones were disrupted by internal conflicts that could be related to governance (U.S. Department of Education Office of Educational Research and Improvement [OERI], 1998, p. 104).

Unlike business boards, charter (and other nonprofit) boards are not obligated to put the interests of stockholders (who care mainly about a return on their investment) above those of management, workers, and clients. Without a stockholder group to represent, nonprofit board members tend either to focus on their personal concerns or to act as representatives of management, workers, or clients. Current parents dominate many charter boards, a fact that can lead to high degrees of conflict and rapid changes of focus as children graduate and parents leave (U.S. Department of Education OERI, 1998, pp. 99–100). As a 2006 report on charter school quality by Rainey and Harvey noted:

> Some nonprofit boards are agenda driven and wind up trying to micromanage the schools . . . Many have weak governing boards; they have little capacity to oversee the school . . . Most, even the nonprofits established by profit-making vendors, have trouble distinguishing between the oversight function of a board and running the school (p. 10).

Thus, board-management relations appear as crucial, and even more problematic, for charter schools as for businesses. So do succession issues, of two kinds. First, for new charter schools, the departure of founders is a profoundly important event that can either give the school new life or destroy it.

In the future, one difference between charter schools and businesses might become more important. Charter schools experience a high degree of customer turnover caused by the inevitable graduation of their students. Customers might patronize a business or supplier for a very long time, and though most businesses serve an individual customer much less intensely than a charter school does, a given customer can patronize a particular business from time to time for many years and never stop being a customer.

Because of relatively rapid customer turnover, charter schools might be forced to revise their marketing and adapt to the needs of a changing customer base relatively often. This could mean a charter school could go through a deep set of changes every few years; in the case of businesses, they change only when competition or secular changes in consumer tastes require it.

CHARTER STARTERS' EXPERIENCE

We contacted individuals who had started charter schools, including leaders of organizations that start and manage multiple schools, for conversations. These included telephone calls, face-to-face interviews, and email exchanges. Our response rates and numbers of respondents were low, numbering in the mid-teens, but the respondents were highly informed. The results helped us understand all the ways in which some charter schools mature, but they did not help us develop any standard model of charter school maturation. As our informants insisted, a given school can resolve a number of maturation issues almost instantly, if its founders are clear about what they want to accomplish. Some schools open with virtually nothing resolved while others are very clear about every issue that can possibly be addressed before a school is in operation.

Respondents confirmed that the main groups of issues identified were all important, but they could not agree on a set sequence or time line for resolving them. The issue groups included:

Instruction: Curriculum, instructional methods, standards for student performance, and methods of self-assessment

Students: Expectations for student work and deportment, methods of socializing new students into the school and maintaining a climate conducive to learning

Teachers: Ideas about the right mix of teacher skills, standards and priorities for teacher hiring, expectations for teacher work ethic, collaboration, and responsibility for events outside the classroom

Administration and facilities: Arrangements to obtain pay for and maintain facilities, account for funds, collect funds owed by the state and district, make required reports, and pay salaries and benefits

Internal governance: Ideas about the right set of skills to be represented on the board, clear and distinct roles for board and management, agreed criteria for hiring and evaluating the school head (principal), stability in the principalship

Marketing and parent relations: Ability to describe the school's instructional program and climate accurately, ideas about the attributes of families to which the school will appeal, a defined marketing strategy, expectations for parent support of student learning

We expected to find that some of these groups of issues (e.g., administration and facilities) were more concrete and easier to resolve from the start than others, but according to our respondents that is not necessarily the case. People who start charter schools come from many different backgrounds.

People with business or legal backgrounds would not try to open a school unless the administrative and facilities issues were resolved, but they might not understand how much must be resolved about students and instruction. On the other hand, educators have often dealt with the administrative and facilities issues last, and only then when something went very wrong. People with public school backgrounds, accustomed to having human resource and student assignment issues decided by district central offices, can be late in resolving those sets of issues.

Our respondents agreed that new charter schools have serious maturation issues, but none felt there was a canonical development process. Schools started by management organizations (called CMOs if they are nonprofits and EMOs if they are for-profit) and schools that have worked with an incubator before opening might be quicker to identify all the related issues. CMOs and EMOs in particular resolve the administrative and facilities issues early and provide a good deal of structure about curriculum and methods of instruction. But their schools still have significant maturing to do after they open.

Thus, the idea of creating a simple maturation scale on which all schools' progress could easily be rated seems more difficult than we had hoped. It probably does not make sense for evaluators of charter schools to take fine measures of the degree to which schools have resolved all the issues above or to use the scores of controls in statistical analysis. Our analysis might help us understand what charter schools must pass through, but it does not help identify a normative pathway or rate of progress.

However, respondents were much more consistent about the three groups of educational issues that charter schools probably share with all other school issues, which we labeled instruction, students, and teachers. These issues appear to affect all start-up schools, even those that have a decent handle on the leadership, board relations, and financial issues.

New schools must take teachers from many different backgrounds and mold them into a functioning team. This is analogous to the formation of an expansion team in baseball: the new players have different levels of skill, and some of them might turn out to be very good. But it takes time for the management to figure out how to maximize the overall productivity of the new team and work around its weaknesses (sometimes by making trades). New teams are seldom top-level competitors immediately after they are formed, but some win pennants after only a few years.

Teaching teams mature as they come to agreement about three things:

What is to be taught and how
What teachers can expect of one another
What work effort and performance should be expected of students

Maturation of the teaching team also supports clarification of the school's relationships with parents and students. Charter schools that know what and how they will teach are then able to help parents determine whether the school is the right place for them. Similarly, schools with clear expectations for students can construct students' expectations and increase the school's own leverage on students who try to evade expectations (see Hill, 1996).

These forms of maturation take time, but they are not simply a function of years since a school first opened. As Anthony Bryk has suggested, charter schools that add one grade a year for several years might have "newness" problems for years after they open. Every year a new group of teachers have to be brought on and informed about the school's values and methods. To a degree the school must also accommodate itself to the preferences and abilities of the new teachers, at least the ones it needs to keep. These accommodations can happen quickly or take years. Businesses might have similar issues, with the opening of new facilities or hiring people to expand into new markets. Compared to businesses, which can continue expanding for decades, charter schools can only add grades for a few years—never more than eleven.

The instructional maturation process might also stop at some point. Though there is evidence that new charter schools have special problems in the first few years after they open, there is no reason to think that schools inevitably continue improving the older they get. Some new charter schools apparently go from bad to worse, lasting for a turbulent year or two until teachers, parents, or administrators give up on them. Moreover, schools that have operated in the same place for a long time can experience good and bad years, and some go through major upheavals and staffing changes that can make them, in effect, new again despite their years.

INSTRUCTIONAL MATURATION
IN THE EDUCATION LITERATURE

For good reason, the educational literature contains little about schools maturing as businesses: until charter schools arose the vast majority of schools were bureaus in a larger governmental administrative structure, not self-governing organizations.

There is, however, a literature related to a school's development as an instructional organization, which is one aspect of school maturation. The focus of this literature is on schools' *instructional coherency*. As Fred Newmann first defined it, a school is coherent if it has a common instructional framework that guides teaching, student work, performance assessment, social climate, teachers' peer interactions, hiring and teacher rewards, and the use of time and money (see, for example, Newmann, Smith, and Bryk, 2001). School coherency has three key elements:

> *Instructional focus*: Teachers must agree that instruction is their job and share a conception of good instruction and good student performance. This must be evident enough to parents so they know what to expect—and not expect—if they choose the school for their child.
>
> *Trust*: Teachers must be able to rely on one another to work hard, provide good instruction, and share responsibility. Parents must believe that adults in the school will keep their promises about climate and instruction and take individual students seriously.
>
> *Coordination*: A school must have mechanisms for enforcing norms, selecting and socializing new members, correcting mistakes, restoring unity when it frays, and maintaining focus despite external threats and pressures. Parents must be able to expect the school to take responsibility for their child's progress from course to course and grade to grade and be stable over time.

Together these elements provide a good description of a mature charter school. There is literature about each of these elements of coherency, but little on how they fit together.

Fred Newmann has written extensively about instructional program coherency but did not try to explain how it depends on trust or coordination (Newmann, Smith, and Bryk, 2001). Anthony Bryk and Barbara Schneider (2002) have published a book about trust as an element of school coherency, but they did not explain how trust leads to instructional coherency or how schools high in trust maintain their focus despite distractions. Hill, Foster, and Gendler (1990) wrote about how schools maintain a "social contract" that defines individual and joint responsibility and enforces norms but did not explain in detail how this interacts with the social and instructional aspects of schools.

All these results share the weaknesses of the effective schools literature, which identifies unusually effective schools and asks what distinguishes them from ordinary schools. It provides existence proofs that schools can be effective and identifies some key attributes, like coherency, that meet the test of common sense. However, like the business literature that it imitates (see, for example, *In Search of Excellence*), the effective schools literature says a great deal more about what good examples look like than about how they came to be. It is one thing to identify attributes like unity, trust, dedication to a common mission, and instructional coherency and quite another thing for a school to develop them (Muncey and MacQuillan, 1996).

The literature cited above provides some evidence for links among school coherency, instructional quality, and student learning (Newmann and Wehlage,

1995; see also Newmann, Lopez, and Bryk, 1998). But the strongest argument for the importance of coherency is based on common sense. A student's learning accumulates over time, and though at any moment a student is in only one classroom, what she learns depends, this year at least, in part on what she learned earlier. Teachers who can't count on all students knowing certain fundamentals are often forced to repeat instruction that was supposed to be delivered earlier, wasting time and boring students who have already mastered the material. Individual teachers might be well organized and implement their own instructional plans well, but without coordination among classrooms and over time, students can miss learning key skills and fail to understand logical and historical relationships links (see, for example, Smith, Smith, and Bryk, 1991).

Beneath these arguments are assumptions about the roles of school leaders, who must work to ensure that children's experiences accumulate smoothly over time, and parents, who understand and support the school's instructional program and do not disrupt it by irrelevant complaints and do not pull out of the school necessarily.

Beneath these generalities we know a lot less about school maturation than we should. One can only speculate about why school maturation has received so little attention in the literature focused on district-run schools. One possibility is that education research (with the exception of studies led by Bryk and Newmann) has been focused below the school level, on the skills and practices of individual teachers, and thus missed the "forest" of the school as a whole. Another is that researchers, knowing that district-run schools are subject to disruption through the teacher "bumping" process and abrupt reassignment of principals, have assumed that most schools were always in some sense new. If the latter assumption is correct, the capacity to mature (by stabilizing leadership and retaining key teachers committed to the school's core principles and by socializing new teachers, parents, and students) could be a special advantage of charter schools.

CONCLUSION

If new charter schools typically have performance problems right after they open, but progress steadily over time, newness should be a factor in any performance assessment. A study that ignored school newness and inadvertently compared a group of new schools with a group of well-established schools could mistakenly attribute performance differences to schools' charter status when they were in fact due to school age (see, for example, Nelson, Rosenberg, and Van Meter, 2004). Similarly, a study that distinguished high-performing versus low-performing charter schools could miss the fact that some schools whose current performance was low might soon, simply with the passing of time, get much better.

Studies of Charter Outcomes

However, until we have a strong research-based model of school maturation, large-scale studies of charter school outcomes cannot take full account of the phenomenon. In the short run, people conducting studies of large numbers of charter schools should make sure they have measures of the years a charter school has been in operation and, if possible, the number of years since a school opened its highest grade. These measures might not have a linear relationship with school performance, but school age under three or five years should, if the maturation evidence we have seen holds any water at all, have an inverse relationship to student performance.

Smaller scale studies that are able to look more deeply into individual schools might reasonably ask additional questions about

- Number of years since the last change in the principalship
- Teacher turnover rate[5]
- Student turnover, particularly the proportion of students who stay in the school one year or less

If possible, it would also make sense to measure the degree to which a school is building a steady clientele; e.g., the proportion of all families who have more than one child in the school.

Informing Authorizer and Funder Judgments

The forgoing measures might also be useful for charter school authorizers and for foundations and other supporters trying to decide whether a school is worth additional investment. Accountability schemes for charter schools surely need to take account of maturation. New schools can be expected to have some rough edges and take some time to develop stable staffs and coherent instructional plans. However, as schools age they can be expected to stabilize staffing and operations, develop relationships of trust and confidence with families, and deliver more coherent instructional programs. These attributes do not guarantee school effectiveness, but they are almost certainly precursors to it; thus, charter authorizers or other oversight bodies can use them as leading indicators of performance (or their absence as advance indication of trouble).

For authorizers, evidence of school maturation could never overshadow the importance of test scores and other student outcomes. However, evidence about maturation could justify authorizers taking a hard look at a school that is not maturing and giving an obviously maturing school more time.

Need for In-depth Studies

Researchers conducting in-depth studies in charter schools have additional options. Bryk and others at the Consortium on Chicago School Research have used teacher surveys to measure mutual trust and the existence of collaborative environments (Bryk and Schneider, 2002). Newmann has also developed survey-based measures of instructional program coherence. It might also be possible to code a school's marketing material on the specificity of its description of the instructional program and expectations for student effort.

One argument for charter schools was that they could escape the regulations and teacher-union contract provisions that make it difficult for district-run schools to be coherent. Charter schools, it was argued, can hire teachers who agree with one another about instructional methods and can reward effective collaboration. A complementary argument was that charter schools had a strong incentive to be coherent because they needed to make and keep promises to parents about what and how children would learn.

However plausible these arguments are, it is now clear that not all charter schools are coherent in the ways theorized. There is a need for more direct studies of the processes of school maturation, stagnation, and decline. Such studies would require longitudinal observation of significant numbers of new schools over several years. It is vital for this research to be designed to distinguish maturation from natural selection: if the most internally divided schools are the likeliest to fail because staff members and parents decide to go elsewhere, older schools could be more coherent even if no individual school becomes more coherent over time. Thus, researchers need to do more than identify long-lived charter schools and identify their common characteristics. They must start with a broad sample of charter schools and ask whether those that survive develop differently than those that fail.

The results, if they lead to a robust model of normal maturation, could eventually strengthen both outcome studies and charter authorizers' use of leading indicators to identify troubled schools.

NOTES

1. Studies that compare students randomly assigned to different treatment groups can sometimes escape this criticism, but for the most part they too must show that randomization produced similar groupings for comparison.

2. In 2007 the National Charter School Research Project will mount a series of studies of charter school instruction and staffing that should tell us a great deal about how charter schools differ from district-run schools and from one another.

3. Abigail Schumwinger (2000) has reviewed business incubators and suggested the desirability of similar institutions for schools.

4. See, for example, "50 Percent of Founders Get Fired," http://www.detroitstartups.com/startup-advice/50-of-founders-get-fired/ (downloaded May 7, 2009).

5. NCSRP has just started a study of charter school human resource strategies that will explore how charter schools manage turnover. The results should produce a more nuanced distinction between strategic versus destabilizing turnover.

REFERENCES

Adizes, I. (1979). Organizational Passages: Diagnosing and Treating Lifecycle Problems of Organizations. *Organizational Dynamics* (Summer), 3–25.

Bifulco, R., and Ladd, H. F. (2005). The Impacts of Charter Schools on Student Achievement: Evidence from North Carolina. *Education Finance and Policy* 1, 50–90.

Booker, K., Gilpatric, S. M., Gronberg, T., and Jansen, D. (2004). The Impact of Charter School Attendance on Student Performance. PERC Working Paper #0410. College Station, TX: Texas A&M University, Private Enterprise Research Center.

Bryk, A. S., and Schneider, B. L. (2002). *Trust in Schools: A Core Resource for Improvement.* New York: Russell Sage Foundation.

Gill, B., Hamilton, L. S., Lockwood, J. R., Marsh, J. A., Zimmer, R., Hill, D., and Pribesh, S. (2004). *Inspiration, Perspiration, and Time: Operations and Achievement in Edison Schools.* Santa Monica, CA: RAND.

Greiner, L. (1972). Evolution and Revolution as an Organization Grows. *Harvard Business Review* (July-August), pp. 37–46.

Hanushek, E. A., Kain, J. F., and Rivkin, S. G. (2004). Disruption versus Tiebout Improvement: The Costs and Benefits of Switching Schools. *Journal of Public Economics* 88, 1721–46.

Hanushek, E. A., Kain, J. F., Rivkin, S. G., and Branch, G. F. (2005). Charter School Quality and Parental Decision Making with School Choice. NBER Working Paper No. 111252. Cambridge, MA: National Bureau of Economic Research. Downloaded June 3, 2009, from http://papers.nber.org/papers/w11252.pdf.

Hill, P. T. (1996). The Educational Advantages of Choice. *Phi Delta Kappan* 77, 671–76.

Hill, P. T., Foster, G. E., and Gendler, T. (1990). *High Schools with Character.* Santa Monica, CA: RAND.

Hill, P. T., and Lake, R. J. (2003). How Charter Schools Develop Internal Accountability. In *Charter Schools and Accountability in Public Education.* Washington, DC: The Brookings Institution.

Loveless, T. (2003). Charter Schools: Achievement, Accountability, and the Role of Expertise. In *The 2003 Brown Center Report on American Education: How Well Are American Students Learning?* Washington, DC: The Brookings Institution.

Muncey, D. E., and MacQuillan, P. (1996). *Reform and Resistance in Schools and Classrooms: An Ethnographic View of the Coalition of Essential Schools.* New Haven, CT: Yale University Press.

Nelson, F. H., Rosenberg, B., and Van Meter, N. (2004). *Charter School Achievement on the 2003 National Assessment of Educational Progress.* Washington, DC: American Federation of Teachers.

Newmann, F. M., Lopez, G., and Bryk, A. S. (1998). *The Quality of Intellectual Work in Chicago Schools: A Baseline Report.* Chicago: Consortium on Chicago School Research.

Newmann, F. M., Smith, B. A., and Bryk, A. S. (2001). *School Instructional Program Coherence: Benefits and Challenges.* Chicago: Consortium on Chicago Schools Research.

Newmann, F. M., and Wehlage, G. G. (1995). *Successful School Restructuring.* Madison, WI: University of Wisconsin, Center on Organization and Restructuring of Schools.

Rainey, L., and Harvey, J. (2006). *High-quality Charter Schools at Scale in Big Cities.* Seattle: National Charter School Research Project.

Ryan, W. P., Chait, R. P., and Taylor, B. E. (2003). Problem Boards or Board Problem? *The Nonprofit Quarterly* 10: 2 (Summer).

Schumwinger, A. (2000). *Stimulating the Supply and Building the Capacity of New Schools and School Developers: Recommendations for the Design and Implementation of a New Schools Incubator.* Seattle: Center on Reinventing Public Education.

Smith, J. B., Smith, B. A., and Bryk, A. S. (1991). *Setting the Pace: Opportunities to Learn in Chicago's Elementary Schools.* Chicago: Consortium on Chicago School Research.

Teske, P., Fitzpatrick, J., and Kaplan, G. (2007). *Opening Doors: How Low-income Parents Search for the Right School.* Seattle: Center on Reinventing Public Education.

U.S. Department of Education Office of Educational Research and Improvement. (1998). *National Study of Charter Schools Second-Year Report.* Washington, DC: U.S. Department of Education.

Chapter Eight

What Do We Know about Teachers in Charter Schools?

Dominic J. Brewer and June Ahn

INTRODUCTION

What makes a good school? Why do some schools succeed in raising student achievement and others fail? These questions have long interested parents, policy makers, and researchers. The answers, of course, are complex. Undoubtedly, the types of students a school serves, and the community in which it is located, are important. The kind of leader, the curriculum and instructional program, and the resources available may all be factors. Perhaps the crucial ingredient is skilled, motivated teachers.

Over the past decade research has documented that teacher quality is one of the most important educational factors affecting student achievement (Ehrenberg and Brewer, 1994; Goldhaber and Brewer, 1997; Hanushek, 1997; Hanushek, Kain, and Rivkin, 2004; Nye, Konstantopoulos, and Hedges, 2004). Although it has proven extremely difficult to relate observable characteristics of teachers to student achievement, No Child Left Behind demands that every student have a "qualified" teacher.

How to recruit and retain, educate and retrain, and motivate and reward excellent teachers, particularly in underperforming schools, has been a major issue in educational policy. States have developed alternative routes to certification and offered incentives for teachers to acquire more demanding certification (Ballou and Podgursky, 1998; Goldhaber and Brewer, 2000; Goldhaber, Perry, and Anthony, 2003). University Schools of Education have undertaken an array of programmatic reforms (e.g., with Carnegie Corporation's "Teachers for a New Era," see Kirby, McCombs, Barney et al., 2005), some districts have experimented with "pay for skills" or outcomes-based pay (Odden and Kelley, 2001), and new national schemes to encourage smart young people to enter the teaching profession (e.g., Teach for America, Troops to Teachers; see Glazerman, Mayer, and Decker, 2006) have blossomed.

For all the reform around teachers in traditional public schools, the system retains a "one best system" character in which uniformity and hierarchy are emphasized. For example, despite some changes at the margin, the vast majority of teachers in the United States are trained in state college teacher preparation programs, are recruited and allocated to schools by school districts, receive tenure after several years, are paid according to a uniform salary schedule that rewards years of experience and degrees rather than any explicit measures of on-the-job performance, and receive state-governed pensions. In most settings, seniority rules and other collectively bargained contractual provisions ensure that teachers have considerable job autonomy, influence over their assignments, and are rarely fired. Within the public educational sector, there is little variation in the critical policies and practices affecting teachers—with the exception of charter schools.

Charter schools are an exception to the "one best system." Charter schools are schools of choice: educators, parents, and students choose to be there rather than being assigned by a district office, and these stakeholders have considerable autonomy to decide the school mission, who will be hired, how students will be taught, and how resources will be used. These schools can be started by educators, parents, community groups, or others who enter into a performance contract with an authorizing agency, usually a local school district (Brewer and Wohlstetter, 2006). Forty states and the District of Columbia permit charter schools, and they serve more than a million students across the country. Many states allow existing public schools to convert to charter status, and laws also allow charter schools to start from scratch. The school's performance contract spells out how the school will be organized and governed, methods of instruction to be used, and the performance goals that will be achieved at the end of the contract period.

The theory of action underlying the charter school concept proposes that if schools are empowered to make their own decisions (through school-site autonomy and deregulation) and they are schools of choice that must attract educators to work in them and families to attend, then the schools will work to innovate—to improve teaching and learning. In many ways, then, one of the most potentially radical reforms in regard to teachers over the past decade has been the emergence of charter schools. Since these schools are typically outside many of the regulatory and contractual provisions that govern who teaches and how they must work, charter schools provide a rich environment both to understand how teachers impact school performance and to explore promising and innovative strategies in regard to teacher recruitment, training, and rewards.

The kinds of teachers attracted to charter schools, and the conditions under which they work (e.g., degree of professional autonomy, compensation), could—in principle at least—be an important part of understanding charter school effects on student achievement, either positive or negative. Charter schools are typically smaller than regular public schools, with teachers having a potentially greater say and more flexibility over curriculum, instructional, and organizational issues. On the other hand, charter schools may not be able to attract top-quality teachers due to concerns about workload, salary, and job stability.

Although it is extremely difficult to trace direct linkages between charter school teacher characteristics and student achievement, it is clearly important to understand teachers in charter schools, both who they are and how they work, and in particular how these differ from other settings, because this will aid in interpreting evidence on student achievement. Increasingly, as the charter movement matures, concerns are being raised about perceived "burnout" among charter school teachers and high attrition rates, sparking renewed interest in promising practices and innovative strategies to ensure high teacher quality and a stable workforce. Similarly, as the debate about charters moves from "good or bad?" to "how can we help charters succeed?" and "what can conventional public schools learn from charters?", we will need a much richer picture of the ways in which charter schools attract and use resources, teachers being perhaps the most crucial.

Finally, an interesting aspect of the public debate about charter schools has been the evolution in attitudes toward them from teachers' organizations. In 1988, Albert Shanker (president of the American Federation of Teachers) was one of the first to introduce the notion of charter schools to the nation. He saw the creation of charter schools as a way to improve education for all students and envisaged that they would be created by groups of teachers, or parents with teachers, who wanted to develop a new curriculum or teaching strategies to improve student learning. Although there is continuing interest in the notion of teacher-operated schools as well as attempts to unionize teachers in charter schools, teachers' unions are at best skeptical about charters.

Given the potential importance of variation in teacher policies in charter schools and the central role of teacher quality in understanding student achievement effects, examining teachers in charter schools would seem to be a fruitful endeavor. The purpose of this chapter is therefore to synthesize the current research literature concerning teacher characteristics and work conditions in charter schools. In the next section we explore state charter school laws as they pertain to teacher policy. Charter laws and teacher requirements vary from state to state, and we examine how current state requirements may restrict or widen what charter schools can do in terms of teacher policy. In the third section, we build on an earlier thorough review by Malloy and Wohl-stetter (2003) to examine the existing literature on charter school teacher characteristics and experiences in areas such as teacher certification, salary and compensation, work experience, job security, and tenure.

These two analyses reveal a remarkably slight research base, and one which—despite progress in student achievement studies (Betts and Hill, 2006)—gives us a very incomplete picture of who teaches in charter schools and why. In other words, the current evidence on charter school teachers, which is largely descriptive, is not sufficient for use in evaluation and policy development. Clearly, research that links charter teacher characteristics and the ways teachers are used in these schools to student achievement is needed. That research needs to be longitudinal and sustained to track the development of charters from start-up to maturity given that teacher qualities may change over that maturation process. Finally, as charters experiment with recruiting and compensating teachers in different ways, we may have the opportunity to find other measures of quality (i.e., career changers with subject knowledge, graduates of highly competitive colleges, etc.) that will be linked to student achievement.

STATE CHARTER LAWS AND TEACHERS

Charter schools are creatures of state policy, and charter laws differ greatly from state to state. These laws may cover the nature of charter schools' contracts, such as the performance period, authorization and renewal procedures, what aspects of existing state legislation must be complied with, who can operate a school and under what conditions, what students can attend, the school's financing and governance structures, and so on. Laws vary widely in the extent to which they prescribe school operations and hence the extent to which they impact who can work in a charter school and how they should work. This variation in teacher policy across charter school laws is undoubt-edly the result of a complex historical and institutional context in each state, including the origin of legislation, party control of the legislature and general ideology of the state, the strength of teacher organizations and collective bar-gaining provisions, and the perceived health of traditional public schools.

What kinds of teachers are able to work in charter schools? Table 8.1 shows the distribution of states according to teacher certification require-ments. Many states, nineteen out of forty-one, require teacher certification for all teachers in a school. However, there is great diversity in certification requirements across states: twelve states require certification for varying per-centages of teachers, four states have no regulations, four states offer waivers,

Table 8.1. State Teacher Certification Requirements for Charter Schools

Teacher Certification Required (19 Total)	Teacher Certification Waived (4 Total)	Teacher Certification Required for Specified Percentage of Teachers (12 Total)	Teacher Certification Requirements Set in Charter Application (2 Total)	Teacher Certification Required but May Be Waived in Certain Circumstances (4 Total)
Alaska	Arizona	Connecticut (50%)	Georgia	Arkansas
California	District of Columbia	Delaware (65%)	Oklahoma	Colorado
Hawaii	Illinois	Louisiana (75%)		Florida
Idaho	Texas	Mississippi (90%)		Kansas
Indiana		Missouri (80%)		
Iowa		Nevada (70%)		
Maryland		New Hampshire (50%)		
Massachusetts		New York (30%, no more than 5 uncertified in a school)		
Michigan				
Minnesota		North Carolina (75% in elementary, 50% in secondary)		
New Jersey				
New Mexico		Oregon (50%)		
Ohio		Pennsylvania (75%)		
Rhode Island		South Carolina (90 % in conversion, 75% in start-up)		
Tennessee				
Utah				
Virginia				
Wisconsin (special license available if no candidate can be found)				
Wyoming				

Source: Center for Education Reform, "Charter School Laws Across the States," 2008, http://www.edreform.com/About_CER/Charter_School_Laws_Across_the_States/?Charter_School_Laws_Across_the_States.

and two states allow individual charter schools to specify their own policies in the charter application.

Although teacher certification in most states is not an intellectually demanding barrier to entry, it can be a time-consuming one (Ballou and Podgursky, 1998). The evidence that traditional forms of certification are tied to student achievement is weak at best (Goldhaber and Brewer, 2000; Walsh, 2001) and on newer forms of certification only just emerging (e.g., Goldhaber et al., 2003). It certainly is unlikely that requirements on charter schools to hire certified teachers will have much effect on student achievement; it may, however, be the case that charter schools in states *without* such restrictions have an opportunity to employ different kinds of teachers than in traditional settings. Plausibly these teachers could be young, smart, and enthusiastic or they could be hopelessly unqualified to face children in classrooms. Without much more refined data, there is no way to know for sure how these state legislative requirements play out in practice.

Teacher salaries are another key area of state charter school policy. States have generally split between using collective bargaining agreements to drive charter teacher salaries and allowing individual charter schools to determine their own salary levels (Education Commission of the States, n.d.). As table 8.2 shows, the majority of states have given full autonomy to charter schools to determine their own teacher salaries. Twenty-five of the forty-one states allow individual charter schools to develop their own salary policies, while nine states require charters to follow collective bargaining agreements. California and Ohio allow the choice of either collective bargaining or school-level autonomy.

Four states make distinctions by type of charter school. For example, in Connecticut local charter schools must follow collective bargaining agreements, but state charter schools have full autonomy to determine their own salary policy. Finally, New Jersey has enacted a policy that gives autonomy to charter schools but specifies teacher salaries cannot go beyond the minimum and maximum levels set by respective school districts. Similar to the variety in state laws regarding teacher compensation, the research literature to date has shown a diversity of teacher salary results. Some teachers, for example in California and Arizona, report competitive or higher salaries compared to their public school counterparts (Malloy and Wohlstetter, 2003). Still, other examples, such as Michigan, report substantially lower salaries for charter school teachers (Harris, 2006). Again, the linkages between either how teacher salaries are set or their levels and student achievement is not clear from previous research (see, for example, Eberts and Stone, 1984; Hanushek et al., 1999, 2004; Hanushek, 1997; Hoxby, 1996).

Table 8.2. How Are Teacher Salaries Determined?

Collective Bargaining Agreement (9 Total)	Individual Charter Schools (25 Total)	Either Collective Bargaining Agreement or Charter School (2 Total)	Stipulations based on Type of Charter School (4 Total)	Other Policies (1 Total)
Alaska	Arizona	California	Arkansas	New Jersey
Hawaii	Colorado	Ohio	(Conversion charter schools, the	(A charter school shall
Iowa	Delaware		existing salary schedule. For open	not set a teacher
Kansas	District of Columbia		enrollment charter schools, the	salary lower than
Louisiana	Florida		charter school.)	the minimum teacher
Maryland	Georgia			salary pursuant to
Nevada	Idaho		Connecticut	state law nor higher
Rhode Island	Illinois		(Local charter schools collective	than the highest step
Virginia	Massachusetts		bargaining agreements. For state	in the salary guide
	Michigan		charter schools, the charter schools.)	in the collective
	Minnesota			bargaining agreement
	Mississippi		Indiana	that is in effect in the
	Missouri		(Conversion charter schools,	district in which the
	New Hampshire		collective bargaining agreements.	charter school is
	New Mexico		For start-up charter schools, either	located.)
	North Carolina		charter schools or collective	
	Oklahoma		bargaining agreements.)	
	Oregon			
	Pennsylvania		New York	
	South Carolina		(In conversions, collective	
	Tennessee		bargaining agreements. In	
	Texas		start-ups, charter schools.)	
	Utah			
	Wisconsin			
	Wyoming			

Source: Education Commission of the States, http://mb2.ecs.org/reports/Report.aspx?id=113.

Charter laws concerned with teacher leave and retirement benefits also vary on a state-by-state level. As table 8.3 shows, some states require that public school teachers obtain a leave of absence from their school districts in order to teach in a charter school, while others offer full freedom from this requirement. Twenty states do not require a leave of absence for teachers who choose to work in a charter. Of the seventeen states that require a leave of absence, the time limits typically range from one to five years (Education Commission of the States, n.d.). Furthermore, four states specify unique rules that determine the relationship between the teacher and district. For example, teachers in Oklahoma require school-district approval to obtain a leave, while teachers in Indiana may receive a two-year leave of absence but can apply for longer leaves if they work in a start-up charter school.

States have also generally allowed charter teachers access to the public school retirement system. Thirty-six states offer charter teachers the opportunity to participate in the public school teachers' retirement system (table 8.4). The five states that do not offer access to retirement benefits have differing regulations concerning teacher access to public school retirement systems. For example, Washington, D.C., only allows participation in public school retirement systems if the teacher has transferred from a public school. Florida requires that the charter school be organized as a public employer, while Wisconsin charters must be a part of a school district in order for teachers to participate in retirement plans. Despite these different charter laws, the majority of states allow charter school teachers to participate in the retirement systems of their public school peers.

Malin and Kerchner (2007) observe that early advocates of charter schools envisioned autonomous, flexible organizations that would be able to pursue innovative practices in areas such as instruction, governance, and teacher qualifications. With autonomy, market pressures, and accountability, charter schools would be able to pursue and hire high-quality teachers. However, a cursory analysis of charter laws show that states vary in the level of autonomy and power given to individual charter schools. From teacher certification to salary policies, charter schools will vary in their ability to pursue alternative and innovative strategies for hiring, compensating, and retaining teachers.

For example, Podgursky and Ballou (2001) find that when freed from regulations, charter schools are more likely to pursue alternative and innovative personnel policies. Charter schools may hire more uncertified teachers but value individuals from competitive undergraduate institutions or those with deep subject matter expertise. Charter schools also employ other strategies such as one-year contracts, regular evaluations of teachers and dismissal for poor performance, and innovative compensation approaches such as merit-based pay or bonuses.

Table 8.3. Do States Require School Districts to Grant Teachers a Leave of Absence to Teach in Charter Schools?

No Leave Required (20 total)	Leave of Absence Required (17 total)	Leave of Absence Required—Other (4 total)
Alaska	Colorado (Up to 3 years)	Delaware (1 year for the charter school's first year of operation only or such leave as is provided in the collective bargaining agreement of the school district.)
Arizona	Connecticut (Up to 4 years)	
Arkansas	District of Columbia (2 years, unlimited extensions)	
California	Illinois (Up to 5 years)	Indiana (A local school board must grant a transfer of up to two years and may grant a transfer for longer than two years to teach at a start-up charter school.)
Florida	Louisiana (Up to 3 years)	
Georgia	Massachusetts (Up to 2 years)	
Hawaii	Minnesota	Oklahoma (3 years with school district approval)
Idaho	Nevada (Up to 3 years)	
Iowa	New Jersey (Up to 3 years)	Wyoming (Up to 3 years, after which school district determines relationship between teacher and district.)
Kansas	New Mexico (1 year, renewable to 2 years)	
Maryland	New York (Up to 2 years)	
Michigan	North Carolina (1 year)	
Mississippi	Ohio (Minimum 3 years)	
Missouri	Oregon (Minimum 2 years)	
New Hampshire	Pennsylvania (Up to 5 years)	
Tennessee	Rhode Island (2 years, renewable another 2 years)	
Texas	South Carolina (Up to 5 years)	
Utah		
Virginia		
Wisconsin		

Source: Education Commission of the States, http://mb2.ecs.org/reports/Report.aspx?id=113.

**Table 8.4. Do Teachers in Charter Schools Have
Access to the Public School Teachers' Retirement System?**

Yes *(36 total)*	*No / Other* *(5 total)*
Alaska	Washington, D.C.
Arizona	(Yes, if they transfer from a public school. Otherwise, no.)
Arkansas	
California	Florida
Colorado	(No, unless the charter school is organized as a public employer.)
Connecticut	
Delaware	Michigan
Georgia	(No. Employees hired by charter school board are eligible for
Hawaii	state retirement benefits. Employees hired by for-profit
Idaho	corporation contracting with a charter school are not.)
Illinois	
Indiana	Utah
Iowa	(No. While on leave, a teacher may retain seniority accrued
Kansas	in the school district and may continue to be covered by the
Louisiana	benefit program of the school district if the charter school and the
Maryland	school district mutually agree.)
Massachusetts	
Minnesota	Wisconsin
Mississippi	(No. Retirement benefits extend only to charter school teachers
Missouri	whose charter schools are part of a school district.)
Nevada	
New Hampshire	
New Jersey	
New Mexico	
New York	
North Carolina	
Ohio	
Oklahoma	
Oregon	
Pennsylvania	
Rhode Island	
South Carolina	
Tennessee	
Texas	
Virginia	
Wyoming	

Source: Education Commission of the States, http://mb2.ecs.org/reports/Report.aspx?id=113.

These alternative practices along with increased teacher involvement and empowerment create charter schools that Malin and Kerchner (2007) would categorize as high-performance workplaces. High performance organizations rely on flexibility, autonomy, innovation, and participation at all levels—from administration to teachers—to achieve positive results such as student achievement. In their legal analysis, Malin and Kerchner assert that policies such as collective bargaining agreements inherently follow an industrial model of organizations that favor regulation and top-down management. When applied to charter school labor policies, "there is not much in traditional collective bargaining law that encourages charter schools to become high performance workplaces" (pp. 932–33). They recommend a redevelopment of charter labor policies to free charter schools to pursue innovative personnel practices.

Similarly, Podgursky (2006) observes that charter schools, employing market- and performance-based personnel strategies, are more likely to recruit "teachers with better academic credentials as compared to traditional public schools" (p. 17). He analyzed the 1999–2000 Schools and Staffing Survey data supplemented by administrative data from Kansas City, Missouri. Podgursky posits that several factors may affect charter schools' abilities to undertake new and innovative hiring practice. First, market conditions should promote more performance-based personnel policies as well as diversity in compensation levels. Second, the small size of charter schools promote a more *team*-based approach, where local organizations can better evaluate their teachers and alter personnel policies to suit their unique conditions. School districts, working under collective bargaining agreements, are essentially very large, bureaucratic firms that cannot adapt quickly to personnel issues. Third, teacher certification requirements can hinder charter schools' ability to hire along other desirable characteristics.

Podgursky (2006) finds that in charter schools with flexible or waived certification requirements, "school administrators are willing to 'trade off' certification for other desirable teacher attributes" (p. 9). Similar to Malin and Kerchner's recommendation, Podgursky asserts that regulatory freedom, small organizational sizes of charter schools, and a competitive market environment will encourage more market- and performance-based personnel policies.

State charter laws constrain or allow what charter schools can do in terms of their daily operation. Policies such as collective bargaining agreements may affect a myriad of areas. For example, charter schools that follow collective bargaining agreements may pay their teachers on par with public school teachers. However, those charter schools may also be limited in hiring policy, the ability to provide incentives for good performance, and implement alternative workplace strategies. The diversity of charter school law and the varying ability for charter schools to employ new or novel hiring practices ensures that charter schools will differ widely in the composition of their teaching force. A fruitful area for future research would be to examine types of charter schools and their personnel policies.

RESEARCH FINDINGS ON CHARTER SCHOOL TEACHERS

Whatever the impact of particular legislative provisions, charter schools across the nation are a heterogeneous collection of institutions that have varied origins, purposes and goals, educational philosophies, and organizational structures and resources. Given the significant variation, it is difficult to interpret differences between characteristics of charter school teachers on *average* and those in other kinds of schools. This is, however, what most of the limited existing—and almost entirely descriptive—research has attempted to do.

The current research literature typically compares charter school teacher characteristics with those of their public school peers. Scholars have generally examined charter school teachers along several major dimensions: experience, certification, other qualifications such as colleges attended or subject matter knowledge, salary and compensation, job security and teacher attrition, and teacher perceptions. The research on teacher perceptions examines the motivations for working in charter schools as well as satisfaction with school operations and working conditions. One would expect contrasting findings concerning teacher characteristics due to the differences and unique contexts of individual charter schools, and this is indeed what one finds. However, some general trends can be discerned from the research base, which we broadly summarize in table 8.5. Then, in the following section, we provide a brief overview of the literature and try to highlight the general themes that emerge.

Much of the research on charter school teachers come in the form of descriptive studies such as survey data, case studies, and state evaluations. One of the sole nationally representative sources of data on charter school teachers comes from the Schools and Staffing Survey (SASS), and as such many analyses use that data. The SASS tracks information on the nation's schools and school personnel, including teacher and administrator characteristics and school conditions as well as "data on many other topics, including principals' and teachers' perceptions of school climate and problems in their schools; teacher compensation; district hiring practices and basic characteristics of the student population" (National Center for Educational Statistics, n.d.). The 1999–2000 SASS cycle employed a separate Charter School Questionnaire as well as questionnaires specifically geared toward charter teachers and administrators. However, the 2003–2004 SASS administered a standard survey instrument to both charter and traditional public schools.

The public SASS reports from the two cycles provide cursory data on various teacher characteristics on a national scale. For example, the number of teachers in charter schools rose dramatically from 17,477 teachers in 1999–2000 to 42,100 teachers in the 2003–2004 SASS (National Center for

Table 8.5.   Themes from Research on Charter Teachers

Characteristic	Summary
Experience	Charter school teachers are generally less experienced than their public school peers.
Certification	Charter school teachers are less likely to be certified.
Other Qualifications	Evidence suggests that charter school teachers are more likely to have graduated from elite undergraduate institutions—but findings vary.
Teacher Compensation	Evidence concerning salary varies—some salaries are competitive, other charter teachers make considerably less than their public school peers.
	Compensation differences may be explained by experience, certification, and varied compensation strategies from charter schools.
Job Security	Compared to public school teachers, charter school teachers are
	Less likely to have been granted tenure.
	More likely to work under short-term contracts.
	More likely to be dismissed for poor performance.
Work Environment	Charter teachers generally report high satisfaction with professional working conditions.
	Less satisfaction with facilities.
	Some evidence of staff burnout, stress, and turnover.

Educational Statistics, n.d.). The 1999–2000 SASS reports that only 62.2 percent of charter schools use a set salary structure to determine teacher compensation, and the average age for charter school teachers was 37.4. Teachers in the 1999–2000 SASS were required to work in their schools an average of 39.5 hour per week, but they also typically worked approximately twelve hours per week on tasks outside of school.

The 2003–2004 public report highlighted other aspects of teachers in charter schools (National Center for Educational Statistics, n.d.). For example, charter schools reported the most trouble in recruiting and hiring teachers in the areas of special education, mathematics, and sciences. Charter schools in that survey had higher percentages of minority teachers when compared to public schools, with 29.8 percent of charter teachers coming from minority groups versus 16.7 percent in traditional public schools. The average age for charter school teachers in 2003–2004 was 37.9 years old. A higher percentage of charter school teachers had three years of experience or less when compared to public school teachers; 43.4 percent of charter teachers versus 17.5 percent of public school teachers. Charter teachers also made an average of $7,500 less than public school teachers in the 2003–2004 SASS. Table 8.6 highlights some of the common data areas in the 1999–2000 and 2003–2004

**Table 8.6. Comparison of Charter School Teachers from
Overviews of 1999–2000 and 2003–2004 SASS**

	1999–2000 SASS	*2003–2004 SASS*
Number of Teachers	17,477	42,100
Average Age	37.4	37.9
Hours Required per Week in School	39.5	39.2
Total Hours Worked per Week (In and Out of School)	51.7	53.6

Source: National Center for Educational Statistics, http://nces.ed.gov/quicktables/result.asp?SrchKeyword=
    charter+school+teachers&topic=All&Year=2005
http://nces.ed.gov/pubsearch/pubsinfo.asp?pubid=2002313.

SASS overview publications. Unfortunately, the format of the data from public releases to date do not permit simple comparisons across years. Thus, even these national data are not ideal for trying to understand teachers in charter schools.

Teacher Experience

Research typically shows that charter school teachers are younger and less experienced than their peers in public schools. For example, a study of Michigan charter schools in the 1997–1998 school year found that charter school teachers averaged 7.1 years of experience compared to fifteen years for public school teachers (Khouri, Kleine, White et al., 1999). Harris and Plank (2003) also find that the majority of Michigan charter school teachers have five years of experience or less.

Case study reports in Arizona observed that charter schools tend to hire less experienced teachers with the expectation that they would be easier to train and assimilate into new school environments (Gifford, Phillips, and Ogle, 2000). An evaluation of Pennsylvania charter schools also found younger teachers, as approximately 72.9 percent of charter teachers were in their twenties or thirties. This study also found that teacher experience levels had increased to 6.27 years of experience, up from 4.75 years of teaching experience in their 1998–1999 survey (Miron, Nelson, and Risley, 2002). A similar evaluation of Connecticut charter schools found that teachers in that state had more experience than charter teachers in other states. Charter teachers in Connecticut had approximately 7.29 years of teaching experience, but this was a decline from a previous evaluation finding of 8.04 years. The authors found a general trend of charter schools hiring younger and less experience teachers over time in Connecticut (Miron and Horn, 2003). An analysis of the 1999–2000 Schools and Staffing Survey (SASS) found that charter school teachers were typically less experienced than their public school peers. For example, 62 percent of charter school teachers reported five or fewer years of teaching experience compared to 26 percent of public school teachers (Burian-Fitzgerald, Luckens, and Strizek, 2003).

In some respects, the fact that charter school teachers appear to be younger is hardly surprising since the schools are newer institutions. The average experience level does not tell us anything about the stability or turnover of the teacher labor force or whether the more youthful staff results from other factors. Charter schools may have a deliberate educational philosophy about what kinds of teachers are most effective or operate under economic constraints that affect the types of teachers they hire and retain. For example, in a SASS-based study conducted by Policy Analysis for California Education (PACE), researchers found that "charter schools face tighter *financing* overall than regular public schools, displaying scarce resources that directly support teachers and classrooms" (Fuller, Gawlik, Gonzales et al., 2003, p. 8). Similarly, it is impossible with available data to know whether the salary and working conditions offered by charter schools attract younger teachers or deters older ones.

Teacher Certification and Qualifications

In addition to being less experienced, charter school teachers are less likely to be certified. About 70 percent of Pennsylvania charter teachers in 2002 were certified, which was a decline from approximately 82 percent in a similar 1998–1999 evaluation (Miron et al., 2002). Harris and Plank (2003), in their analysis of 1999–2000 data from the National Center for Educational Statistics, also find that Michigan charter school teachers are less likely to have certification than their public school counterparts in the state. Burian-Fitzgerald et al. (2003) found in the 1999–2000 SASS that 72 percent of charter school teachers were certified compared to 93 percent of public school teachers. They also note that "charter school teachers in states that grant waivers to charter schools for teacher certification are less likely to be certified than public school teachers in those states" (Burian-Fitzgerald et al., 2003, pp. 20–21). Another SASS-based study of 1,010 charter schools in the United States during the 1999–2000 school year reports that "just under 9 percent of regular public school teachers are working without a credential, compared to 43 percent of charter school teachers" (Fuller et al., 2003, p. 8). The researchers also found that urban charter schools had a higher concentration of teachers without a credential as compared to suburban charters, but this finding mimics the same pattern as in traditional public schools.

Some research findings suggest that charter school teachers bring other qualifications and characteristics that are valued by charters. Early case study reports of Arizona charter schools found that charters hired teachers with outside experience in relevant subject matter areas. For example, musicians, artists, or engineers were hired to teach music, art, and science classes. Charter schools in the study also often accepted alternative certification (Gifford et al., 2000). Hoxby (2002) found that in general charter school teachers had completed more math and science coursework than their public school peers. In her sample, charter schools seemed to value and demand teachers with such coursework in addition to such characteristics as responsibility and effort. However, national data paints a diverse picture. In the 1999–2000 SASS approximately 38 percent of charter school math teachers majored or minored in math compared to 51 percent of public school teachers and 42 percent of private school teachers. In science, 60 percent of teachers had a major or minor in science in all school types—charter, public, and private (Burian-Fitzgerald et al., 2003).

These findings are potentially important because teacher subject matter preparation, at least in mathematics and science, has been shown to be one of the few measured teacher characteristics that is related to student achievement (Brewer and Goldhaber, 1996; Goldhaber and Brewer, 1997).

Concerning college graduates, Hoxby (2002) finds that charter school teachers were more likely to have graduated from competitive colleges and had slightly higher SAT scores than public school teachers. Evidence from the 1999–2000 SASS also suggests that charter school teachers are more likely to have graduated from selective colleges than their public school peers (Burian-Fitzgerald et al., 2003). Baker and Dickerson (2006) find that charter schools tended to hire more teachers from competitive undergraduate universities as compared to conventional public schools. In addition, they find a correlation between the relaxation of state teacher certification policies and the likelihood that charter schools will hire teachers from competitive undergraduate institutions. Again, because there is some research evidence that teacher ability as proxied by college attended does affect student achievement (Ehrenberg and Brewer, 1994), these findings might be suggestive of higher teacher quality in charter schools. Nevertheless, individual cases have shown differing findings, preventing any general conclusion. For example, Harris and Plank (2003) have found that Michigan's charter school teachers are more likely to have graduated from less competitive or noncompetitive undergraduate institutions than traditional school teachers.

TEACHER SALARY AND COMPENSATION

Salary and compensation levels are another major area of comparison for charter school teachers. Malloy and Wohlstetter (2003), in their synthesis of charter school teacher research, found that compensation levels vary tremendously across states. They note that charter schools are less likely to use salary schedules for teachers compared to traditional public schools. Their review of the research literature also showed that charter schools differed widely in teacher salary levels, ranging from paying their teachers significantly less than their peer public schools to competitive or higher levels of compensation.

Various studies mimic these diverse findings. For example, a survey of California charter schools reported teacher pay for charter teachers to be on par with their traditional public school peers (Riley, 2000). However, Pennsylvania's charter teachers were found to make significantly less than their traditional public school peers. The average charter salary was $34,400 compared to $52,333 in traditional public schools (Miron et al., 2002).

Some studies have attempted to explore the reasons behind salary differences between charter and public school teachers. For example, statistics from the 1999–2000 SASS shows that a Michigan charter school teacher earns over $15,000 less in salary than the average public school teacher (Harris, 2006). In his analysis, Harris (2006) attributes two-thirds of the salary discrepancy to lower levels of teacher attributes such as less experience and lack of certification. He also concludes that charter schools in Michigan seem to use their autonomy to hire and reward a variety of other teacher qualifications.

Podgursky (2006), in his analysis of 1999–2000 SASS data, finds that charter schools show considerable variation in teacher pay and are less likely to use set salary schedules. His analysis of charter schools in Kansas City not only finds considerable variation in teacher compensation between schools but also within schools. He states that charter schools, in that city at least, seem to be valuing, recruiting for, and rewarding various measures of teacher quality.

Finally, statistics from the 1999–2000 Schools and Staffing Survey suggest that newer charter schools are more likely to use financial incentives to recruit teachers that have National Board Certification and can teach in subject areas with personnel shortages (e.g., math and science). In addition, younger charters are more likely to dismiss teachers for poor performance. Similarly, the SASS data has shown that charters converted from private schools are more likely to reward excellence in teaching than public-conversion charters (National Charter School Research Project, 2007).

Teacher Work Environments

Job security and teacher attrition findings generally show that staff turnover is a significant issue for charter schools. Increased administrative and governance responsibilities and burnout from being stretched too thin are common themes, although direct evidence is scant. In addition, charter schools are less likely to grant tenure while being more likely to use short-term contracts and dismiss poorly performing teachers.

In a qualitative study of seventeen California charter schools, researchers found that teachers' main concerns included heavy workloads and fear of burnout due to a large number of overwhelming responsibilities (Charter Schools Development Center, 1998). A state study in Michigan found that charter schools typically used one-year teacher contracts, and rates of attrition were widely varied. However, the researchers found that most teacher turnover generally occurred in the first year of a charter school's operation (Khouri et al., 1999). Other reports have also observed the prevalent use of short-term contracts for teachers as well as the stressful responsibilities of governance and committee work undertaken by teachers in charter schools (Hill et al., 2001; Johnson and Landman, 2000).

In general, charter school teachers are less likely to hold tenure while charter schools are more likely to use at-will employment or one-year teacher contracts (Malloy and Wohlstetter, 2003). As a whole, charter schools appear to have higher rates of teacher attrition as compared to public schools (National Charter School Research Project, 2007). Whether this is detrimental to the educational quality of a school is hard to discern without further evidence. Undoubtedly staff turnover is disruptive and costly. On other hand, if the teachers who are leaving are of poor quality or because they find they do not fit well with the mission of the school, then turnover could be a net positive in terms of student achievement.

Scholars exploring staff motivation for working in charters generally find that charter school teachers seek out school characteristics such as allowing professional autonomy, the opportunity to work with like-minded peers, an educational mission for the school that matches their personal philosophy, and interest in education reform. For example, a qualitative study of seventeen California charter schools observed that teachers valued professional autonomy, small class sizes, and intimate school environments (Charter Schools Development Center, 1998). Another state study in Michigan found similar motivations but also included interest in education reform, expectations of parental involvement, and school safety (Khouri et al., 1999). Other studies also find that charter school teachers generally chose to work in charters due to specific educational missions, philosophies, opportunities to collaborate with peers, and the desire to be involved in school governance (Hill et al., 2001; Johnson and Landman, 2000). Malloy and Wohlstetter (2003), in their review of the research literature, note that professional flexibility, school mission and vision, working with like-minded colleagues, and smaller schools were major motivations for teachers in charter schools.

Charter school research has typically found that teachers have high levels of satisfaction with the school work environment but varying levels of dissatisfaction with school facilities. For example, a case study of Minnesota charter schools reported that about 81 percent of teachers were satisfied with their schools and 25 percent reported dissatisfaction with their physical resources and facilities (Center for Applied Research and Educational Improvement, 1998).

In a study of Colorado charter schools, Bomotti, Ginsberg, and Cobb (2000) also found that charter school teachers felt more satisfied with their classroom work conditions than traditional public school teachers but were generally frustrated about the funding and physical plant aspects of their schools. Teachers felt more empowered to pursue flexible practices in their classrooms. However, additional responsibilities such as increased participation in school governance introduce stress on charter teachers as well (Johnson and Landman, 2000).

Charter teachers generally work longer hours when compared to their public school peers, and charter teachers in start-up schools tended to work more hours than those in conversion schools (Malloy and Wohlstetter, 2003). Malloy and Wohlstetter further summarize by noting that "Overall, research suggests that teachers in charter schools are a relatively satisfied group despite some difficult working conditions" (p. 227).

CONCLUSION: A LONG WAY TO GO

Reviewing the literature on charter school teachers is a surprisingly frustrating experience. As we argued in the introduction, there are many reasons parents, policy makers and researchers might want to know about teachers in charter schools. The primary reason is that of all school-based characteristics, teacher quality is the one factor most strongly tied to student achievement. Explaining student achievement effects, be they positive or negative, requires knowing something about teacher quality. Further, understanding how charter schools—free of many of the restrictive regulations faced by traditional public schools—hire, train, compensate, and organize the work of teachers is potentially one of the few sources of innovation in public schools.

The evidence, such as it is, is almost entirely descriptive. It reflects a paucity of data collection, along with the highly varied contexts in which charter schools operate. There is some evidence that charter schools employ different kinds of teachers than traditional public schools, reward them differently, and value some characteristics (such as ability and subject matter preparation) that are likely to contribute to improved student achievement. However, teachers are on average less experienced and are also paid less, although no study has adequately determined if, *other things equal,* that charters pay less. Undoubtedly there are "compensating differences" both positive and negative that play an important role in attracting teachers to charter schools. Knowing much more about who teaches in charters and why would clearly be beneficial both for understanding why charters succeed and fail and also for helping us to understand what policies might be effective in the K–12 sector more broadly.

As charter schools continue to grow in number, it will be important to track how charters affect the teacher labor market. In some cities, for example, where charter schools have begun to enroll a large fraction of the students, one would expect that the overall dynamics of the teacher labor market, including hiring strategies, pay bargaining, benefit packages, and so on, could have been affected in traditional public schools. Similarly, as existing charters mature, it is important to understand whether the initial enthusiasm that often surrounds the establishment of a new school, both among educators and parents, wanes. Many charters are able to operate on lower ADA funding than their traditional public school counterparts because they have less experienced teachers who are paid less. However, if those teachers continue to work in the same school, they are likely to become more expensive—although in the absence of step salary schedules, it may be that years of additional experience are not automatically rewarded. Over time, patterns of attrition among charter school teachers will clearly be critical.

Finally, the descriptive research on charter teachers to date, combined with evidence of the importance of teacher quality on student achievement, provide a useful foundation to discern the potential uses of teacher information for evaluating charter school progress, quality, and effectiveness. The current information on charter school teachers is insufficient for use in evaluating charter schools, but what information do policy makers, parents, and other stakeholders need? The key questions for policy makers will be:

1. For what teacher characteristics are charter schools recruiting, hiring, and compensating?
2. Which of those teacher qualities are positively correlated with student achievement?

Research linking charter teacher qualities and student achievement must be sustained and track longitudinal trends. Charter schools affect teachers in starkly different ways as they evolve from start-up to maturity, and thus it will be useful for policy makers and researchers to understand those effects on teacher quality and student achievement. A potential benefit of this research direction could be the emergence of new measures of teacher quality, as charter schools value and hire for different teacher characteristics. For example, teacher characteristics such as professionals who enter teaching mid-career (with relevant subject matter experience), young teachers who enter teaching from elite undergraduate institutions, or school characteristics such as teacher burnout or increased administrative responsibilities for teachers could be linked to student performance. These themes are currently descriptive in the research literature, but when linked to school performance could allow policy makers and researchers the opportunity for richer discussions of charter schools that help shape the legislative environment in which they operate as well as provide learning opportunities for traditional public schools.

We conclude with several points and recommendations for policy makers and other stakeholders interested in exploring the link between teacher quality and student achievement in charter schools:

- Charter schools provide an opportunity to experiment and innovate within the public school system.
- Relaxed personnel regulations and charter laws allow charter schools to value and hire for a diverse range of teacher qualities.
- The current evidence on charter school teachers is largely descriptive, concerned with comparing who teaches in charters versus other schools.
- The evidence is insufficient for use in evaluating charter school quality or performance.
- Future research needs to understand not only what kinds of teachers are in charters but also what teacher qualities and school qualities related to teachers are correlated with higher performance. The most convincing work will link individual students and teachers.

The ideal use of research on teacher quality and student achievement would be a dynamic cycle of evaluation—research linking teacher qualities to student performance (ideally through random assignment, which is highly unlikely or rigorous quasi-experimental methods, as detailed in Betts and Hill, 2006), dissemination of information, subsequent action and evolution of hiring practices by charter schools—leading to new trends and further evaluation. In this process of evaluation, teacher characteristics and their link to school performance could be powerful indicators for evaluating and improving charter schools.

REFERENCES

Baker, B. D., and Dickerson, J. L. (2006). Charter Schools, Teacher Labor Market Deregulation, and Teacher Quality: Evidence from the Schools and Staffing Survey. *Educational Policy* 20:5, 752–78.

Ballou, D., and Podgursky, M. (1998). The Case against Teacher Certification. *The Public Interest* 132, 17–29.

Betts, J., and Hill, P. T. (2006). *Key Issues in Studying Charter Schools and Achievement: A Review and Suggestions for National Guidelines.* Seattle: Center on Reinventing Public Education.

Bomotti, S., Ginsberg, R., and Cobb, B. (2000). Teaching in Charter Schools: Is It Different? *Teaching and Change* 7:3, 273–98.

Brewer, D. J., and Goldhaber, D. (1996). Educational Achievement and Teacher Qualifications: New Evidence from Microlevel Data. In B. S. Cooper and S. T. Speakman (Eds.), *Optimizing Education Resources* (pp. 389–410). Greenwich, CT: JAI Press.

Brewer, D. J., and Wohlstetter, P. (2006). Charter Schools Come of Age. *Urban Ed* (Fall/Winter), 15–19.

Burian-Fitzgerald, M., Luekens, M. T., and Strizek, G. A. (2003). Less Red Tape or More Green Teachers: Charter School Autonomy and Teacher Qualifications. In K. E. Bulkley and P. Wohlstetter (Eds.), *Taking Account of Charter Schools: What's Happened and What's Next?* (pp. 11–31). New York: Teachers College Press.

Center for Applied Research and Educational Improvement. (1998). Minnesota Charter Schools Evaluation. Minneapolis: University of Minnesota.

Center for Education Reform. (n.d.). Charter Schools. Downloaded December 14, 2006, from http://www.edreform.com/index.cfm?fuseAction=stateStatsandpSectionID=15andcSectionID=44.

Charter Schools Development Center. (1998). *Beyond the Rhetoric of Charter School Reform: A Study of Ten California School Districts.* Los Angeles: Charter Schools Development Center, University of California Los Angeles.

Eberts, R. W., and Stone, J. A. (1984). *Unions and Public Schools: The Effect of Collective Bargaining on American Education.* Lexington, MA: Lexington Books.

Education Commission of the States. (n.d.). State Profiles Charter Law. Downloaded December 14, 2006, from http://ecs.org/ecsmain.asp?page=/html/educationIssues/ECSStateNotes.asp.

Ehrenberg, R., and Brewer, D. J. (1994). Do School and Teacher Characteristics Matter?: Evidence from High School and Beyond. *Economics of Education Review* 13:1, 1–17.

Fuller, B., Gawlik, M., Gonzales, E. K., and Park, S. (2003). *Charter Schools and Inequality: National Disparities in Funding, Teacher Quality, and Student Support.* Berkeley, CA: Policy Analysis for California Education.

Gifford, M., Phillips, K., and Ogle, M. (2000). *Five Year Charter School Study.* Phoenix, AZ: Goldwater Institute Center for Market Based Education.

Glazerman, S., Mayer, D., and Decker, P. (2006). Alternative Routes to Teaching: The Impacts of Teach for America on Student Achievement and Other Outcomes. *Journal of Policy Analysis and Management* 25:1, 75–96.

Goldhaber, D., and Brewer, D. J. (1997). Why Don't Schools and Teachers Seem to Matter?: Assessing the Impact of Unobservables on Educational Productivity. *Journal of Human Resources* 32:3, 505–23.

Goldhaber, D., and Brewer, D. J. (2000). Teacher Certification and Student Achievement. *Educational Evaluation and Policy Analysis* 22:2, 129–45.

Goldhaber, D., Perry, D., and Anthony, E. (2003). NBPTS Certification: Who Applies and What Factors Are Associated with Success? Seattle: Center on Reinventing Public Education.

Hanushek, E. (1997). Assessing the Effects of School Resources on Student Performance: An Update. *Educational Evaluation and Policy Analysis* 19:2, 141–64.

Hanushek, E. A., Kain, J. F., and Rivkin, S. G. (1999). *Do Higher Salaries Buy Better Teachers?* Cambridge, MA: National Bureau of Economic Research Working Paper 7082.

Hanushek, E. A., Kain, J. F., and Rivkin, S. G. (2004). Why Public Schools Lose Teachers. *Journal of Human Resources* 39:2, 326–54.

Harris, D. C. (2006). Lowering the Bar or Moving the Target: A Wage Decomposition of Michigan's Charter and Traditional Public School Teachers. *Educational Administration Quarterly* 42:3, 424–60.

Harris, D. C., and Plank, D. N. (2003). *Who's Teaching in Michigan's Traditional and Charter Public Schools, Policy Report.* East Lansing, MI: Education Policy Center.

Hill, P. T., Lake, R., Celio, M. B., Campbell, C., Herdman, P., and Bulkley, K. (2001). *A Study of Charter School Accountability.* Washington, DC: U.S. Department of Education, University of Washington Center on Reinventing Education, and Office of Educational Research and Improvement.

Hoxby, C. M. (1996). How Teachers' Unions Affect Education Production. *The Quarterly Journal of Economics* 111:3, 671–718.

Hoxby, C. M. (2002). Would School Choice Change the Teaching Profession? *Journal of Human Resources* 37:4, 846–91.

Johnson, S. M., and Landman, J. (2000). Sometimes Bureaucracy Has Its Charms: The Working Conditions of Teachers in Deregulated Schools. *Teachers College Record* 102:1, 85–124.

Khouri, N., Kleine, R., White, R., and Cummings, L. (1999). *Michigan's Charter School Initiative: From Theory to Practice.* Lansing, MI: Michigan Department of Education.

Kirby, S., McCombs, J. S., Barney, H., and Naftel, S. (2005). *Reforming Teacher Education: Something Old, Something New.* Santa Monica, CA: RAND Corporation.

Malin, M. H., and Kerchner, C. T. (2007). Charter Schools and Collective Bargaining: Compatible Marriage of Illegitimate Relationship? *Harvard Journal of Law and Public Policy* 30:3, 886–937.

Malloy, C. L., and Wohlstetter, P. (2003). Working Conditions in Charter Schools: What's the Appeal for Teachers? *Education and Urban Society* 35:2, 219–41.

Miron, G., and Horn, J. (2003). *Evaluation of Connecticut Charter Schools and the Charter School Initiative, Final Report.* Kalamazoo, MI: The Evaluation Center.

Miron, G., Nelson, C., and Risley, J. (2002). *Strengthening Pennsylvania's Charter School Reform: Findings from the Statewide Evaluation and Discussion of Relevant Policy Issues, Year Five Report.* Kalamazoo, MI: The Evaluation Center.

National Center for Educational Statistics. (n.d.). Schools and Staffing Survey (SASS). Downloaded February 6, 2007, from http://nces.ed.gov/surveys/sass/.

National Center for Educational Statistics. Characteristics of Schools, Districts, Teachers, Principals, and School Libraries in the United States: 2003–04 Schools and Staffing Survey. Downloaded February 6, 2007, from http://nces.ed.gov/pubsearch/pubsinfo.asp?pubid=2006313.

National Center for Educational Statistics. (n.d.). Characteristics of Schools, Districts, Teachers, Principals, and School Libraries in the United States: 1999–00 Schools and Staffing Survey. Downloaded February 6, 2007, from http://nces.ed.gov/pubsearch/pubsinfo.asp?pubid=2002313.

National Charter School Research Project. (2007). *Inside Charter Schools: A Systematic Look at Our Nation's Charter Schools, Project Update.* Seattle: Center on Reinventing Public Education.

Nye, B., Konstantopoulos, S., and Hedges, L. (2004). How Large Are Teacher Effects? *Educational Evaluation and Policy Analysis* 26:3, 237–57.

Odden, A., and Kelley, C. (2001). *Paying Teachers for What They Know and Do: New and Smarter Compensation Strategies to Improve Schools.* Thousand Oaks, CA: Corwin Press.

Podgursky, M. (2006). Teams versus Bureaucracies: Personnel Policy, Wage-setting, and Teacher Quality in Traditional Public, Charter, and Private Schools. Paper presented at the National Conference on Charter School Research, Vanderbilt University.

Podgursky, M., and Ballou, D. (2001). Personnel Policy in Charter Schools. Washington, DC: Thomas B. Fordham Foundation.

Riley, P. A. (2000). *A Charter School Survey: Parents, Teachers, and Principals Speak Out.* San Francisco: Pacific Research Institute for Public Policy.

Shanker, A. (1998). Restructuring Our Schools. *Peabody Journal of Education* 65:3, 88–100.

Walsh, K. (2001). *Teacher Certification Reconsidered: Stumbling for Quality.* Baltimore, MD: The Abell Foundation.

Part II

HOW POLICY MAKERS CAN
MAKE BETTER USE OF EVIDENCE

Chapter Nine

The State of State Charter School Research

Robin J. Lake and Larry Angel

INTRODUCTION

National studies of charter school achievement garner much media attention but are nearly useless to most state policy leaders. As Rhode Island's Commissioner of Education has said, research on charter schools in other states is meaningless to him because the Rhode Island charter law and implementation is substantially different from any other state. Educational environments vary from state to state, and every state law authorizing charter schools is its own creature reflecting the politics and preferences of that state. As a result research outcomes can be expected to vary.

State charter research also tends to carry the greatest consequences for the schools themselves. Many state charter studies are commissioned by state agencies and legislatures seeking to inform high-stakes policy decisions, such as whether to expand the number of charter schools allowed in a state. Yet very little attention has been paid to the quality of state-specific charter school evaluations.

This chapter investigates how states are assessing the effectiveness of their charter schools. We begin with an overview of the types of research states are undertaking to assess their charter schools and the quality of that research. We argue that although there are many examples of very strong state-level charter evaluations, the majority of states are not assessing charters in a way that can tell them 1) whether students are better or worse off by attending charter schools and 2) which charter schools are doing better than others and why. We conclude by making a series of recommendations for states that could improve their evaluations to achieve those goals.

All states assess individual charter schools, but we were interested in knowing how states evaluate the academic success or failure of the charter schools created as a result of the state laws authorizing and the implementation of that law.

To understand the state of state-based charter research, we reviewed twenty-six charter school studies conducted or commissioned by states between 2000 and 2006. We also reviewed state charter laws to learn what requirements they set for state evaluations and conducted interviews with legislative staff from three states. We wanted to know:

- Who initiates and conducts the state charter evaluations?
- What are states trying to learn through their evaluations?
- How often are states conducting evaluations of their charter programs?
- What is the quality of the achievement research?

OVERVIEW OF THE CHARTER
ACHIEVEMENT RESEARCH STATES CONDUCT

Evaluations of state charter programs are driven mainly by legal imperative or by controversy. The vast majority of state charter evaluations are commissioned or conducted by a state agency or office, mainly in response to a requirement in the state's original charter school legislation. As a result, the analyses are almost always crafted to comply with the requirements of the Request for Proposals (RFP) or the charter school law itself. This section is devoted mainly to these state-sponsored charter school studies.

Of those states that do analyze charter school performance separately from other public schools, there are three primary approaches to evaluation:

Many states conduct annual evaluations of charter schools (sixteen states require this by law). These annual evaluations sometimes simply provide state-mandated test results for individual charter schools (e.g., Virginia and Nevada). However, most (e.g., Colorado) go on to aggregate results for all charter schools statewide to show how they perform as a group. Some provide some growth analysis (e.g., New York), and most make *some* comparison to other public schools.

Other evaluations are conducted periodically, anywhere from every few years (two states) to one mandated evaluation a certain number of years after the law was enacted (ten states). These evaluations tend to be much more complex both in the types of questions being asked about the charter program and the methods employed. In this type of evaluation, academic achievement is normally just one outcome among many being assessed.

Rarely, states conduct or commission an evaluation focused only on the topic of charter school academic achievement.

Enormous Variation in Quality, but Poor Methods Typically

We used the same criteria as described in chapter 1 to rate the method of outcome evaluation used in state-sponsored charter studies (Charter School Achievement Consensus Panel, 2006). We found as much variety in the quality of state-sponsored charter evaluations as one would expect given the diversity of state charter school laws and implementation. Figure 9.1 provides a summary of the ratings we gave state studies. The appendix provides detail on how each study was rated and for what reasons.

The National Charter School Research Project's Consensus Panel on Charter School Achievement rates "poor" those studies that simply provide average score comparisons between charter schools and other public schools, especially those that rely on schoolwide data rather than data for individual students. These "average-to-average" comparisons make it next to impossible to say whether the charter schools' scores are a result of actions by the school or are simply a reflection of the prior learning and experiences that

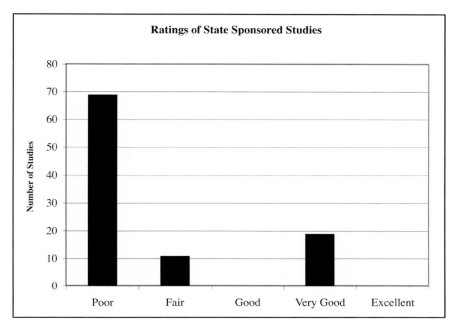

Figure 9.1. Ratings of State-sponsored Studies

the charter school students brought with them to the school. Furthermore, using statewide averages of average school scores, a common method in state evaluations, can mask important variability in the performance of individual students and schools.

Slightly better, but still "poor," approaches include making the comparison group a nearby district, rather than the state, or using several years of data to compare test score changes over time, not just one year of data. Without controlling for student characteristics such as poverty and race (known to correlate with student achievement), test scores differences (positive or negative) may be almost entirely a function of the students' particular character or experiences at home or at the school he or she previously attended.

Eighteen of twenty-six (69 percent) of the state-sponsored studies we reviewed used what we consider "poor" methods for understanding whether or not students benefit from attending charter schools. Most studies simply compared average passage rates on the state exam in charter schools to passage rates statewide or in nearby districts. In three states (Oklahoma, Nevada, and Virginia), what passed for a state report on charter school achievement was simply a school-by-school accounting of charter school test scores.

By accounting for appropriate school characteristics, it is possible for researchers to improve on the shortcomings described above while still using school-level data. For instance, a researcher working with school average test scores might look for trends over several years, factoring into the analysis school characteristics such as demographic composition, enrollment, student-teacher ratio, free and reduced-price lunch participation, and teacher salaries. By our assessment, such a study would be labeled as "fair," the highest possible rating for research using school-level data. Three (11 percent) of the studies we reviewed fell into this category.

The studies rated "good" use student-level data, look at growth over time, and include at least some controls for student characteristics. None of the studies we reviewed fell into this category.

The "very good" category includes methods such as fixed-effects or hierarchical linear modeling (HLM), which are sophisticated analyses of changes in student-level data over a number of years. Nineteen percent (five) of the studies we reviewed fell into this category.

The most effective, or "excellent," methods for understanding whether students benefit from a particular school environment are experimental or quasi-experimental studies. Such studies generally use students on the school's wait list as a comparison group to control for family or student self-selection biases.

There were no experimental studies (using as the comparison group the performance of students who applied to the school but did not get in). For practical reasons, statewide experimental studies may not always be feasible. Such research could only include oversubscribed schools, which are likely a subset of charter schools in the state and likely not representative of the other charters.

About half the states with charter school laws have not conducted or commissioned *any* achievement evaluation since 2000. All but nine state-sponsored studies used less than four years of data to draw their conclusions.

It should be noted that from the point of view of a state evaluating its charter schools, several topics other than student achievement will likely be of interest, such as the demands oversight requirements place on schools and authorizers, teacher characteristics, and parental satisfaction. However, academic achievement is perhaps the most objective measure by which to judge school performance, and it ultimately gets to the heart of the charter bargain to provide a quality educational alternative.

Eight out of twenty-six studies look at some form of achievement indicators other than test scores, such as graduation rates or college acceptance.

In general, then, state agencies do not seem to be getting nearly the information they would need to accurately assess whether students in the state benefited academically by attending charter schools. With a few exceptions, most states are simply taking gross measures of student achievement in charter schools. We hesitate to even refer to such analyses as studies. They are really just quick comparisons of data. That approach may be fine for states that intend to take the long view of their charter school policies, waiting to see if many years down the line, charter school students are obviously outperforming or underperforming other public schools. But for states that wish to know how much current charter school test score performance is due to abilities or experiences students brought with them to the school, the current methods being used fall seriously short.

Little Guidance for Policy and Improvement

Of equal concern is the fact that only one state-sponsored study provides any real insight into the question of what types of charter schools are more successful than others.

Just two state-sponsored studies that we reviewed break down achievement results by school type. The RAND study commissioned by the California Legislative Audit Committee (Zimmer et al.) provides analysis of achievement results for new charter schools versus public school conversions, and online charter schools. Similarly, two state studies (NYSED and Miron CT) analyzed whether charter school achievement in the state seems to improve as a function of the age of the school. No studies provided any analysis of how charter school achievement varies according to what agency (school district, etc.) oversees it.

In all, states do not seem to be playing a role in using evaluation research to guide charter school improvement. A few studies identify charter schools that seem to be performing at very high levels (e.g., Colorado, 2006), but they do not provide any assessment of why that may or may not be the case.

Some of the Best Studies Are the Result of Ongoing Collaboration between the State and a Local University

The vast majority of state-sponsored charter evaluations are either

- performed by a state agency itself (e.g., Ohio's Legislative Office of Education Oversight);
- conducted by the agency in collaboration with a third-party researcher or firm; or
- commissioned through a procurement process such as a Request for Proposals.

In general, the middle category, a collaborative effort between a state agency and an outside researcher or firm, produced higher-quality methods than the other two approaches. In particular, one study conducted by Duke University researchers in collaboration with the North Carolina Department of Education was the result of a long-standing data analysis agreement, allowing Duke researchers access to confidential data and the freedom to craft their own research design. The Michigan Evaluation Center has also conducted a number of strong state evaluations. Contracting out the data analysis function often allows state agencies to get much higher-quality research design and analysis than if they had tried to do the evaluation themselves.

Independent Research—An Additional and Effective Source of Information for States

In addition to reviewing studies paid for by states, we reviewed state-specific charter school studies conducted by researchers, usually university-based, and most often paid for by local foundations. Examples include studies of charter schools in Florida by Tim Sass at Florida State University; in Wisconsin by John Witte at the University of Wisconsin; and in Texas by the Texas Public Policy Foundation.

In general, here we found a more consistently high-quality approach to evaluation. In fact, as our broader review of national charter school studies has shown, these studies are generally of very good quality.

We can only speculate as to why these studies are higher quality. It may be that the studies are better funded so can be more thorough. It may also be that independent researchers are more likely to seek out good data sources that would allow strong causal inferences. We suspect, however, that there are other factors at play that work against high-quality state-sponsored studies. The following sections describe those possibilities.

FACTORS THAT MAY EXPLAIN
LOW-QUALITY STATE EVALUATIONS

Thin State-Level Data and Expertise
Limit Possible Methods and Scope of Analysis

The most common complaint among those who conduct state-sponsored evaluations is that they had insufficient data with which to work. Researchers complained both that states were not requiring charter schools report information necessary for complete evaluations and that charter schools were often simply not providing information when it was required.

The December 2003 charter school evaluation conducted by the New York Board of Regents encountered both these problems. Because not all of the New York charter schools serve grades in which the required statewide exams are given, less than half of New York charter schools submitted data for the evaluation. The researchers went on to try to piece together an analysis based on the tests that were being used, but because there were so many different tests being used—so many schools switching metrics from one year to the next, so many different ways of reporting the results, etc—the researchers were unable to do more than present average test scores and growth scores for a subset of schools and compare those scores to the average scores of schools in the nearest public school district.

A recent study conducted by Jon Christensen of the National Charter School Research Project reviewed the types of data states collect and confirmed the paucity of reliable charter school information. Christensen found major data obstacles in carrying out quality assessments of student achievement. Nearly half of all states with charter schools reported that incomplete or inaccurate reporting of data is a problem. Timeliness, completeness, and accuracy were typically mentioned together as issues. These issues were typically attributed to relatively lean staffing and higher staff turnover at charter schools compared to traditional district schools. While this issue was not always unique to charter schools, it presents a challenge to research in any school. Moreover, it appears that while most states have collected several important data elements, much more data should be collected to accurately assess charter quality in the states, in particular data on individual students that would allow longitudinal analysis of achievement.

For states that have relied on state agency staff, those agencies' capacity to perform complex analyses probably also comes into play. State agencies often lack funding to staff research studies and have a hard time competing with the private sector for staff with strong technical expertise, especially with the rise of the testing industry. In many cases, state agency staff also are not familiar with the specific policy issues surrounding charter schools or do not know how to commission effective studies of such a diverse and complex policy area.

Trying to Answer Too Many Questions

State-sponsored charter school evaluations too often try to answer too *broad* a research question or simply ask too *many* research questions. As a result, researchers can only provide superficial analysis. The 2003 study conducted by Ohio's Legislative Office of Education Oversight (LOEO), for example, identifies as its "focus" the "academic achievement of [charter] schools; student attendance rates, parental choice and satisfaction; and the degree to which [charter] schools are being held accountable." Each one of these topics really warrants its own deep treatment in order to develop a rigorous analysis and meaningful results. Instead, the LOEO report devotes twelve pages of a sixty-two-page report to academic achievement, using methods that should, in no way, be considered informative.

The tendency of these studies to take on more than they can honestly answer is at least in part driven by legal requirements. The parameters of many state evaluations are determined in the original state charter law. The state charter school laws (when evaluation is addressed) point to four main reasons for the research (some laws include more than one reason):[1]

- measure effectiveness of the charter school approach (ten states),
- compare charter school performance to other public school students (fourteen states),
- provide recommendations for improving the law (four states), and
- measure the impact of charter schools on public school districts (four states).

With few exceptions, state laws describe extremely broad and high-stakes research questions. For example: Idaho's law says the "state board shall review the educational effectiveness of charter schools." Pennsylvania's law requires an independent consultant to conduct an "evaluation of the charter school program" and provide recommendations regarding the continuation, modification, expansion, or termination of the program. Some state charter laws are much more specific about the purpose of the evaluation and even point to the measures that should be used. Texas requires the use of precharter and postcharter school test scores. New Jersey requires assessment of charter students' progress toward meeting state content standards. But no state provides specific, measurable benchmarks for statewide charter performance to guide an evaluation.

The broad research questions are even more difficult to answer considering that most states have multiple, and sometimes potentially conflicting, stated goals or purposes of their charter school laws. It is common for states to include innovation, improved accountability, new professional opportunities for teachers, and new choices for parents as stated purposes in addition to improving student performance that would presumably have to be considered in addition to academic results in evaluations of charter effectiveness.

As a result, most state evaluations end up being a mile wide and inch thick, only tapping the surface of any of these topics. Even when the studies are confined to academic achievement, researchers struggle with what measures they should use to define academic success. In just a sample of six of the studies we reviewed, academic achievement was defined as including:

- Performance of charter schools compared with "similar" traditional public schools (leaving it to the researchers to define what is meant by similar).
- Performance of charter schools compared to the accountability plans in their contracts with their sponsors.
- Performance gains of charter schools compared to other public schools.
- The long-term positive or negative effects on students and parents associated with attending or sending a child to a charter school.
- Performance or at-risk students who attend charter schools compared to those attending other public schools.
- Meeting the requirements of the state accountability system.
- Meeting the requirements of the federal No Child Left Behind law.

With such vague and sometimes contradictory definitions of achievement, researchers are often left to present basic comparative information and let policy makers and the public come to their own conclusions. Even the most sophisticated studies will fail to provide meaningful insights without a clear definition of what level of achievement, and what measures of achievement, are expected of charter schools.

Some States May Not Care To Know

The variation in quality of studies among states is not entirely surprising given the wide variety of approaches to charter laws and implementation of those laws across the states. States that have considered chartering a small-scale experiment tend to either not have any required evaluation or simply review basic data analysis on existing charter schools through their state departments of education. Conversely, the best studies have come out of states with large numbers of charters. This is understandable given that the success or failure of the charter policy affects a greater proportion of public school students, and the potential positive or negative impact of chartering on students attending traditional public schools is greater in these states. We argue, however, that all states with charters should want to know whether or not the experiment is working in order to inform whether it should be expanded or not, and reasonably sophisticated evaluations are the only way to honestly inform that question.

RECOMMENDATIONS TO SUPPORT HIGHER-QUALITY STATE-BASED CHARTER SCHOOL RESEARCH

Deeper Analysis of Fewer Topics

As difficult as it may be to resist the idea that one study can provide definitive answers to the effectiveness of a state charter law, useful results can only come from narrowly defined research questions that focus on measurable outcomes. Such questions may be the following:

- Are students benefiting academically from attending charter schools in the state?
- Are students benefiting in ways other than can be measured with state test scores? (See Laura Hamilton and Brian Stecher's chapter in this volume for more detail on what states might wish to measure.)
- Are schools doing better than others, and why?
- In what ways could the state charter program be improved in order to increase academic success? Such a study would attempt to trace the impact of provisions of state law (e.g., levels of autonomy, funding, and oversight/accountability) to results.
- What systemwide impact is the state charter program having, and why?

Smaller-scale achievement questions states might pursue include whether charter schools are cost-effective and whether charter schools are innovating in ways policy makers had hoped they would.

A good statewide study cannot answer more than one of these questions at a time without a significant budget. States that wish to pursue many or all of these questions (as they probably should) might consider a sequence of studies that build on each other, as Massachusetts is doing.

A Research Infrastructure That Supports Good Charter and Noncharter Achievement Research

As noted above, many of the state charter school achievement studies conducted to date have tried to use whatever data they could find and make the best use of it as possible. In far too many cases, as Hill and Betts described in a paper on the subject, the data too often have incomplete student records, weak information on student characteristics, or weak links to school and teacher characteristics, making it "impossible to measure gains in achievement for individual students." It is in the interest of all states to commit to building sets of data that will allow for sophisticated performance evaluations of all schools, not just charters.

An investment in stronger databases comes with a cost, but it can make the cost of future charter evaluations quite low. State evaluations can be costly if the state does not keep a good central database of key information (California spent $600,000 on the RAND evaluation), but evaluations can be much less costly if the data just need to be accessed and analyzed.

Charter schools themselves should also give more thought to what data will be needed in the future to resolve the questions of interest to policy makers and practitioners. As the New York Board of Regents noted in its report, "Charter schools (in New York) have not made an effective effort to organize and present their data to make a case for their academic effectiveness." The increased state attention to better accountability systems and student-level data will assist any such efforts.

More Evaluations Focused on Helping Charter Schools Improve

It would not take a great deal more effort for state evaluations to identify what kinds of schools are working well and what kind are not, as the RAND California charter school study did. A good researcher should be able to define categories of possible variation with the state charter school community. Some obvious possibilities include: new starts; conversions; schools run by management companies; older schools versus newer schools; schools following a particular whole-school design or curriculum; and online schools.

More ambitious research might look to factors that contribute to or impede performance, such as the level of funding, the type of oversight, etc. A legislative staffer in California indicated interest in knowing much more than bottom-line achievement numbers, such as the link between achievement and individual teachers (especially in nonunionized schools) and the impact of innovative instructional programs. Such a research focus would not only provide charter schools with a roadmap for improvement but also would allow other public schools to learn from the charter school experience.

BETTER STATE GOVERNMENT CAPACITY TO COMMISSION AND CONDUCT STRONG EVALUATIONS

Though policy makers look to many sources of information to learn about charter school performance, state agencies are often the most trusted source and are generally responsible for conducting or commissioning evaluations. Given this central role, states, foundations, and even the federal government have an interest in ensuring that departments of education, auditors, and analyst offices at least fully understand the charter school concept, the intent of the law, and the most appropriate methods for the evaluation of charter school achievement effects. Specific trainings or "boot camps" could cover:

- how to design a state evaluation and an RFP
- how to evaluate proposals
- how to get the data to support high-quality achievement studies

More Long-Term Research Partnerships

As discussed above, there appears to be a real advantage for states that partner with a local university to act as their data center and evaluation partner. Especially for small states that do not have large, in-house data analysis capacity, a university can often perform more sophisticated studies, especially if the analysis is over a number of years so the right data can be assembled if needed. A contract for independent analysis also can provide a political buffer from the whims of politicians who might wish to add research questions or otherwise broaden the scope of the evaluation. In the case of RAND's California charter study, the LAO was able to steer the researchers toward the most critical policy issues facing lawmakers.

Foundations should also consider filling holes in state research needs. Foundation-funded studies offer researchers greater flexibility to design their ideal study without bureaucratic RFP constraints and may provide an additional buffer from politics.

Clear Performance Goals for the State Charter School Program

It is past time for state officials to become clear about their expectations of charter schools. State legislators or state departments of education would do evaluators and charter schools a great service by becoming clear about the academic and nonacademic outcomes for the state charter program. The goals should be specific, realistic, and developed with input from existing charter schools. There might be a ten-year goal and a five-year goal. The goals could be nonacademic or academic, but they must be measurable. Such a set of goals would allow for more focused research and would provide the charter school community with a clear set of guideposts for improvement.

Evidence That Is Relevant to Policy

Finally, it would be naïve to assume that producing better studies will alone lead to more evidence-based state-level policy decisions. As Jeff Henig's chapter makes clear, it is not entirely clear that politicians actually want better evidence or pay attention to it, especially when the methods are very complex. Our state-level interviews, however, provide reason to believe that rigorous research does influence charter policy and that politicians, especially those in the middle of the political spectrum, will pay attention to nuanced findings. To make sure complicated and balanced research gets the attention it deserves, researchers and those interested in evidence-based decision making would do well to:

- *Make sure research is written in a way that lay people can understand and that includes clear recommendations for policy.* The people we interviewed recognized the propensity for lawmakers to embrace simplistic numbers in defense of their own biases but also argued that important votes come from lawmakers who are open to evidence. Those moderates understand and sympathize with ideas such as seeing how school results play out over several years and taking into account the types of students that attend the schools, but even they need help with translation. RAND's California evaluation benefited greatly by the LAO writing its own summary report of the study with clear recommendations for lifting the charter cap and other policy implications.
- *Get state charter advocates and associations on board.* If charter advocates and foes can agree that independent, rigorous research is in everyone's interest, it will be easier to build a case for large state investments in data collection and analysis.

CONCLUSION

If the real action in state charter evaluation must be within states, this analysis has shown that the quality of state-sponsored analysis should generally be considered far from adequate to inform policy. There are too many studies providing only rough estimates of the academic value charter schools may add to a given state's public education offerings, and there is almost no achievement information being gathered by states that *ought* to be used to inform important decisions by policy makers, such as these: What types of schools are doing better than others? Are charter schools helping to close the minority achievement gap?

In reality, though, some of the least sophisticated state-sponsored studies get quite a bit of policy attention inside and outside the state, often playing important roles in high-stakes decisions, such as whether to lift legislative caps on the number of charter schools allowed or whether to impose new regulations on charters. Often this is despite strong cautions by the studies' authors about the limitations of the study due to lack of data or other barriers. The reality is that legislators, the media, and the general public are impatient to learn whether charter schools in their states are working and are happy to accept simple measures that most researchers find irresponsibly simplistic.

Our interviews with analysts and lawmakers show that there is openness and even interest in "better" studies, but the responsibility for making that happen falls squarely on charter school advocates and associations. They must insist that states invest in higher quality studies, and, as the New York State Education Department has suggested, must present a proactive and unified approach to improving the quality of data and developing strong, long-term evaluations.

Appendix Table 9.1. State-by-state Charter School Law Summary

State	Evaluation?	Who?	How often?	How specific?	Description/notable:
AK	No				
AZ	No				
AR	Yes	State department	Annual	Evaluation includes but not limited to seven factors ("student scores on assessment instruments")	Factors include "student scores on assessment instruments"
CA	Yes	Neutral evaluator	On or before July 1, 2003	Evaluation of "effectiveness of charter school approach" includes fifteen factors	One of most extensive list of factors of all states (NJ, TX); factors include "if available, pre- and postcharter school test scores"
CO	Yes	State department	Every three years	Evaluate "success or failure of charter schools . . . and suggested changes in state law" to strengthen charter program	State board compiles local board evaluations to determine whether releases from state law assisted or impeded charter schools
CT	Yes	State commissioner	Annual	Review "operation of" charter schools; report includes four factors	Factors include statutory changes, compilation of school profiles, assessment of adequacy of funding and facilities; school profiles include report on "educational progress of students"
DE	Yes	State department	Annual	Report on "success or failure of charter schools and propose changes in state law" to improve charter program	One of the least specific provisions
DC	No				
FL	Yes	State department	Annual	Analysis and comparison of "overall performance of charter school students" versus comparable public schools students	Comparison based on scores from statewide assessment programs

Appendix Table 9.1. (*Continued*)

State	Evaluation?	Who?	How often?	How specific?	Description/notable:
GA	Yes	State board	Annual	"The state board shall report . . . on the status of the charter school program."	The least specific of all state evaluation provisions
HI	No				
ID	Yes	State board	Not later than July 1, 2004	"The state board shall review the educational effectiveness of charter schools"	One of the least specific provisions
IL	Yes	State board	Annual	Compile annual evaluations from local school boards and prepare annual report that: (1) compares academic performance of charter and noncharter students, (2) determines if exemptions assisted or impeded charter schools, (3) suggests changes in charter law	In addition, state board of education does "periodic evaluations of charter schools that include evaluations of student academic achievement"
IN	No				
IA	Yes	State board	Annual	Evaluate the state's charter school programs generally; report shall include seven factors	Language almost identical to MI law; factors include "aggregate assessment test scores"
KS	Yes	State board	Annual	State board shall "review, assess and compile" evaluations of charter schools submitted by local boards	Local board "shall evaluate the impact the charter school has had on the educational system of the district"
LA	Yes	State board	No later than January 1, 2001	Report shall compare performance of charter students with comparable groups in other schools	
MD	Yes	State board	On or before October 1, 2006	Report "shall address the advisability of the continuation, modification, expansion, or termination of the program."	

MA	Yes	Independent evaluator	By December 1999	Primary research questions: (1) is charter school initiative presenting parents and students with significant educational choices? (2) Is charter school initiative affecting district schools?	Evaluation conducted by MA Education Reform Review Commission
MI	Yes	State board	Annual	Evaluate charter schools generally; report shall include six factors	Language almost identical to IA law; factors include "aggregates assessment test scores"
MN	No (but see) comment				*But see* Sec. 124D.10 (subd. 15): State department must review and comment on evaluation, by sponsor, of performance of charter school before charter school's contract is renewed
MS	Yes	State board	Annual	Report on "status of the charter school program"; report includes five factors	Factors include: comparison of academic performance of charter school students with comparable groups; "assessment of the students' academic progress in the charter school as measured, where available, against the academic year immediately preceding the first year of the charter school's operation" (similar to NC)
MO	Yes	Contractor	Not clear (impact study every two years; performance study not specified)	Two studies: (1) performance of charter students in comparison with comparable group; and (2) impact of charter schools upon the districts in which they are located	

Appendix Table 9.1. (*Continued*)

State	Evaluation?	Who?	How often?	How specific?	Description/notable:
NV	No (but see comment)				*But see* NRS 386.605 (legislative accountability bureau "may" authorize a consultant to review and analyze charter school accountability information)
NH	No (but see comment)				*But see* Sec. 194-B:21: Joint legislative oversight committee "shall monitor the effect of this chapter" and make recommendations for changes to charter law
NJ	Yes	Independent study	By October 1, 2001	Evaluation of charter school program based upon public hearings and independent study; evaluation includes twelve elements	One of most extensive list of factors of all states (CA, TX); elements include comparison (for charter and noncharter students) of "student progress toward meeting the core curriculum content standards as measured by student results on statewide assessment tests"
NM	No				
NY	Yes	Board of regents	Annual progress reports and review of effectiveness by December 31, 2003	Report annually re: "the academic progress of students attending charter schools, as measured against comparable public and nonpublic schools wherever practicable"	Also, "review the educational effectiveness of the charter school approach . . . and the effect of charter schools on the public and nonpublic school systems" and report by December 31, 2003; report to include "student performance on standardized assessment tests"

NC	Yes	State board	By January 1, 2002	Evaluate "the educational effectiveness of the charter school approach . . . and the effect of charter schools on the public schools in the [district] in which the charter schools are located"; evaluation based primarily on four factors	Factors include "student academic progress in the charter schools as measured, where available, against the academic year immediately preceding the first academic year of the charter schools' operation" (similar to MS)
OH	Yes	State department	Annual	Report "regarding the effectiveness of academic programs, operations and legal compliance and of the financial condition" of all charter schools	One of the least specific provisions
OK	Yes	State board	Annual	Report "outlining the status of charter schools in the state"	Report shall include . . . information on "enrollment, testing, curriculum, finances and employees"
OR	No				
PA	Yes	Independent consultant	Five years following effective date of law	"Evaluation of the charter school program," which shall include recommendation re: continuation, modification, expansion, or termination of program	One of the least specific provisions
PR	No				No information on Puerto Rico
RI	No				
SC	Yes	State board	During fifth year after effective date of law	Review "implementation and effectiveness of this chapter" and "comprehensive reports issued by local school boards concerning successes or failures of charter schools"	State board shall compare the academic performance of charter school pupils with comparable groups

Appendix Table 9.1. *(Continued)*

State	Evaluation?	Who?	How often?	How specific?	Description/notable:
TN	Yes	Office of Educational Accountability	By February 1, 2008	Comprehensive study of charter schools across TN to (1) evaluate each school's status in achieving purposes established in the law and (2) recommend measures for improvement	Report shall include "comparison of any relevant test data" from public traditional and charter schools; report shall also include information on other states' charter school legislation and corresponding results
TX	Yes	Impartial organization	Annual	Evaluation must include consideration of seven items before and after implementing the charter, as well as three other items	Items include "students' scores on assessment instruments" administered under state law
UT	Yes	Charter school governing board	Annual	Charter school board provides progress report to legislature; report to include a minimum of four factors	Report to include "a narrative describing the school's progress toward achieving its goals" and "the school's annual state performance report" pursuant to state law
VA	Yes	State board	Annual	Board "shall report annually its findings and evaluations of" charter schools	State board shall review local school board evaluations of charter schools; local boards shall submit a comparison of the performance of charter and noncharter school students
WI	No				
WY	No				

Appendix Table 9.2. Summary of State-sponsored Charter School Achievement Research, Covering Research Released between 2001 and 2006

	Quality of Research in Principle	Student-Level or School-Level	Value-Added or Levels	FE, HLM, C, P, N	#	Identity
Experiment	E	St	V	C	–	
	E/VG	St	V	None	–	
	VG/G	St	L	C or None	–	
	F	Sch	V	C or None	–	
	F	Sch	L	C or None	–	
	VG	St	V	(F, C) or H	3	Buddin and Zimmer (2003)*, Florida Department of Education (2004)*, Florida Department of Education (2006)
Observational	VG	St	V	F or P	2	Miron (Year 1, 2004)*, Miron (Year 2, 2006)
	G	St	V	C	2	Noblit and Corbett (2001)*, Michigan DOE (2005)
	F	St	V	None	2	Idaho DOE (2004), Colorado (2006)
	F	St	L	F, (F, C) H or P	1	Miron, Nelson, Risley, and Sullins (2002)*
	F	St	L	C		
	P	Sch	L	None	6	Miron and Horn (2002)*, Missouri DOE (2003), Missouri (2006), Texas (2005), New Jersey DOE (2001), Oregon (2005)
	F	Sch	V	C		
	P	Sch	V	None		
	P	Sch	L	C	10	Colorado Department of Education (2003)*, LOEO (2003)*, NYU (2003)*, Virginia DOE (2005), Georgia DOE (2006), Illinois DOE (2006), Nevada DOE (Draft), Oklahoma (2006), Arkansas (2004), Louisiana (2004)
	P	Sch	L	None		

NOTES

1. A complete table listing evaluation provisions of state laws is listed in the appendix.

REFERENCES

Charter School Achievement Consensus Panel. (2006). *Key Issues in Studying Charter Schools and Achievement: A Review and Suggestions for National Guidelines.* NCSRP White Paper Series, No. 2. Seattle, WA: Center on Reinventing Public Education.

Christensen, J. (2006). *Charter School Data: What States Collect, State Data, and Implications for Research.* NCSRP Research Brief. Seattle, WA: Center on Reinventing Public Education.

Colorado Department of Education. (2003). *The State of Charter Schools in Colorado: 2001–02: The Characteristics, Status and Performance Record of Colorado Charter Schools.* Download at http://www.cde.state.co.us/cdechart.

Colorado Department of Education. (2006). *The State of Charter Schools in Colorado 2004–05: The Characteristics, Status, and Performance Record of Colorado Charter Schools.* Download at http://www.cde.state.co.us/cdechart/download/Final_Study_2005.pdf.

Florida Department of Education. (2004). Florida Charter Schools: 2002–2003 Annual Accountability Report. August 17, 2004. Download at http://www.fldoe.org/board/meetings/2004_08.../Charter_ExecSum.pdf.

Florida Department of Education. (2006). Florida's Charter Schools: A Decade of Progress. Download at http://www.floridaschoolchoice.org/Information/charter_schools/files/Charter_10Year_Book.pdf.

Gallant, F. (2004). Idaho's Charter School Students' Achievement. Download at http://www.sde.idaho.gov/site/charter_schools/research_reports_docs/Idaho%20Charter%20School%20Student%27s%20Achievement%202004_Dr.%20Frank%20Gallant.pdf.

Georgia Department of Education. (2006). 2005–2006 Annual Report on Georgia's Charter Schools. Prepared by Kathy Cox, State Superintendent of Schools. Download at http://www.doe.k12.ga.us/pea_charter.aspx?folderID=8383&m=links&ft=Downloads.

Hill, P., and Betts, J. (2006). Improving State and Local Assessment of Charter School Performance. In R. Lake and P. Hill (Eds.), *Hopes, Fears, & Reality: A Balanced Look at American Charter Schools in 2006.* Seattle, WA: Center on Reinventing Public Education.

Illinois State Board of Education. (2006). Illinois Charter School Annual Report. Download at http://www.isbe.net/charter/Default.htm.

KPMG. (2001). Evaluation of the New Jersey Charter Program, September. Download at http://www.nj.gov/njded/chartsch/evaluation/.

Legislative Office of Education Oversight. (2003). Community Schools in Ohio: Final Report on Student Performance, Parent Satisfaction, and Accountability. Download at http://www.ode.state.oh.us/GD/Templates/Pages/ODE/ODEDetail.aspx?Page=3&TopicRelationID=662&Content=79301.

Louisiana Department of Education. (2006). Framework for the Evaluation of Louisiana Charter Schools. Download at http://www.louisianaschools.net/.

Michigan Department of Education. (2006). *Public School Academies, 2006–07: Michigan Department of Education Report to the Legislature.* Download at http://www.michigan.gov/documents/mde/Item_I1_217074_7.pdf.

Miron, G. (2004). *Evaluation of the Delaware Charter School Reform: Year 1 Report.* Kalamazoo: The Evaluation Center Western Michigan University. Download at http://www.wmich.edu/evalctr/charter/de_cs-eval_year1_report.pdf.

Miron, G., and Horn, J. (2002). *Evaluation of Connecticut Charter Schools and the Charter School Initiative.* Kalamazoo: The Evaluation Center Western Michigan University. Download at http://www.wmich.edu/evalctr/charter/ctcharter.html.

Miron, G., Nelson, C., Risley, J., and Sullins, C. (2002). *Strengthening Pennsylvania's Charter School Reform: Findings from the Statewide Evaluation and Discussion of Relevant Policy Issues.* Kalamazoo: The Evaluation Center Western Michigan University. Download at http://www.wmich.edu/evalctr/charter/pa_5year/5_year_report_pa_cs_eval.pdf.

Miron, G., Wygant, B., Cullen, A., and Applegate, B. (2006). *Evaluation of the Delaware Charter School Reform: Year 2 Report.* Kalamazoo: The Evaluation Center Western Michigan University. Download at http://www.wmich.edu/evalctr/charter/de_cs-eval_year2_report.pdf.

Nevada Department of Education. (2005). *Status of Charter Schools in Nevada.* Carson City: Nevada Department of Education.

New York Board of Regents. (2003). *Report to the Governor, the Temporary President of the Senate, and the Speaker of the Assembly on the Educational Effectiveness of the Charter School Approach in New York State.* Download at http://www.emsc.nysed.gov/psc/5yearreport/fiveyearreport.htm.

Noblit, G. W., and Dickson, C. (2001). *North Carolina Charter School Evaluation Report.* State Board of Education: Evaluation Section Division of Accountability Services Instructional and Accountability Services.

Oregon Department of Education. (2005). *Oregon Charter Schools: 2004–05.* Download at http://www.ode.state.or.us.

Texas Center for Educational Research. (2005). *Texas Open-Enrollment Charter School: 2003–04 Evaluation.* Prepared for Texas Education Agency, February 2005. Download at http://www.tea.state.tx.us/index2.aspx?id=3010.

Virginia Department of Education. (2005). *Annual Report on Public Charter Schools in the Commonwealth of Virginia.* Prepared by Office of Program Administration and Accountability Division of Instruction, Virginia Department of Education. Download at http://www.doe.virginia.gov.

Zimmer, R., Buddin, R., Chau, D., Daley, G., Gill, B., Guarino, C., Hamilton, L., Krop, C., McCaffrey, D., Sandler, M., and Brewer, D. (2003). *Charter School Operations and Performance: Evidence from California.* Santa Monica: Rand. Download at http://www.rand.org/publications/MR/MR1700/.

Chapter Ten

Would Better Research Lead to Better Schools?

Jeffrey R. Henig

INTRODUCTION

This collection of papers, and the white paper that preceded it (Betts and Hill, 2006), underscore two simple points. First, not all studies are equal; in the realm of charter school research, as elsewhere, some studies employ stronger designs and better measures than others. Second, to the extent that they have the tools to do so, government, foundations, and researchers themselves should strive to increase the ratio of stronger studies to weaker ones.

But there is a third point implied, and this one is more problematic. We want to believe that better research will lead to better policy and therefore better schools. Logic, surely, suggests that this should be true. Policy makers face difficult choices, not just about *whether* and *how much* to encourage charter schools but also about specific legislative and regulatory provisions.

Solid and reliable knowledge about how existing charter school programs are functioning is not the only thing that policy makers need in order to wend their way intelligently through the briar of choices they confront; they also need the good judgment to translate knowledge into specific proposals appropriate to their constituencies and the political will and capacity to convert good policy ideas into programs that are implemented and work. But incorporating the best research into the process seems likely to be a necessary, or if nothing else, a precursor to making the right decisions.

Although consensus is elusive in the hot-button world of school-choice research, people on both sides can probably agree on one truism: the devil is in the details. How specific and how exacting should be the prerequisites for obtaining a charter? Should some kinds of charter sponsors be encouraged and others discouraged? How high should be the per-pupil public support

179

and should this vary by student needs? Should charter schools receive capital funds? What information should charter schools be required to compile? When should authorizers be prepared to close charter schools? What is the responsibility of authorizers to help students find alternative placements if their charter schools are closed?

These are just a handful of the questions that policy makers need to visit, and often revisit, as they shape their state and district policies.

The answers they arrive at may depend on the answers to questions that empirical research can answer. Do charters encourage resegregation? Do they lead to higher test scores? What are their influences on other kinds of outcomes, such as parental satisfaction, student turnover, dropout rates, college attendance, and productive reform within the conventional public school system? And how do the answers to these questions vary depending on local context (growing population versus declining; deeply dysfunctional traditional schools versus others; whether charters are started by national for-profits or local community-based organizations)?

Policy makers armed with good answers to questions like these should be more able to fine-tune policies to their local contexts, less wedded to ideologically defined premises, and less at the mercy of lobbyists—unions or education providers—who will attempt to sway them with selective claims about what the evidence shows.

One of my goals in this chapter is to counsel against naïve optimism about how much good research will affect policy decisions. You can nail a proclamation about good research design to a legislature's walls, but when it comes to shaping policy decisions, it might still be ignored, misunderstood, dismissed as off point, or simply unable to counteract other factors at play.

The first section discusses this problem, taking into consideration some disheartening recent episodes in the public discourse about charter school research. Here and throughout, I draw on some of the research and thinking I did for my book *Spin Cycle: How Research Is Used in Policy Debates: The Case of Charter Schools.*[1] It uses the 2004 American Federation of Teachers (AFT) charter school study and its aftermath as a lens through which to consider more general issues about the politicization of research.[2] One lesson: Under certain circumstances, bad research can eclipse the good.

While I counsel against naïve faith in the power of good research, I favor a position of guarded optimism. In the second section of this paper I suggest that despite some wrong turns, unnecessary scuffles, and polarized rhetoric, the evolving empirical literature reveals an encouraging arc. Despite the political maneuvering that has surrounded, and at times infected, the research enterprise regarding vouchers, charters, and school choice, I will argue that the quality of research has improved. We know things now that we didn't know before, and as a result our prospects for mapping a policy route to better education have improved.

If political realities mean that the value of high-quality research will not necessarily win the day, the question arises as to what can be done in order to improve the prospects for a more informed policy discourse. That is the focus of the final section. The institutions and values that sustain good research are resilient and not without defense, but arguably they are weakening. Under pressure to be "relevant," researchers at times have been seduced into thinking they must be speedy, speak simply, and project undaunted confidence. Policy makers have many legitimate grievances about overly abstract, impenetrable, slow-to-develop, and politically naïve research, but there is another side to that story as well. I suggest that researchers have been too willing to accept politicians' and advocates' prescriptions for relevance and that they need to play a role in refurbishing the core values of good research.

Researchers must affirm that good things can be worth waiting for, that simple is often simplistic, and that a person without doubts is a person without substance. But exhortation about values is not sufficient, it is also important to look at institutional changes — in funding, in the media, in journals, in universities — that might redirect the incentives researchers face and encourage choices that are more likely to enrich the national policy discourse.

CAUTIONARY TALES

On August 17, 2004, the front page of the *New York Times* prominently displayed a story about a new study of charter schools. "Charter Schools Trail in Results, U.S. Data Reveals," read the headline. It described a report by the AFT using National Assessment of Educational Progress (NAEP) data to compare test scores of charter school students to those in traditional public schools.

Within days of Schemo's front-page article, proponents of charters and vouchers had launched a counterattack. Jeannie Allen of the Center for Education Reform (CER), a Washington-based organization supported by conservative foundations and with an aggressively promarket message, contacted prominent researchers to see whether they would be willing to have their names listed on a protest ad. The full-page ad, the type that typically costs over $100,000, ran just eight days after the article first appeared. Its text read like a primer in research methods, highlighting attributes of good research and criticizing the *Times* for giving prominent coverage to a study that was primitive when measured against such standards.

At the same time, school choice proponents got busy placing editorials, providing supporters with talking points for discussion on television talk shows, and publicizing a report by Caroline Hoxby, a Harvard economist, that reached the opposite conclusion.

Thus began a battle that continues to sputter to this day. On the one hand, this high-profile debate about proper and improper research methods could be taken as a positive sign about the maturation of public discourse. If advocacy groups like the AFT divert organization resources into the production and dissemination of research, doesn't that suggest that they believe policy makers and the public are open to being convinced by objective evidence rather than symbolic appeals and spin? If advocacy groups like CER conclude that the most effective way to counter such findings is by funding a public tutorial on research methodology and trotting out another study that it claims boasts a stronger research design, doesn't that suggest a high level of confidence in the attentiveness of the public and its capacity to disentangle competing evidentiary claims?

Yet, while both the AFT study and the Hoxby study have been widely cited in public debate,[3] neither scores at all well on the criteria identified in the white paper (Betts and Hill, 2006) that emerged from the deliberations of the National Consensus Panel on Charter School Research. The AFT study was, even in the words of its authors, "not really a 'study' in any conventional sense" at all. "There was no research 'design,' no 'methodology . . .'"[4] The AFT researchers had not engaged in their own data collection or analysis but had essentially downloaded basic information from the NCES website using the site's own data extraction tool. The comparison offered between charter schools and traditional public schools was not based on student level data, was not based on longitudinal data, and offered only rudimentary controls for student race, location, and school lunch status.

Referring to the AFT report, Hoxby wrote that "Much attention has been paid to this crude comparison, and many people have incorrectly interpreted it as sound evidence that charter schools reduce achievement." She labeled her own study a "straightforward comparison" of charter schools to regular public schools, arguing that it was superior because it included all charter schools (not just a sample) and relied on direct comparison of average test scores to those of nearby traditional public schools. Her initial release of her data, however, showed every sign of being rushed into the public eye. The original version included several gross errors that substantially overstated the claimed charter school advantage.[5] And her proud assertion that in her study, unlike that of the AFT, "no complicated statistics are used," suggests a possible tension between two legitimate but discrete goals: using advanced but often complicated analytical techniques versus presenting data in a manner that the average citizen finds readily understandable.

The AFT study, the ad that followed, and the critical jousting over the Hoxby study's merits and flaws created an atmosphere of harsh public charges and countercharges in which researchers were sometimes on center stage. Some researchers seemed to embrace this position eagerly, others reluctantly. The terms of the debate ostensibly remained focused on issues of research methodology, but the sharp bite came from charges of shoddiness, hypocrisy, and intimations that data were manipulated for political ends (Carnoy et al., 2005).

Earlier Conflicts over Vouchers

The brouhaha over the AFT study was not an aberration. It occurred against a backdrop of very public and personalized disputes that seem to belie the self-image of research as cool, calm, collected, and collective. In October 1996, an earlier school-choice skirmish reached the front page of the *Wall Street Journal*. Reporting on studies of Milwaukee's school voucher program, Bob Davis, the article's author, wrote: "Education scholars were hoping the Milwaukee experiment would finally settle the question." "Fat chance." The article described the clash between John Witte, a University of Wisconsin political scientist who had concluded the vouchers were not raising test scores, and Paul Peterson, the Harvard political science professor, whose reanalysis using a more quasi-experimental design suggested that they did. Instead of converging on a cooler and clearer understanding of how abstract market-based theories behind vouchers translated into real-world consequences, Davis wrote, research appeared to have done little more than add a new kind of fuel to the fires of ideological debate.

> The Milwaukee voucher plan has become entangled in a brawl between two leading political scientists with clashing egos, ambitions and analyses. They look at the same student data and reach opposite conclusions.

Although the *WSJ* article delved into some of the methodological issues that may have accounted for the differences in findings, readers could not be blamed for concluding that research was less a light of illumination than a snowball in a schoolboy spat. "The two men have come to despise each other, with Mr. Witte at the Milwaukee university calling his foe a 'snake' and Mr. Peterson shooting back that Mr. Witte's work is 'lousy'" (Davis, 1996).

Hoxby versus Rothstein

Nine years after the Witte versus Peterson altercation, in October 2005, readers of the *Wall Street Journal* were treated to another front-page story on school choice, one with almost eerie parallels. Like the 1996 article, it gave an impressive prominence and space to intricate matters of measurement and research design. And like the earlier one, the 2005 article featured drawings of the principal opponents, lacing the description of social science methodology with comments about their personalities and backgrounds.

This one pitted two economists, rather than political scientists, against one another: Caroline Hoxby of Harvard against Jesse Rothstein of Princeton. And, once again, charges of bias and a tone of vitriol were prominent. On the well-regarded National Bureau of Economics Research (NBER) website, Rothstein had posted a paper that raised questions about the accuracy of the data and the substance of the claims Hoxby had made in a highly cited article about the positive effects of interjurisdictional choice on educational outcomes (Rothstein, 2005). After attempting to replicate Hoxby's analysis, Rothstein concluded "that Hoxby's positive estimated effect of interdistrict competition on student achievement is not robust," and that "a fair reading of the evidence does not support claims of a large or significant effect."

Hoxby replied in kind. In a paper also posted on the NBER website, she stated that she had reviewed every Rothstein claim "of any importance" and that "every claim is wrong." She charged him with being confused, relying on innuendo, presenting her original work as his own, making bad decisions "repeatedly," and worse. "It should surprise no one," Hoxby wrote, "that if a person makes a determination to change data and specifications until a result disappears, he will eventually succeed . . ." (Hoxby, 2004). The WSJ article reported on the subsequent back-and-forth in which Rothstein complained of Hoxby's "name-calling" and "ad hominem attacks" while Hoxby accused Rothstein of "ideological bias" (Hilsenrath, 2005).

The Inevitability of Dueling Studies

Suffice it to say for now that anyone who believes in the potential for social science research to fuel a more reasoned and informed democracy, the track record in the area of school choice and charter schools is, at least at first glance, hugely disillusioning. Based on what they read in the newspapers or hear from competing political candidates on Sunday morning news shows, informed citizens attempting to make sense of the school choice research can be forgiven if they are tempted to throw up their hands and say "it's all politics."

"In a perfect world," writes political scientist Kevin Smith, "policy makers more interested in fashioning effective programs than in scoring partisan points could turn to academics to help cut through the rhetorical brawling. Unfortunately, it has not turned out that way" (Smith, 2005). Rather than dampening the histrionics by displacing symbol with facts and simplification with nuance, research—at least as it has stepped onto the public stage—has seemed to replicate or even amplify the strident and destructive forms of ideological trench warfare. The dynamic can become self-sustaining. As one researcher put it to me, "Once somebody else brings a knife to the fight, you have to bring a knife to the fight too."

What's notable here is not so much the fact that there is disagreement and debate. Only the most unsophisticated adherents to the notion of the policy sciences imagine that research proceeds in a steady parade of scientific consensus, like a marching band with each member in step and in tune. Tales about the intrigue and competition that marked the pursuit of major scientific studies like deciphering the double helix of DNAs or mapping the human genome make it clear that the enterprise of enlarging our knowledge base is a messier and more contentious operation than that. Good research often challenges existing presumptions, and good researchers often show jealousy and zealotry in the pursuit of their vision of what is true.

What is puzzling, though, and disturbing as well, is the fact that this highly personalized and politically polarized public discourse about charter school research takes place even when other studies—and better studies—are bringing into focus a clearer picture of the charter school phenomenon. For example, there has been a series of studies using state databases that permit the kinds of longitudinal student-level analysis ranked high by the Betts and Hill white paper (Bifulco and Ladd, 2004; Booker, Zimmer, and Buddin, 2005; Hanushek et al., 2005; Hanushek and Raymond, 2004; Sass, 2006; Zimmer and Buddin, 2006), but for reasons we will explore, these have not been as prominent in the national policy debate as studies of unambiguously weaker research designs.

WHY WEAK RESEARCH CAN TRUMP STRONGER RESEARCH WHEN IT COMES TO PUBLIC DEBATE

An idealized view of the role of research in democratic politics and governance presumes that leaders and the voters who put them into office believe that better research generates better policies and that they are attentive enough and sufficiently informed to recognize and appreciate distinctions based on the quality of research designs. Somewhat less lofty expectations of the research itself might suffice if other institutions (the media, universities, academic journals, governmental agency experts, funders) serve as intermediaries, sifting through research to identify that which is important, lending a stamp of approval to research designs that meet high standards, clarifying the findings and implications in ways that are accurate and unbiased. But can we be confident that either the ideal or its back-up holds in the real world?

Polarized Politics

Beginning in the late 1960s or early 1970s, liberal Republicans and conservative Democrats became more and more of an oddity, making the parties simultaneously more ideologically homogenous internally and more ideologically different from one another. This showed up in the substantial dwindling of cross-party alignments on House and Senate roll call votes. This ideological polarization between the parties was *not* driven by polarization within the American public; mass public opinion changed very little from the 1960s into the 1990s. The average voter became slightly more conservative over this time period, but the center of gravity remained very nearly halfway between the left and the right with most Americans adhering to a moderate position (Jacobs and Shapiro, 2000).

A combination of demographic shifts and gerrymandering of legislative boundaries, however, tended to create more homogenous and politically extreme electoral districts even when the overall population had more mixed or moderate views. With fewer competitive elections, politicians in safe Democratic or safe Republican districts had less incentive to adopt moderate positions. As the general elections became less important (because their results were more preordained), the internal processes by which the parties select their candidates became proportionally more important.

As explained by political scientists Lawrence Jacobs and Robert Shapiro, "The implications are significant: the combination of fewer legislators outside their party's ideological mainstream and growing policy differences between the parties on social issues and economic issues increased the costs of compromising the policy goals of partisans" (Jacobs and Shapiro, 2000). To maintain the loyalty of ideologically purist elements among their parties' activists, elected leaders are frequently forced to adopt more one-dimensional and extreme positions than the average citizens might prefer.[6]

A national environment in which politics is sharply polarized based on party and ideology can increase the possibility that weaker studies could trump stronger ones.

Elsewhere I have written about the high-stakes, high-reverberation politics surrounding school choice. Pragmatic positions that recognize nuance and contingency are difficult to sustain when opponents on both sides of the ideological aisle believe that acknowledgment of complexity provides encouragement to an opposition intent on pursuing radical change (Henig, 2005). In such a context, studies that fail to fit the purist framings preferred by partisan activists may simply lack an audience.

Timing

Scholars who consider the diffusion of research into the policy process have distinguished between types of impact (Weiss, 1979), direct and indirect. The indirect kind of impact is accumulative, slow, working its influence through a gradual shifting of ideas and understandings. Ultimately, it may be that this kind of impact is the more important. And arguably it responds more to elements of research design—as better studies stand up more to subsequent scrutiny.

It is the direct kind of impact, however, that is more commonly discussed. It is seen when a particular study features prominently in policy debate and appears to have some causal impact—either by changing the minds of key actors, providing political standing to groups that had previously been on the margins, or shifting perceptions among the large number of generally disengaged third parties, thereby altering the preexisting balance of power (Baumgartner and Jones, 1993). Direct impact of this kind appears to depend substantially on timing. As John Kingdon famously argued, events occasionally create "windows of opportunity" when problems, policy ideas, and politics align (Kingdon, 1995). That is when the potential for individual studies to migrate into public debates is greatest.

Legislative, judicial, and regulatory agendas march based on their own logic, however, not the tune played by researchers. When Congress is ready to vote on reauthorization of ESEA, when a court is set to rule on whether racial concentration attributable to school choice policy is unconstitutional, when a state agency must decide whether to make charter schools central in reformulating a nonperforming school district, that is when there will be attentive eyes and open ears. In principle, the legislature, court, or agency involved could scan existing studies using sophisticated criteria for determining their reliability and validity and only attend to the best of the lot.

But the worlds of politics and policy making often exhibit a reverse telescopic view of the past—studies released more than a year or two ago can seem obsolete; events of more than one election cycle ago all seem ancient. In that context, a fresh study with weak design has the potential to overshadow a better study that seems less current—despite the fact that the older study will have been around long enough to hazard critique and replication, while the newer one may not have had the time to undergo any careful scrutiny.

SPEED AND THE NEW TECHNOLOGIES—
AND NEW NORMS—OF DISSEMINATION

The influence that matters of timing may have on policy research and its uptake may be increased by the prevalence of new technologies that make it possible to get research findings immediately from the first data runs to the eyes of policy influentials easily and inexpensively. Although there have always been exceptions, at one point the normal cycle for policy research included submission to a peer-reviewed journal, a double-blind review, often requirements for revision, nine months or more from acceptance to publication, and then—if the researcher or funder or university public relations office was eager for impact—dissemination of a press release. Researchers who worked in similar areas might hear about forthcoming work at conferences, if they happened to attend the right ones and the right panels, but except in special cases there was often a reluctance to publicly cite and respond to conference papers until they had been vetted through the slower and more meticulous processes of peer review.

Today, blogs, electronic newsletters, email, and websites mean that studies—and even preliminary findings—often get tremendously broad dissemination within incredibly short periods.

Consider the NCES-funded study to compare the effectiveness of public and private schools using hierarchical linear modeling (Braun, Jenkins, and Grigg, 2006). The study was released on Friday, July 14, 2006. It was reported on the front page of the *New York Times* the next day. Within just two weeks, Paul Peterson and Elena Llaudet of Harvard released a rebuttal that not only critiqued the methodology of the original report but also offered a reanalysis of the same data using different indicators and models and coming up with dramatically different results.

The NCES study had gone through months of internal reviews. The rebuttal could not possibly have received the same pre-release attention. Yet the rebuttal received about as much public attention as the original study. A month later, Peterson and Llaudet presented their paper at an academic conference, but by that point the paper had been revised; indeed, they indicated that some of the tables presented were based on runs completed the day before the conference. The changes were substantial enough that the panel discussant was somewhat taken aback and expressed some uncertainty about whether her planned comments would still apply.

Researchers' willingness to bypass traditional peer review is controversial (Greene and Peterson, 2000; Muir, 1999, 2000). But while technology is making it more possible to get studies out quickly to broader audiences, the willingness of researchers to go this route depends also on changing norms about what is appropriate behavior for scholars who want to both do good work and have their work be relevant. To those who believe that what they are studying is important and that policy makers need and want the latest information, the notion of sitting tight until one's work percolates through the notoriously slow and sometimes idiosyncratic process of scholarly peer review can seem untenable. It is possible, such researchers argue, to get critical feedback from others using the less formal process of soliciting input. That is probably true, although relying for honest feedback on those with whom one has cordial ties and eliminating the double-blind aspects of academic review undoubtedly comes with costs as well.

When researchers buy into the notion that speed is critical, normal processes for refining, checking, and simply deliberating about evidence get short-circuited.

KEEP IT SIMPLE

A number of years ago, when working with some foundations on the release of some research, I was asked to attend a media training session. Lots of matters were covered, but one thing was repeated over and over again. Keep the message simple—no more than two or three bullet points—and stay on the message regardless of whatever questions might be asked.

There are at least three arguments behind this mantra of keeping the message simple. The first has to do with theories about the limitations in the capacity of the public to understand complex messages (Jones, 1995). The second has to do with theories about how to attract the attention of the media and to crack their standards for what is and is not newsworthy. The third has to do with estimations of what competing interests might do in order to blunt, twist, or spin messages that are not straightforward and declarative.

In the long run, and for the sake of serious and informed public discourse, it makes a difference whether estimates of the public's limited interest and capacity are accurate, whether the media really does tend to favor studies that make strong and confident claims over those that admit limitations and uncertainties, and whether findings that admit ambiguities inevitably lose traction in high-stake political debates.

But in the short term, it seems to be the case that the media training mantra is infiltrating the arena in which research results are communicated to broader audiences. That is partly because those funding and disseminating research, like the foundations that supported my research several years ago, increasingly are hiring such firms to coordinate their strategies for influencing public policy. This is not necessarily nefarious; in a crowded arena, those who want to get their message heard feel pressure to work with professionals to craft that message accordingly. But it can work to screen some kinds of studies in and others out of public discourse based on factors other than their method-ological strength.

Some of the research approaches that rank high on methodological grounds also have the kind of simplicity that makes for easy communication. Argu-ably, some of the current push behind randomized field trials is attributable to their straightforward logic. The core message—we delivered this treatment to one of two randomly selected groups and the experimental group did this much better—after all is not very different from the kinds of evidence cited in an average TV commercial for laundry detergent or cold remedies. But other strong designs—for example, models with fixed effects or propensity scores—fail to meet what has been referred to as the elevator test: can the author, in an elevator, get across the essence of the message to someone standing outside before the doors completely close?

THE DIFFERENCE BETWEEN HERE
AND THERE: PLACE, RELEVANCE, AND MEDIA FIT

Most discussion of research methodology centers on questions of inter-nal validity. Social scientists are more confident passing judgment about whether a study has managed to isolate the causal relations it claims to than they are commenting in a more than ad hoc manner about its external validity: whether its findings, generated in one setting, can be generalized to another. The Betts et al. white paper did a service by bringing issues of external validity into the discussion, but it too is less detailed and confi-dent in handling that set of issues. But in the world of political response to policy research, informal criteria for external validity play an important role.

Although I know of no systematic research on this topic, localism and sense of place seem to play a role in how citizens evaluate the relevance of research to their own lives. Studies of charter schools in Arizona, for instance, do not have much bite in District of Columbia debates. Ad hoc standards of "similarity" come into play, with large and diverse central cities, for example, more likely to credit studies that were conducted in comparable locales. A police official once told me that a study of preventive patrolling that was done in Kansas City had no relevance to his city because his city had fewer hills. Indirect evidence that informal perceptions of similarity affect judg-ments about the relevance of experience in other places comes from studies of policy diffusion among states, which historically have found a tendency by states to import policies from neighboring rather than from more distant policy innovators (Gray, 1973; Walker, 1969).

To the extent that this is true, studies with a national database might have more impact than those limited to state and local data, even when the latter might be methodologically stronger. Indeed, this appears to be the case in the charter school arena, where the best data currently can be found in some state administrative records. The studies based on these rich, student-level databases are methodologically among the most powerful, but they have, as noted earlier, lacked the public visibility of studies like that of the AFT or Caroline Hoxby, which had weaker designs but seemed more generally applicable because they used national data.

This phenomenon may get an additional twist because of the particular structure of much of the nation's media. Newspapers and local television stations tend to have local markets. Magazines and network news programs have national markets. Very few of the major media identify their markets as aligning with state boundaries. Thus, once again, criteria other than the quality of the study *per se* can easily enter into the equation in determining which studies get an audience and which do not.

REASONS FOR GUARDED OPTIMISM THAT BETTER RESEARCH MIGHT GENERATE BETTER OUTCOMES

In conducting research for *Spin Cycle*, I interviewed many of the researchers who work in charter schools. The researchers differed in discipline, in seniority, in the methodological tools they use most frequently, and in their base-level orientation toward market-based strategies for meeting public needs. But on at least two broad points the interviews elicited common responses.

First, a large majority of those with whom I spoke felt that the area of charter school research was highly politicized—which is to say that they felt that issues relating to partisan tactics, ideology, and political interest helped to determine how research is funded, attended to, and used. Asked how politicized they feel education policy research is in the United States today, on a scale from one to five (with one meaning almost completely evidence-based and five meaning almost completely driven by political and ideological factors), the average score was 3.9; not one of the twenty researchers I interviewed gave a score of less than three.

Second, and the reason for my guarded optimism, is that despite their sense that the area was highly politicized, when asked, "What is your current reading of the available evidence on charter schools?," this varied group of researchers offered very similar responses. This leads me to conclude that what has been politicized is more the way research is used in public debate and not the core workings of the research enterprise.

Despite media portrayals of school choice and charter school research as partisan and polarized, there has actually been meaningful convergence of knowledge about charter schools. We know considerably more now about marketlike mechanisms than we did ten years ago. The emerging picture is a more nuanced, tentative, and contingent on time and place than were the interpretations advanced by the most assertive proponents and opponents in the early days of the charter school debate. It does not support the rosy predictions of leaping test scores and contagious competitive effects offered by some of the early advocates, but neither does it reinforce the worst fears of the charter skeptics about creaming, resegregation, and dire effects on the schools and students left behind.

There is no room here to summarize the many specific points of emerging agreement, but I can highlight some broad themes.

Charter Schools Are Not All Alike

When I asked researchers to characterize what we currently know about charter schools, their most common first response was to struggle against the invitation to generalize. More and more, it is becoming apparent that the term *charter school* is a broad umbrella under which are huddled schools that differ among themselves in important ways.

Researchers have begun discovering differences in behavior and outcomes between start-up charters and existing schools that convert to charter status; between charter schools started by for-profit firms and those started by non-profit and social service agencies; between those targeting "median" students and those seeking to serve "niche" populations with special needs; between those that are classroom-based and those that provide home-schooling and distance learning.

Regardless of their basic orientation on the school choice issue overall, researchers are in near agreement on the fact that there are some very good charter schools and some very bad ones and that the simple sector-versus-sector comparison is not as stark or illuminating as it was once expected to be.

Time Matters

In the early days of charter school research, all the schools under the magnifying glass were young and green and works-in-progress. Today, the early cohorts have been around for ten years or more. Years in operation can change charter schools in many ways, both for the better and for the worse. As the Hill and Rainey chapter in this volume shows, there are good reasons to expect positive maturation effects, as teachers and administrators find their way, as funding becomes more regularized and assured, as families become more familiar with different types of schools and better able to select the one that best fits their needs. But there are also possibilities that some things may change less favorably. Schools may lose momentum as the original founders burn out or move on, as the early funders begin to pull back on their support, as routines get more routinized, as enthusiasm wanes. Evidence suggests that the passage of time can be associated with changes in student composition, levels of satisfaction, and academic performance.

Place Matters

Some charter schools are in central cities, some are in suburbs, and some (a markedly smaller number) are in rural areas. Some are in places where the population is booming; some, where it is in decline. Some are in racially and ethnically mixed communities, while others are in more homogenous settings; some are in districts with reasonably strong public schools, and others are not.

Here again, the point is not simply that variation exists but that the evidence is accumulating that these variations make a difference in terms of the way that charter schools behave and perform, their effect on racial and economic composition of student bodies, and the way that existing schools, districts, and political actors respond to charter schools.

Governance Matters

Like so many other domestic policies in our federal system, charter school programs differ based on differing state laws, regulations, and implementation. Some states have passed laws designed to make the chartering process slower and to set a ceiling on charter school expansion. Others have worked as hard as they can to set ground rules that make it easier for charters to form.

States differ in the rigor and frequency of their reauthorization processes, the amount of funding they provide, the kinds of rules and regulations they impose, the extent to which they favor certain types of charters, and more. These state differences are meaningful; charter schooling, as a phenomenon, can look and be quite different depending upon where one lives.

Student Background Still Matters . . . A Lot

One of the strongest and most consistent findings in education research is the powerful role of family, community, and peer background as it affects student test score performance. The original Coleman report nailed this point and radically changed the way subsequent researchers have analyzed and talked about school effects. Since then, the battle to account for differences in student test scores has been fought at the margins. The question among researchers is whether some factors relating to schools *also* matter and in more than a minor way. Debates over how to measure and control for family background historically have bedeviled efforts to gain consensus on whether private schools outperform public schools and if they continue to do so today (Lubienski, 2003, 2004; National Center for Education Statistics, 2005). The same issues now account for much of the stalemate and polarization around the question of charter school effects. But just to be clear: the debate is not over whether family background matters. That is a given.

Despite the fact that researchers know very well that family background and peer effects are powerful, public discourse about education generally and charter schools specifically has recently deemphasized this fact. Reciting the catchphrase "all children can learn," advocates on both the right and the left have adopted the posture that admitting to the role of class is tantamount to lowering expectations for the poor and to making excuses for the schools. Either in response to this or because they just plain believed it, many early charter school advocates promulgated the belief that charter schools would be able to quickly and dramatically raise test scores above and beyond what would be predicted based on student demographics alone.

Sharp clashes over the methodological details of recent charter schools studies like that of the AFT, Hoxby, and the subsequent ones by NCES should not obscure the fact that the new charter school research has reconfirmed that class matters a great deal. For example, the challenge that Peterson and Llaudet level at both the Lubienskis and the NCES HLP studies of private schools and public schools is primarily over competing notions of how to control for class, not whether it is necessary to do so. Indeed, in all three sets of studies various indicators of student and family class and race have stronger and more consistent power to predict test scores than do the school sector variables.

That school sector nonetheless remains the focus of the policy debate appears to reflect a general, albeit problematic, acceptance of the fact that inequalities in socioeconomic status are an immutable backdrop against which policy decisions are made (Rothstein, 2004).

That there are signs that research is clearing away some misconceptions and generating some convergence in our understanding of charter schools does not mean that consensus on policy responses is sitting just around the corner. It does, however, dilute some of the fuel that has been thrown on the fire of the school choice debates. Better research will not wash away hard lines of ideological conflict, but it can potentially soften the edge of disputes, help dissipate alarmist rhetoric and its consequences, and facilitate a focus on pragmatic solutions.

CONCLUSION: WHAT CAN BE DONE TO INCREASE THE CHANCES THAT BETTER RESEARCH WILL CONTRIBUTE TO BETTER POLICY

Over the past three decades, researchers interested in conducting policy relevant to education research have been subjected to at least two distinct visions of reform. The first arose in response to initial disappointment with the perceived minimal impact of the emerging field of "policy science." Researchers, it was concluded, needed to make their product more user-friendly to decision makers. That meant picking topics that were already on the governmental agenda, speeding the process of getting research in the field and completed, communicating findings directly to policy makers in terms they could understand, avoiding ambiguous "on the one hand . . . on the other hand" interpretations, and linking findings to specific policy recommendations.

The second reform vision emerged in reaction to the perceived low quality of education research and was manifested in the birth of the Institute of Education Sciences and the NCLB emphasis on scientific- and evidence-based educational decision making. Researchers, this wave of thinking suggested, needed to conduct studies with better research designs. A small number of high-quality studies would be much preferable to a large number of weaker studies. As interpreted by IES, the gold standard in designs would be randomized field trials (RFTs).

While recognizing the advantages of RFTs, the Betts/Hill white paper argued that fixed-effects analyses using student-level and longitudinal data also had distinct advantages, especially in external validity.

Both of these reform visions have something of value to contribute, but there is unacknowledged tension between the two and, based on the assessment I have presented here, a case can be made that both share some limitations. The tension between the two relates primarily to the issue of timing and simplicity.

The stronger research designs emphasized most recently are not well adapted to the earlier reform movement's push to make policy research more user-friendly. RFTs simply cannot be done well and done quickly. Student-level longitudinal and fixed-effects models can be done well and relatively quickly, but only if collection, maintenance, organization, and availability of the appropriate data have been institutionalized. RFTs can in principle meet some of the consumer-friendly standards of the earlier reform movement; policy makers do not need to understand sophisticated statistical techniques in order to appreciate the simple logic of an experimental design if it is well structured and carried out as envisioned.[7]

But even when researchers use relatively simple graphics to make findings derived from fixed-effects models more clear and dramatic, the underlying analyses are unavoidably complex and based on nested assumptions that, when acknowledged, make the storyline more complicated, results more problematic, and interpretations more open to challenge.

What both visions share, although each expresses it differently, is an overly simplistic, overly optimistic notion about the power of research to steer policy.

Policy makers, the media, and the public want research to provide sharp, universal, and speedy answers; more than that, they want these answers un-ambiguously to point to specific policy directions, despite the fact that the most potent policy conflicts are not caused simply by insufficient information but are grounded in conflicts of values and interests.

Policy researchers know that knowledge takes time to accumulate, that confidence comes from the aggregate weight of multiple studies rather than the definitive findings of any one study, that even clear and consistent find-ings can involve small effect sizes, that context matters, and that part of the contribution of research is to sharpen questions in ways that may end up mak-ing the value conflicts more apparent rather than making them disappear.

In an effort to make policy research more accessible, researchers may unintentionally contribute to the politicization of research. By speeding the transmission of findings into public discourse, bypassing peer review, gloss-ing over the technical details, and boiling down interpretation into sound bites delivered without caveats, researchers may have missed a chance to explain and defend some of the characteristics of the scientific enterprise that consti-tute the core of its long-term value.

The more recent emphasis on scientific rigor in one sense represents a needed correction of this course. But it, too, overpromises. While emphasiz-ing the importance of strong research design and good data, it arguably has overemphasized the potential for the "killer study." The term *killer applica-tion* emerged in the software industry as a way to characterize wildly popular new computer programs that not only sell well but also redefine the market and lift the underlying hardware to new levels of credibility.

In the context of charter school research, the prospect of a "killer study" encourages public and private funders to concentrate available resources on one or two truly superior—and highly expensive—studies in the expectation that these can answer central questions once and for all. That this is likely to be an empty promise gets some support from the recent history surrounding the HLM charter school study. During the years between its initiation and final release, many saw the prospect of a nationwide, multilevel study using the known and respected NAEP data as the kind of watershed project that would resolve the question of whether differences in public and charter school performance were attributable to differences in the populations they served.[8] But its ultimate release caused a ripple and no more. Indeed, its authors and sponsoring agency took great pains to emphasize how inappropriate it would be to draw bold conclusions from it (Cavanagh and Robelen, 2006; Robelen, 2006).[9]

I've argued here that the demands and dictates of politics make it problematic whether good research will trump weaker studies. I've also argued that, despite the very personalized, polarized, and politicized uses of research in the public charter school debate, research has been converging on some general new understandings of the phenomenon that highlight how much its impact depends on such particulars as types, time, and place. What this suggests to me is that the core challenges have less to do with the production of research—which has been, as it should be, improving through accumulation, refinement of theory, improvements in data, replication, and critical exchange—than with the particular ways that research gets taken up within public forums.

Researchers have some responsibility in remedying this but, ironically, they need to do so by framing their claims about the importance of research more realistically, which means more modestly. At the same time we sound the call for improved research designs and investment in the infrastructure of data, we need to be educating the media, funders, policy makers, and the public more about the limitations of research. When policy makers say they need the information and they need it now, we must sometimes be ready to tell them honestly that the information they want does not yet exist. When funders or the media say they need a sharp and definitive and broadly stated lesson, we sometimes need to hold our ground and say that available evidence only permits tentative, contingent, and qualified conclusions.

To some, this might sound like a recipe for irrelevance. But two points are worth considering. First, the pressure for fast, simple, and confident conclusions is generated by the needs of politicians—not necessarily the needs of the polity. There is a difference, for example, between "political time" and "policy time." Political time is defined by election cycles, scheduled reauthorization debates, and the need to respond to short-term crises or sudden shifts in public attention. But a consideration of the history of public policy suggests that societal learning about complex problems and large-scale policy responses takes place on a much more gradual curve. The issues on the table in today's debates about vouchers, charter schools, and school choice more generally are in many key respects the same issues that were presented—with urgency—ten and fifteen and twenty years ago. Arguably, we would now be better off if we had then set a research agenda designed to provide better answers today, rather than rush various findings into the public discourse too soon—before the phenomenon had come into clear focus, before the range of variability been recognized, before the longitudinal data been collected.

The second point is that failing honestly to present the challenges and complexities of research carries its own risks of irrelevance as well. The current course of action has been eroding the impact of good research by erasing the distinction between, on the one hand, strong methodology and nuanced findings, and, on the other hand, compelling talk. It is exhilarating for researchers to be on the public stage and to feel themselves a part of serious discussions about serious matters. We would be better off bearing politicians' irritation with our tentativeness and disdain for our deliberateness than losing touch with the norms and procedures that over the long run set research apart and give it what authority it deserves.

NOTES

1. New York: Russell Sage Foundation, 2008.

2. The author wishes to thank the Spencer Foundation, the Russell Sage Foundation, and the Century Foundation for their support of the larger research project on which this chapter draws.

3. A Google Scholar search yielded fourteen scholarly citations for the AFT Study (Nelson et al., 2004) and twelve for the Hoxby study, but searching the same terms on the Web generally produced 839 for the former and 103 for the latter.

4. Howard Nelson, Bella Rosenberg, and Nancy Van Meter, in a letter to the editor in response to *Education Week*'s article ("Release of Unreviewed Studies Sparks Debate," May 18, 2005).

5. The most egregious errors involved the data from Washington, D.C., where she inadvertently omitted all of the charter schools authorized by one of the district's two authorizing bodies and used test scores that employed much more demanding definitions of "proficiency" for regular public schools than for the charter schools. For the AFT's review of these issues, see Nelson and Miller (2004).

6. Jacobs and Shapiro identify four factors in addition to partisan polarization that make it easier and more tempting for legislators to be unresponsive. The others — institutional individualization, incumbency bias, interest group proliferation, and divisive interbranch relations — are less consistently relevant to the politicization of research.

7. This "if" statement can be important. In practice, most policy experiments are much messier than the initial design predicts, and the strategies researchers use to adjust for deviations (participant dropouts; changing policy contexts; other unpredicted external "shocks") can gradually reintroduce most of the kinds of problematic assumptions and complicated analyses that undermine the definitiveness and clarity of studies employing less elegant designs.

8. When news of the AFT charter school study first broke, Robert Lerner, then Commissioner of Education Statistics, suggested that the HLM study-in-waiting would provide much stronger and potentially different results. As reported in the *New York Times,* Lerner indicated that NCES would be releasing "a larger analysis that would adjust results for the characteristics of charter schools and their students." He characterized the AFT "raw comparison of test scores" as "the beginning of something important," and said, "What one has to do is adjust for many different variables to get a sense of what the effects of charter schools are." (Schemo, 2004).

9. Arguably, the NCES efforts to downplay the significance of the study's findings was in part attributable to its perceived political volatility. While not a "killer study" in the sense I discuss here, my expectation is that this report will stand as a major contribution to the literature and our understanding of what charter schools can and cannot be expected to accomplish.

REFERENCES

Baumgartner, F. R., and Jones, B. D. (1993). *Agendas and Instability in American Politics.* Chicago: University of Chicago Press.

Betts, J., and Hill, P. (2006). *White Paper: Key Issues in Studying Charter Schools and Achievement: A Review and Suggestions for National Guidelines.* National Charter School Research Project. Seattle: Center on Reinventing Public Education.

Bifulco, R., and Ladd, H. F. (2004). *The Impacts of Charter Schools on Student Achievement: Evidence from North Carolina.* Terry Stanford Institute of Public Policy, Duke University.

Booker, K., Zimmer, R., and Buddin, R. (2005). *The Effect of Charter Schools on School Peer Composition.* Santa Monica, CA: RAND.

Braun, H., Jenkins, F., and Grigg, W. (2006). *Comparing Private Schools and Public Schools Using Hierarchical Linear Modeling (NCES 2006-461).* U.S. Department of Education, National Center for Education Statistics, Institute of Education Sciences. Washington, DC: U.S. Government Printing Office.

Carnoy, M., Jacobsen, R., Mishel, L., and Rothstein, R. (2005). *The Charter School Dust-Up: Examining the Evidence on Enrollment and Achievement.* Washington DC: Economic Policy Institute.

Cavanagh, S., and Robelen, E. W. (2006). NCES Calls for Sticking to the Stats: Study of Charter Scores Latest to Be Questioned. *Education Week* (August 30).

Davis, B. (1996). Class Warfare: Dueling Professors Have Milwaukee Dazed over School Vouchers—Studies on Private Education Result in a Public Spat about Varied Conclusions—Candidates Debate the Point. *Wall Street Journal* (October 11), A1.

Gray, V. (1973). Innovations in the States: A Diffusion Study. *American Political Science Review* 67, 1174–85.

Greene, J. P., and Peterson, P. E. (2000). If the Peer Review Attack Fails, Attack Something Else. *PS: Political Science and Politics* 33:2, 229–31.

Hanushek, E. A., and Raymond, M. E. (2004). *Does School Accountability Lead to Improved Student Performance?* Cambridge, MA: National Bureau of Economic Research.

Hanushek, E. A., Kain, J. F., Rivkin, S. G., and Branch, G. F. (2005). *Charter School Quality and Parental Decision Making with School Choice.* National Bureau of Economic Research, Working Paper 11252.

Henig, J. R. (2005). Understanding the Political Conflict over School Choice. In J. R. Betts and T. Loveless (Eds.), *How School Choice Affects Students and Families Who Do Not Choose.* Washington, DC: Brookings.

Hilsenrath, J. E. (2005). Making Waves: Novel Way to Assess School Competition Stirs Academic Row to Do So, Harvard Economist Counts Streams in Cities; A Princetonian Takes Issue. *Wall Street Journal* (October 24), A1.

Hoxby, C. M. (2004). *Competition Among Public Schools: A Reply to Rothstein.* National Bureau of Economic Research [cited]. Download at http://www.nber.org/papers/w11216.

Jacobs, L. R., and Shapiro, R. Y. (2000). *Politicians Don't Slander: Political Manipulation and the Loss of Democratic Responsiveness.* Chicago: University of Chicago.

Jones, B. D. (1995). *Reconceiving Decision-Making in Democratic Politics: Attention, Choice, and Public Policy.* Chicago: University of Chicago.

Kingdon, J. W. (1995). *Agendas, Alternatives, and Public Policies.* 2nd ed. Boston: Little, Brown & Company. Original edition, 1984.

Lubienski, C. (2003). *School Competition and Promotion: Substantive and Symbolic Differentiation in Local Education Markets.* New York: National Center for the Study of Privatization in Education Teachers College, Columbia University.

Lubienski, C. (2004). Charter School Innovation in Theory and Practice: Autonomy, R&D, and Curricular Conformity. In K. Bulkley and P. Wohlstetter (Eds.), *Taking Account of Charter Schools.* New York: Teachers College Press.

Muir, E. (1999). They Blinded Me with Political Science: On the Use of Nonpeer Reviewed Research in Education Policy. *PS: Political Science and Politics*, 762–64.

Muir, E. 2000. Social Science Should Be a Process, Not a Bloody Shirt. *PS: Political Science and Politics* 33, 235–37.

National Center for Education Statistics, NCES. (2005). *The Nation's Report Card. America's Charter Schools: Results from the NAEP 2003 Pilot Study.* Washington DC: U.S. Department of Education, National Center for Education Statistics.

Nelson, H., and Miller, T. (2004). A Closer Look at Caroline Hoxby's "A Straightforward Comparison of Charter Schools and Regular Public Schools in the United States." Washington DC: American Federation of Teachers.

Nelson, F. H., Rosenberg, B., and Van Meter, N. (2004). *Charter Achievement on the 2003 National Assessment of Educational Progress*, Washington, DC: American Federation of Teachers.

Peterson, P., and Llaudet, E. (2000). *On the Public-Private School Achievement Debate*. Paper presented at the Annual Meetings of the American Political Science Association. August 31–September 3, 2006, Philadelphia, PA.

Robelen, E. W. (2006). Reanalysis of NAEP Scores Finds Charter Schools Lagging, Study Initiated by NCES Revisits Data Underlying Controversy in 2004. *Education Week* (August 30).

Rothstein, J. (2005). *Does Competition Among Public Schools Benefit Students and Taxpayers? A Comment on Hoxby (2000).* In NBER Working Paper #11215 (March 2005). Forthcoming, American Economic Review.

Rothstein, R. (2004). *Class and Schools: Using Social, Economic, and Educational Reform to Close the Black-White Achievement Gap.* Economic Policy Institute (Washington, DC) and Teachers College, Columbia University (New York, NY), (Eds.).

Sass, T. R. (2006). Charter Schools and Student Achievement in Florida. *Education Finance and Policy*, Winter 2006, 91–122.

Schemo, D. J. (2004). Charter Schools Trail in Results, U.S. Data Reveals. *New York Times* (August 17).

Smith, K. (2005). Data Don't Matter? Academic Research and School Choice. *Perspectives on Politics* 3:2, 285–99.

Walker, J. (1969). The Diffusion of Innovations Among the American States. *American Political Science Review* 63, 880–99.

Weiss, C. H. (1979). The Many Meanings of Research Utilization. *Public Administration Review* 39:5 (September–October), 426–31.

Zimmer, R., and Buddin, R. (2006). *Making Sense of Charter Schools.* Santa Monica, CA: Rand.

Chapter Eleven

Conclusions about Charter School Policy and Research

Julian R. Betts and Paul T. Hill

INTRODUCTION

Maturation, the subject of one of our chapters, is also the theme of this concluding chapter. Just as we argued that individual schools mature, charter school research and policy are maturing as are the public school system's response to charter schools.

As we will discuss:

- Charter school research is improving slowly but steadily. Though many studies are still poor, the number using more advanced methods (which as Betts, Tang, and Zau show in chapter 2 are likely to give much more valid results) is growing. Moreover, the quality of data on student achievement and school characteristics is also growing, thus allowing good studies that simply were not possible before.
- Charter school policy is becoming more stable and sophisticated, at least in some states and localities. States are, though with difficulty, raising the caps on the numbers of charter schools allowed and are moving toward more rigorous charter school oversight.
- Public school systems are treating charters as one among many legitimate ways of providing public schools. Some school districts (e.g., Chicago, New Orleans, Denver, and New York) are encouraging charters as a way to create options for children in need. Under pressure from No Child Left Behind, the same localities and others (e.g., Hartford and Baltimore) are also developing charterlike forms of performance-based oversight for all their publicly funded schools.[1]

This is not to say that all the battles about charter laws and policy are over or that questions about charter school performance are even close to being resolved. But it looks like charter schooling will play an increasingly important role in public education. The Obama administration's apparent support for NCLB's accountability provisions is extremely important. It means that consistently underperforming schools must be restructured from a menu of options, including conversion of the schools to charter status. These provisions are likely to accelerate the charter movement even further over the next five years.

Even more significant for the charter school movement, President Obama has directly signaled support for charter schools as an instrument of education reform. Speaking to the Hispanic Chamber of Commerce, President Obama stated in March 2009:

> One of the places where much of that innovation occurs is in our most effective charter schools. And these are public schools founded by parents, teachers, and civic or community organizations with broad leeway to innovate—schools I supported as a state legislator and a United States senator. But right now, there are many caps on how many charter schools are allowed in some states, no matter how well they're preparing our students. That isn't good for our children, our economy, or our country. Of course, any expansion of charter schools must not result in the spread of mediocrity, but in the advancement of excellence. And that will require states adopting both a rigorous selection and review process to ensure that a charter school's autonomy is coupled with greater accountability—as well as a strategy, like the one in Chicago, to close charter schools that are not working. Provided this greater accountability, I call on states to reform their charter rules, and lift caps on the number of allowable charter schools, wherever such caps are in place (Obama, 2009).

The call for an expansion in the number of charter schools is helpful to the prospects of the charter school movement. President Obama's warning that we must not only open new charter schools but also close failing charters raises serious questions about whether school districts and other authorizers of charter schools have the capacity to discern successful from failing charter schools.

Frankly, we don't believe that at present district or state education policy makers typically have the data required to make accurate judgments about which schools are succeeding because they tend to rely on test score levels rather than longitudinal measures of individual student progress. This problem encompasses both charter and traditional public schools. Under NCLB we have equated the quality of a school with the percentage of students who are proficient on state tests. But because students embark on their public school education with markedly different preparation, socioeconomic status of students remains the best predictor of a school's average test scores. Low test scores are no more a sign of poor teaching than high scores guarantee excellent teaching. We will need more sophisticated value-added measures of student learning to identify schools that are truly successful.

The remainder of this chapter elaborates our conclusions about charter school research, charter school policy, and charter schooling's consequences for the future of public education.

ON CHARTER SCHOOL RESEARCH

Despite the noisy fights over specific studies, research on charter schools is showing the normal development of a new scientific inquiry. Dueling findings are normal even in more mature fields like medicine and environmental policy. Disputes over methods and interpretation of mixed findings normally advance, rather than retard, understanding.

Thus, in charter school research we are coming to understand that mixed findings have important uses. They produce clues about how things really work (e.g., that charter schools become more effective after a tough first year and that charter schools are heterogeneous) and lead researchers to seek understanding about what causes variations in outcomes. Mixed findings can also point out the need for changes in governmental policy and oversight, for example as Betts and Tang suggest, more rigorous pruning of the lowest-performing charter schools.

Later studies often show that earlier ones were wrong (e.g., they missed an important factor that explains differences in outcomes). However, the later studies would not have been done so well if the earlier ones had not sparked controversy and gone down some blind alleys.

At the same time, further progress in our understanding of the effects of charter schools is far from automatic. It requires that researchers eschew weaker methods of inquiry that predominated in the early studies in favor of stronger methods. In particular it means abandonment of crude comparisons among all children in charter schools and all children in a set of traditional schools, without controls for student attributes and prior levels of performance.

Such a shift will not occur automatically. Scholarly exchanges and debates will move research in this direction. But it will also require better data and a fuller understanding of the relative strengths and weaknesses of different research approaches among policy makers and the public. State and federal government must play a key role in mandating both better data systems and better evaluations. The media will also need to work at teasing out the most accurate interpretations of the research on charter schools as it develops.

Because charter research does not and should not take place in a vacuum, we return to the roles of key constituencies at the end of this chapter.

On the research front, we are also starting to understand the strengths and weaknesses of different approaches to charter school performance assessment. As Julian Betts, Emily Tang, and Andrew Zau show in chapter 2, more sophisticated nonexperimental approaches that use students as their own controls are more likely to register positive charter school effects. Even more convincing than the best nonexperimental methods, but still too rare, are analyses of lottery data. As Patrick McEwan and Rob Olsen show in chapter 6, there are ways to improve lotteries and thereby increase the numbers of studies that can use randomization. The availability of computer-adaptive testing is allowing some states to test students multiple times each year. As Dale Ballou, Bettie Teasley, and Tim Zeidner (2006) have demonstrated, this will allow studies that compare learning rates for children who switch between charters and other public schools and for students who stay in charter schools.

Zimmer, Gill, Booker, Lavertu, Sass, and Witte (2009) have also demonstrated the importance of measuring outcomes other than test scores, especially for charter high school students who apparently stay in school longer and are more likely to graduate and enter college than students who apply for but lose in charter lotteries. Chapter 4 by Julian Betts summarizes this and other recent evidence on nonachievement outcomes.

Charter school research might eventually gain the degree of nuance and complexity now typical of research in medicine in the hard sciences. But even if it improves to that point there will still be disputes about methods, data, and generalization, just as there are in other fields. Future controversies over charter schools' effects on test scores will be better grounded, but they will be about the same issues as now.

We are also just starting to look more deeply into charter school outcomes other than test scores. Test scores are important because they measure results while children are still in school, while something can still be done for students who are falling behind. But there is no substitute for direct measures of long-term results. Research has shown positive but weak associations between test scores and longer term outcomes such as students' earnings decades after they have left school.

Charter schools offer (or at least can claim to offer) safer and more serene environments[2] whose full effects might be evident only in the long run, for example on student persistence in school and avoidance of course failures. If charter schools motivate students to stay in school longer, work harder, and take more rigorous courses, these results might be visible only near or after the end of high school. The same would be true of important outcomes like college application and attendance and ability to avoid remedial courses in college. Some effects of charter schools might not appear until students are further than college into their adult lives. In chapter 3, Laura Hamilton and Brian Stecher identify some of these longer-term and subtler outcomes, which charter schools might or might not produce. As research takes greater account of such outcomes, it is likely to reflect what Americans care about most, which is how charter schools affect their students' ultimate life chances.

Chapter 4 by Julian Betts shows that recent work that goes beyond test scores is still in its infancy. However, a small number of studies strongly suggest that at least in some areas attending a charter school may boost a student's chances of graduating from high school, of graduating from college, and may also increase attendance and reduce disciplinary incidents. We will need many more studies to conclude that these patterns apply generally, though.

The shallowness of outcome measures for charter schools could help explain Jeff Henig's findings that elected officials are slow to use research on charter schools; and as other chapters show, to date that is probably a good thing. Many of the earlier studies would have led officials to draw the wrong and overly pessimistic conclusion about charter schools' effects on test scores, and even the best studies available could over- or underestimate charter schools' ultimate consequences for the children who attend them.

Even though policy makers rightly avoid using test-score-based research as the sole ground for decisions, in fact the charter community takes it very seriously. Charter operators and funders might not have been totally convinced by earlier mixed and negative findings, but they were worried. As a result they formed new national and state associations focused on providing assistance to schools and limiting new schools' growing pains. Funders also supported independent technical assistance organizations and charter school mutual support networks to improve school quality and charter management organizations to reproduce higher quality schools. Charter advocates also joined with government agencies responsible for charter authorization and oversight to raise standards for approval of charter applications and increase the likelihood that low-performing charters would be transformed or closed.

Indeed, operators of charter schools have become aware that the phrase *charter school* is a brand name to be guarded jealously. The implication is that competing charter school operators will increasingly view their reputations as intertwined with one another. This encourages charter school administrators to band together, for instance, by providing know-how and other assistance to new schools. More dramatically, we may increasingly see charter school associations acting as de facto regulators; for instance, exposing and correcting financial irregularities at a specific charter school. If necessary charter school associations may increasingly even lobby for the closure of a charter school if it is palpably failing in its mission to educate students.

Taking the research seriously, charter operators and funders have also encouraged increasing the number and quality of studies. The National Charter School Research Project, of which this book is one product, directly resulted from a determination among charter schools and philanthropic organizations to get a better handle on what works and what does not.

ON CHARTER SCHOOL POLICY

In most states, the public has moved on from the debate about whether to have charter schools at all. Now the question is how to make charters an effective contributor to children's welfare and to the overall performance of public education.

Some might think this an odd development: after all, the charter schools that have arisen since the first laws were enacted are highly variable in quality. Though some students attending charter schools are arguably better off, many others may have benefited only slightly or not at all. Yet the state laws that allow charter schools to exist offer something that other methods of providing public education do not—and the possibility of continuous improvement through competition, imitation of successful exemplars, and abandonment of models that do not work.

Four Key Features of Charter School Policy Are Developing Rapidly

The first is performance oversight. The government agencies and nonprofit organizations that state laws make responsible for authoring and overseeing charter schools are working hard to develop the capacity to distinguish promising from poor charter applicants and to identify weak charter schools soon enough to intervene before the children in them are hurt. These efforts depend in part on the improvement of charter school performance data and research. Authorizers are also working on ways of closing poor performing charter schools and finding better alternatives for children. Some school districts (for example, Oakland, Chicago, New York, and New Orleans) are adopting kindred approaches such as contracting and performance-based funding to oversight of the schools they run directly.

Charter schools have highlighted the need to judge the performance of individual schools, but they have not created the need out of nothing. It was present all along, but few states or localities had the motivation to pursue it. Now chartering and NCLB school choice options requirements put school effectiveness research on the front burner. The need to study and authorize charter schools depends on data and methods that would also enable valid and informative conclusions about district-run schools.

Policy makers in district and state offices could noticeably improve the quality of charter school evaluations by taking steps to make data from application lotteries more readily available to researchers and/or official evaluators. For instance, Hill and Betts (2006) suggest that charter schools should be required, in return for relative autonomy, to submit lists of lottery winners and losers by year and grade both to the chartering authority (typically a district) as well as the state department of education.

The second area in which policy is evolving concerns caps on the numbers of charter schools. Early state laws put strict limits on the numbers of charter schools allowed in particular states and localities. Due to the popularity of charter schools and to struggling urban districts' need to create new schools to provide options for children trapped in consistently unproductive schools, these caps are being lifted in one state after another, most recently after a prolonged fight in New York State. It is far too soon to say whether every state will continue to lift its cap on charter schools, but the trend is upward. President Obama's March 2009 call for states to ease their numerical caps on the number of charter schools will only strengthen this trend. The policy of numerical caps is likely to evolve along with performance oversight: if performance oversight becomes more rigorous and reliable, there will be less reason for arbitrary limits on charter school numbers.

A third area of charter policy that is changing rapidly involves regulations that affect the supply of new charter schools. Policy decisions in these areas could equally well choke off or accelerate growth of charter schools. Betts, Goldhaber, and Rosenstock (2005) emphasize the idea that opening new charter schools will remain difficult until these schools have adequate access to the credit markets, to unused school district sites, or preferably both. The short period for which a school is granted its charter scares off financial institutions from making the loans that are typically required to obtain land and build a school on it. Alternatively, charter school operators need access to unused public schools so that they can be spared the costs of building from scratch.

There are a few hopeful signs on both fronts. As discussed by Betts in chapter 5, new federal policy has made it possible for charter school sites to be developed through the New Markets Tax Credit. And in California, a new state law requires districts to rent unused district school sites to charter school operators for nominal fees. This law seeks to put charter schools on a more equal financial footing with traditional public schools, which do not have to bear the costs of building new facilities.

A fourth policy area that deserves close scrutiny by policy researchers and state policy makers is institutional factors that limit the mobility of teachers between regular public schools and charter schools. For example, we know of several charter schools that have lost, or come close to losing, some of their most senior teachers when the sponsoring district refused to allow teachers "on leave" from traditional public schools in the district to continue as a regular member of the state teachers' retirement system. In states and urban districts whose teachers and other employees get generously defined benefit pensions, the inability of charter school teachers to accrue service time in the state retirement system creates a powerful deterrent for senior teachers to remain at charter schools. As Dominic Brewer and June Ahn show in chapter 8, there is a great deal to learn, both about charter school teachers today and about the future labor market response to charter schools' needs for teachers with particular values and skills. However, lack of good data from states and the federal government now inhibit research on teachers in charter schools.

ON RESTRUCTURING PUBLIC EDUCATION

Charters and charterlike arrangements are introducing the principle of performance contingency into our public education system. Competition with charters is forcing some districts to adopt features commonly associated with chartering, e.g., decentralization, greater site-level control of resources, new niche schools, and family choice.[3] We also see unions (e.g., the United Federation of Teachers in New York City) using chartering as a way to try out innovations that are attractive to teachers.[4]

Will chartering set the new pattern for all of public education? It is too soon to say. But it is clear that it is a pattern that is broadly imitated, even by people who do not like the title "charter." Charters already clearly have broad influence that transcends their still relatively small share of enrollment nationwide.

The value of charter schools as public policy might ultimately be measured very differently than by the performance of the first few hundred charter schools. Charter schools might usher in an era of continuous improvement, where districts as well as charter authorizers are continually eliminating their lowest performing schools and opening more promising ones, including schools based on instructional models that have proven productive elsewhere. Broadening the frame in this way might look like a rhetorical retreat for charter proponents, and it is; but it is also a retreat to much firmer ground.

The emerging agreement in the research community that we must evaluate charter schools using methods that follow the progress of individual students over time has the potential to lead to better evaluations not only of charter schools but also of traditional public schools. Many of the compelling lessons we have learned in the research and policy communities about the dangers of naïvely comparing average achievement at charter schools and traditional public schools, and about the advantages of following individual student progress over time, could do much to further our understanding of which traditional public schools truly offer the best (and the worst) education.

CONCLUSION

The future of the charter school idea, and charter schools' influence on the broader public education system, depend on the quality of evidence and research available. This book has laid the groundwork for strong recommendations about how states, localities, philanthropies, and researchers can improve the quality of evidence about charter schools. Similarly, the analysis in these pages provides hints about how the media can best assess and popularize the results of charter school research. Recommendations include:

To state legislatures and departments of education:

- Assemble longitudinal student-linked databases including test scores, teacher, and school information for charter students.
- Clarify requirements for charter school lotteries so true, randomly selected control groups can be identified for student outcome studies.
- Require charter schools to submit lists of lotteries and lists of students who won and who lost each lottery by grade and year, both to the chartering authority and the state.
- Increase the ability to track students past high school graduation.
- Commission evaluation as soon as charter school policy is enacted or amended, not post-hoc.
- Seek independent analysis by making rich data available to university and other independent researchers.
- Require ambitious quasi-experimental and experimental research designs, not simple comparisons of means.
- Focus RFPs (Requests for Proposals) on a few questions about performance, not a grab bag of issues.

To local district and city leaders:

- Conduct rich studies of charter schools, including measures of organizational growth and stability. Alternatively, partner with local universities or think tanks to have an independent agent conduct these studies.
- Take advantage of localities' own longitudinal databases.
- Use the same data and methods to evaluate charters and all other public schools.
- Assess competitive effects of charter schools on existing public schools and teacher supply.

To researchers:

- Use the most sophisticated methods possible given data availability.
- Avoid study designs that inherently produce ambiguous results.
- Present the results of both randomized and student value-added analyses whenever possible.
- Return to an earlier tradition of modest claims and appropriate caveats for research findings.
- Emphasize research approaches that focus on factors that make charter schools different from traditional public schools and from each other. In particular, focus on teachers' backgrounds, given that standard measures of teachers' credentials, education, and experience have been shown time and time again to have at best weak positive relationships with student learning. Thus, determine whether charter schools produce better teachers by tapping unusual pools of talent and innovative forms of professional development.

To philanthropies:

- Demand quality evaluations and refuse funding for naïve designs.
- Support new research on charter school maturation.

To journalists and other members of the media:

- Regularly report on studies of the effect of charter schools on academic achievement.
- Consult with two or more outsider researchers to obtain evaluations of the research quality underlying a given report before writing a story on the report.
- Avoid providing undue publicity to poorly designed studies, most notably those that study a student's achievement—or average performance at the school—at a single point in time without taking into account the student's achievement in earlier grades.

Though the future of charter schools is by no means certain, their growth and persistence has refuted predictions that they would soon be absorbed into mainstream public education and leave few traces. It now looks, to the contrary, that charter schools might set a new pattern for public education, especially in big cities, leading to fundamental changes in the missions and functions of school districts. That said, it is by no means certain that future charter schools will all be effective in preparing children for higher education, success at work, or citizenship. No approach to educating our nation's children has been effective enough to earn a free pass; it is essential that civic leaders, elected officials, and scholars continue to measure, assess, and critique charter schools and call attention to failures. There will always be a need for fair and perceptive assessment of charter school performance and for improvements in methods of measurement and analysis. We hope this book, by summarizing the current state of the art, lays the groundwork for further progress.

NOTES

1. On charter-style performance-based oversight of regular public schools, see Hill and Lake (2009).
2. See Hill and Christensen (2007).
3. See, for example, Campbell and DeArmond (2006).
4. See http://www.uft.org/chapter/charter/secondary/, downloaded April 17, 2009.

REFERENCES

Ballou, D., Teasley, B., and Zeidner, T. (2006). *Charter Schools in Idaho*. Manuscript prepared for the National Conference on Charter School Research at Vanderbilt University on September 29, 2006.

Betts, J., Goldhaber, D., and Rosenstock, L. (2005). Supply Side Responses to Systems of School Choice. In Julian Betts and Tom Loveless (Eds.), *Getting Choice Right: Ensuring Equity and Efficiency in Education Policy*. Washington, DC: Brookings Institution Press.

Campbell, C., and DeArmond, M. (2006). *No Longer the Only Game in Town*. Seattle: Center on Reinventing Public Education.

Hill, P. T., and Betts, J. R. (2006). Improving State and Local Assessments of Charter School Performance. In Robin J. Lake and Paul T. Hill (Eds.), *Hopes, Fears, & Reality: A Balanced Look at American Charter Schools in 2006* (pp. 37–47). National Charter School Research Project. Seattle: Center on Reinventing Public Education.

Hill, P. T., and Christensen, J. (2007). Safety and Order in Charter and Traditional Public Schools. In Robin J. Lake and Paul T. Hill (Eds.), *Hopes, Fears, & Reality:*

A Balanced Look at American Charter Schools in 2007 (pp. 53–64). National Charter School Research Project. Seattle: Center on Reinventing Public Education.

Hill, P. T., and Lake, R. J. (2009). *Performance Management in Portfolio School Districts.* Seattle: Center on Reinventing Public Education.

Obama, B. (2009). Remarks by the President to the Hispanic Chamber of Commerce on a Complete and Competitive American Education. Washington, DC: White House, Office of the Press Secretary, March 10.

Zimmer, R., Gill, B., Booker, K., Lavertu, S., Sass, T. R., and Witte, J. (2009). *Charter Schools in Eight States: Effects on Achievement, Attainment, Integration, and Competition.* Santa Monica, CA: RAND Corporation.

Index

Abdulkadiroglu, A., 58
academic: history, 16, 23; success/
    failure, 155–56
academic achievement: primacy of, 33;
    sample definitions of, 163
Academic Performance Index, 16
accountability, 125–26
achievement, 35, 56; academic, primacy
    of, 33; as central importance to
    research, 48; effect of charter schools
    on, 15, 24; effect of Preuss School
    on, 25; evaluation, 159; gains
    vs. levels in, 29–30, *30*, *31*, 58;
    limitations, 40; literature on charter
    schools and, 55–58; misreading of
    average school, 18–19; National
    Assessment of Education Progress,
    data, 18–19; results by school type,
    159–60; sample definitions of
    academic, 163; state-based research,
    156; state-sponsored research
    covering research released between
    2001–2006, *175*. *See also* math
    achievement; student
    achievement
Adequate Yearly Progress, 28–29
administrator, cheating, 109n3
admissions: in Chile, 109n1;
    discrimination in, 2; state regulations

on charter school, for selected states,
    108; from waiting list, 99–100
admissions lottery, 11n3, 24, 83–108;
    audits/monitoring, 108; data, 55;
    data, value of, 59; groups, definition
    of, 91; implementation, 92; losers,
    99; manipulation, 109n3; Preuss
    School, 24; process, 106, 108; rules,
    85; settings, 91; winners vs. losers,
    58–60; on a zip code–by–zip code
    basis, 73. *See also* lotteries
Advanced Placement (AP), 42; exam
    limitations, 39
AFT. *See* American Federation of
    Teachers
age of charter school, 15–16, 192–93.
    See also newness, charter school
Ahn, June, 9
alignment studies, 37–38
Allen, Jeannie, 181
American Federation of Teachers
    (AFT), 180, 191, 199n8; study,
    182–83
Angel, Larry, 9
Angrist, J., 58, 97, 110
AP. *See* Advanced Placement
API, 16; shift-share analysis of sources
    of reduction in, Gap between charter
    and public schools (1999–2005), *19*

Ginsberg, R., 147
goals: charter vs. public school, 33; performance, long term, 167; of public education, 55
Goldhaber, D., 209
governance: internal, 120; matters, 193–94
grades, 37
graduation: high school, 59; middle school, 41; probability of, 8; rates, 40–41, 48–49, 51
Green Dot Public Schools, 73
growth, 117
Guarino, C., 72

Hamilton, Laura, 7, 55, 72, 207
harassment, 114
Harris, D. C., 143–45
Harvey, J., 119
Heckman's method, 74
Henig, Jeffrey, 10, 78, 207
hierarchical linear modeling (HLM), 158
higher education, preparation for, 213
high performance organizations, 138–39
high school, 38; analyses for, 23; graduation, 59; math performance in, 56, 62
High Tech High (HTH), 72–73
Hill, P. T., 123, 190, 209
Hill, Paul, 8, 10
HLM. *See* hierarchical linear modeling
host district, 1
Hoxby, C., 100–1, 105, 108, 144, 182, 191; vs. Rothstein, 184; study by, 182–83
HTH. *See* High Tech High

Idaho charter schools, 56
IES. *See* Institute of Education Sciences
Imberman, S., 61
impacts, 101
improvement: focus on, 165–66; guidance for, 159–60

income, family, 31n2, 75–76, 79, 114, 194; decision to attend charter school and, 66–69; geographic location and, 67–68; representation of, 69. *See also* low-income
incubators, 116
Institute of Education Sciences (IES), 109n2, 110n8
instruction, 120; effective, 46
instructional: focus, 123; framework, 122–23; maturation process, 122–24; support, 47
integrated schools, 76
internal governance, 120

Jacob, B. A., 100–1
Jacob-Almeida, R., 24, 59
Jacobs, Lawrence, 186
journalists, 212

Kane, T., 58
Kansas City charter schools, 145
Kerchner, C. T., 136, 138–39
Key Issues in Studying Charter Schools and Achievement: A Review and Suggestions for National Guidelines (May 2006), 3–4; unresolved, 6
killer application, 196–97
kindergarten students, 66
Kingdon, John, 187
Kleitz, B., 68
Koedel, C. R., 72
Krop, C., 72

Ladd, H. F., 58, 72, 75
Lake, Robin, 9
LaLonde, R., 29
Lavertu, S., 58, 60, 206
law, charter: battles over, 204; teacher requirements and, 131–32. *See also* state charter laws
learning process, 47
Legislative Office of Education Oversight (LOEO), 162
Lerner, Robert, 199n8

About the Contributors

June Ahn is a PhD student at the University of Southern California, Rossier School of Education. His research interests focus on the impact of communication technologies on school reform, education policy, and student academic achievement. His other publications include "Policy, Technology, and Practice in Cyber Charter Schools" (forthcoming, Teachers College Record) and "What Do We Know About Reducing Class and School Size?" (2009, AERA Handbook of Education Policy Research). Prior to his PhD studies, he obtained his BA from Brown University and MA from Columbia University, Teachers College.

Larry Angel is an economics instructor at South Seattle Community College and is also a doctoral candidate at the University of Washington. His research interests include economics of education, educational statistics, and community colleges. Currently, he is working on his dissertation, which focuses on policies that improve retention rates for community colleges.

Julian Betts is Professor of Economics and Chair of the Department of Economics at the University of California, San Diego. He also serves as a Research Associate of the National Bureau of Economic Research and an Adjunct Fellow at the Public Policy Institute of California (PPIC). He has written extensively on the link between student outcomes and measures of school spending, including class size, teachers' salaries, and teachers' level of education. More recently, he has examined the role that standards and school choice play in student achievement. His work includes a theoretical analysis of the impact of educational standards published in the American Economic Review (1998), the coedited book *Getting Choice Right: Ensuring Equity and Efficiency in Education Policy* (Brookings Institution Press, 2005), and the coauthored book *From Blueprint to Reality: San Diego's Education Reforms* (PPIC, 2005). Current research includes a national study of magnet schools and a local study of career and technical education, both for the U.S. Department of Education. He is also a member of the National Charter School Research Project's Charter School Achievement Consensus Panel.

Dominic J. Brewer is Associate Dean for Research and Faculty Affairs and the Clifford H. and Betty C. Allen Professor in Urban Leadership at the Rossier School of Education at the University of Southern California. He holds courtesy appointments in the USC College Department of Economics and in the School of Policy Planning and Development. He is also a Codirector of PACE, Policy Analysis for California Education, a policy research collaboration of USC, UC-Berkeley, and Stanford.

Laura Hamilton (PhD, Educational Psychology and MS, Statistics, Stanford University) is a Senior Behavioral Scientist at the RAND Corporation and an Adjunct Associate Professor in the University of Pittsburgh's Learning Sciences and Policy program. She has directed several large studies, including an investigation of the implementation of standards-based accountability in response to No Child Left Behind and an evaluation of a leadership development program for principals in urban school districts. She has served on a number of national and state panels, including the Brookings National Commission on Choice in K–12 Education, the Center on Education Policy's Advisory Panel on Student Achievement under No Child Left Behind and its Panel on High School Exit Exams, and the APA/AERA/NCME Joint Committee to Revise the Standards for Educational and Psychological Testing.

Jeffrey R. Henig is a professor of political science and education at Teachers College and professor of political science at Columbia University. He earned his PhD in Political Science at Northwestern University in 1978. His most recent book, *Spin Cycle: How Research is Used in Policy Debates; The Case of Charter Schools,* was published by the Russell Sage Foundation/Century Foundation early in 2008.

Paul T. Hill is the John and Marguerite Corbally Professor at the University of Washington Bothell and Director of the Center on Reinventing Public Education. He is a nonresident Senior Fellow at the Brookings and Hoover Institutions and directed the National Working Commission on Choice in K–12 Education. He also chairs the National Charter School Research Project and leads its Charter School Achievement Consensus Panel, which authored the influential white paper, *Key Issues in Studying Charter Schools and Achievement: A Review and Suggestions for National Guidelines* (May 2006). Dr.

Hill's current work on public education reform focuses on school choice, finance, accountability, and charter schools. He works closely with city and state leaders and has written a series of books designed as resources for mayors and community leaders facing the need to transform their urban public school systems, including: *Making School Reform Work: New Partnerships for Real Change* (2004), *Charter Schools and Accountability in Public Education* (2002), *It Takes a City: Getting Serious about Urban School Reform* (2000), and *Fixing Urban Schools* (1998), all published by Brookings. Dr. Hill holds a PhD and MA from Ohio State University and a BA from Seattle University, all in political science.

Robin Lake is Associate Director of the Center on Reinventing Public Education (CRPE) at the University of Washington Bothell where she focuses on charter schools, accountability, and urban district reform. She is Executive Director of the National Charter School Research Project (NCSRP), a multiyear effort to improve the balance, rigor, and application of charter school research. Currently Lake is studying the internal operations and staffing of charter schools, and she is a lead researcher on the National Study of CMO Effectiveness, a three-year initiative on the effectiveness, achievement, and characteristics of Charter Management Organizations. Lake is editor of *Hopes, Fears, & Reality: A Balanced Look at American Charter Schools*, and author of numerous reports, policy briefs, and op-eds. She holds a master's in Public Administration from the University of Washington.

Patrick J. McEwan is an Associate Professor in the Department of Economics and the Whitehead Associate Professor of Critical Thought at Wellesley College. His research focuses on the economics of education, applied econometrics, and education policy in Latin America. It has been published in a wide range of economics and education journals, as well as three books. He has consulted on education policy and evaluation at the Inter-American Development Bank, the RAND Corporation, UNESCO, the World Bank, and the ministries of education of several countries.

Robert Olsen is a Senior Scientist in the Social and Economic Policy Division at Abt Associates, Inc. Dr. Olsen's research has focused on large-scale Randomized Controlled Trials in education, including the methodological issues that these studies face. He has played leadership roles on several large-scale random assignment studies in education, including an evaluation of charter schools, two evaluations of the Upward Bound program, and the design of an evaluation to test major schoolwide and districtwide interventions. In addition, Dr. Olsen is an active contributor to the field on how to conduct impact evaluations in education. His methodological research has included studies of how to address missing data in RCTs, how to boost the external validity of these types of studies, and the consequences of relying on state tests to measure student achievement in studies of educational effectiveness. Dr. Olsen received his PhD in labor economics from Cornell University in 1999, and he held research positions at Mathematica Policy Research and the Urban Institute before joining Abt Associates in 2007.

Lydia Rainey is a researcher at the Center on Reinventing Public Education at the University of Washington Bothell and a doctoral student at the University of Washington's College of Education. Her research interests include organizational theory and school and central office reform.

Brian Stecher is a Senior Social Scientist and Associate Director of the RAND Education program. His research focuses on measuring educational quality and improvement, with an emphasis on assessment and accountability systems. During his nineteen years at RAND, he has directed prominent national and state educational research projects, and he has served on expert panels relating to standards, assessments, and accountability for the National Academies. He has published widely in professional journals and is currently a member of the Editorial Board of *Educational Evaluation and Policy Analysis* and *Educational Assessment Journal*. Dr. Stecher received his bachelor's degree in mathematics from Pomona College, his master's degree in mathematics from the University of Oregon, and his PhD in education from UCLA.

Y. Emily Tang is a Faculty Fellow in Economics at the University of California, San Diego. She obtained her PhD in Economics from UCSD in 2007. Her studies have focused on social issues, including education, crime, and racial tensions. She is a coauthor of *Does School Choice Work: Effects on Student Integration and Achievement* (Public Policy Institute of California, 2006).

Andrew C. Zau is a Senior Statistician in the Department of Economics at the University of California, San Diego. Previously, he was a research associate at the Public Policy Institute of California. His current research focuses on the determinants of student achievement in the San Diego Unified School District. He holds a BS from the University of California, San Diego and an MPH in epidemiology from San Diego State University.